SOCIETY, STATE, & SCHOOLS

SOCIETY, STATE, & SCHOOLS

A Case for Structural and Confessional Pluralism

|20317

by The Fellows of the Calvin Center
for Christian Scholarship, Calvin College

Rockne McCarthy
Donald Oppewal
Walfred Peterson
Gordon Spykman, coordinator

WILLIAM B. EERDMANS PUBLISHING COMPANY
GRAND RAPIDS, MICHIGAN

Printed in the United States of America

Library of Congress Cataloging in Publication Data
Main entry under title:

Society, state & schools.

   1. Education — United States — Philosophy — History.
2. Church and education — United States — History.
3. Education and state — United States — History.
4. Education — United States — Finance — History.
5. Calvinism — History.   I. McCarthy, Rockne.
II. Calvin Center for Christian Scholarship.
LA212.S65   370'.973   81-1238
ISBN 0-8028-1880-3   AACR2

Grateful acknowledgment is made for permission to quote from Sheldon S.
Wolin, "Paradigms and Political Theories," in *Politics and Experience*, ed.
Preston King and B. C. Parekh (© 1968, Cambridge University Press).

CONTENTS

CONTENTS

ACKNOWLEDGMENTS

WE owe a debt of gratitude to the following readers who critically reviewed this manuscript and suggested many helpful revisions prior to its publication: Jack Carloyle, Philosophy Department, Washington State University; Peter De Boer, Education Department, Calvin College; Philip Elve, Government Relations, Christian Schools International; Daniel McGarry, History Department, St. Louis University; Joel Nederhood, Radio Minister, Back to God Hour; John Olthuis, Research and Policy Director, Committee on Justice and Liberty, Toronto; Derk Pereboom, graduate in the Philosophy Department, University of California, Los Angeles; Robert Sandin, Academic Vice-President, North Park College; Clifford Schimmels, Education Department, Wheaton College. We acknowledge with thanks the contributions all these scholars made during the final stages in the production of this book. We also recognize gratefully the diligent labors of our Center secretary, Nelle Tjapkes, and our other secretaries, Jylene Baas and Donna Quist, in typing this manuscript and preparing it for publication.

PREFACE

THIS project appears under the auspices of the Calvin Center for Christian Scholarship. The topic chosen for year-long research in the academic year 1978–79 was "Public Justice and Educational Equity." In the title of this book we have sought to capture the underlying themes of this topic as we came to understand it during months of reading, writing, joint reflection, and discussion. Our common project was shaped by the guidelines of the Center Constitution, which commit its participants to rigorous and creative scholarship that is articulately Christian, dealing with fundamental questions of both theoretical and practical significance. Working as a team proved to be both demanding and delightful. We hope this fruit of our labors makes some contribution to a more peaceful society, a more just state, and a more equitable school system.

In carrying out this research project we, as senior fellows, were ably assisted by our two student fellows, then seniors in philosophy at Calvin College, Gary Knoppers and Thomas Postema.

ROCKNE MCCARTHY, *Lectureship Center, Dordt College*
DONALD OPPEWAL, *Education, Calvin College*
WALFRED PETERSON, *Political Science,*
Washington State University
GORDON SPYKMAN, *Theology, Calvin College (Coordinator)*

CHAPTER 1

INTRODUCTION:
CRISIS
AND RENEWAL

TWO things seem clear. First, our American society continues to go thumping along from crisis to crisis. Second, increasingly these crises relate directly to the very structures of our society and of the state. A sound index to the structural distress of our society and state is our system of schooling. The crisis is real—in our society and its schools. At the center stands the state; at stake is a host of social structures.

A growing body of literature is focusing public attention on these issues. Our study embraces and significantly extends the conclusions of a series of such social studies.

ECLIPSE OF MEDIATING STRUCTURES

Peter L. Berger and Richard J. Neuhaus, two keen observers of the American scene, have proposed a major reform for American society based on their recent public policy research.[1] Reform is needed, they argue, because, while the public is permanently committed to the services of the modern welfare state, at the same time it has a "strong animus against government, bureaucracy, and bigness as such." This antipathy is aimed at all levels of big government as well as against other "megastructures," including ". . . the large economic conglomerates of capitalist enterprise, big labor, and the growing bureaucracies that administer wide sectors of the society, such as education and the organized professions."

Hostility to these megastructures creates "a double crisis." There is the individual crisis of people who must live their private lives struggling to manage alone in the face of the powerful impact of impersonal megastructures. There is also the political crisis caused by the aggregate fear and distrust of the megastructures. How can these crises be resolved or mitigated?

For Berger and Neuhaus the answer is reform, not revolution or reaction. The American public has shown itself inhospitable to the appeals of the revolutionary left or libertarian right. The old left is unattractive because it offers the bigness of the socialist state, and that very bigness, of course, renders this alternative suspect. The new left, now sensitive to that objection, offers a version of socialism that stresses worker control of autonomous industries. Yet its immediate prospect is only one of an unattractive "struggle toward building socialism," which offers hope only in some unforeseeable future day. The libertarian right, on the other hand, is either romantic, yearning to "revoke modernity," a desire whose realization the authors describe as "neither likely nor desirable," or it is blind to the alienation resulting from the image of big business. So, the "ideological baggage of the past" offers no useful course of action.

The alternative paradigm offered by Berger and Neuhaus is the protection and promotion by public policy of "mediating structures" — "those institutions standing between the individual in his private life and the large institutions of public life." Such structures are many, but the authors analyze four in detail: the family, the neighborhood, church, and voluntary association. These structures are the primary elements of a society that promotes community feelings.

The value and function of small community loyalty were lost in the emergence of Enlightenment individualism. This movement stressed the rights of the individual on the one hand and the public order, the universal, on the other. It viewed "anything 'in between' . . . as irrelevant, or even an obstacle to the rational ordering of society." This Enlightenment denigration of communal social values still controls American liberalism. It "may be the Achilles' heel of the liberal state today"; it must be overcome.

Berger and Neuhaus describe both a minimum and a maximum effort that can be directed toward overcoming this inheritance. "Minimally, public policy should cease and desist from damaging mediating structures." For example, tax structures should not make it difficult for the poor family to own an adequate house, nor threaten the survival of voluntary associations. The certification and professionalization of many callings should not limit the capacity of persons working in small groups to assume those callings. Maximally, governments should carry out many of their programs by utilizing mediating structures "wherever possible." Government must avoid co-opting these agencies in ways that destroy the "distinctiveness of their function."

This last point emphasizes the authors' real concern. Berger and Neuhaus are not calling simply for decentralization "within government." They are asking, rather, that some present governmental operations be transferred out of the bureaucracy of the state altogether. Their theme is "empowerment," a theme vividly captured in the title of their study: *To Empower People: The Role of Mediating Structures in Public Policy*. Official empowerments for "people-sized" institutions, more than the bureaucracies of government and other megastructures, "are the principal expressions of the real values and real needs of people in our society."

FAMILY CHOICE IN EDUCATION

The work of John E. Coons and Stephen D. Sugarman may be thought of as an application of Berger's and Neuhaus's maximum strategy to the specific case of American education, although the two sets of writers worked independently of one another. Like Berger and Neuhaus, Coons and Sugarman state their conclusion in the title of their book: *Education by Choice: The Case for Family Control*.[2]

According to Coons and Sugarman, the American public school system has become a megastructure. The child and family must submit to it, for it will not adjust to them. True, for a few there is a costly educational option. For most people, however, there is only "Hobson's Choice: Your Neighborhood Public School, Take It or Leave It" — which is the heading of a major section of the book. Were the public school truly a neighborhood institution, the situation would not be as bad as it is. But the "neighborhood" school is required to fit the requirements of the school district and the state, not the needs of the distinct subgroups that may actually be in the neighborhood. Children attend the public school — take it or leave it. It is this or almost nothing else.

As an alternative Coons and Sugarman call for "education by choice." They believe that children and families differ in a variety of ways — different learning styles, different educational goals, different ideologies. The present educational system is not structured to take account of these differences. The system, moreover, is not neutral with respect to them. Fitting square-peg children and families into round-hole schools alienates the consumers of education from the producers in significant ways. True, some public systems offer a choice of schools, and within some public schools there is some choice of curriculum; but there is far too little real choice.

This situation has grown out of the way in which public education is financed and controlled and the purpose to which it is directed. Public monies are given to public school districts. They in turn spend it by offering universal, free education defined by district and state rules. Such "melting pot" education is designed to promote assimilation and consensus. In a society composed largely of a diverse, multi-lingual, immigrant people, such an end may have served reasonably well. But that society no longer exists in America. Today America must have an educational paradigm that recognizes healthy plurality. The school must teach the child that there is a realizable private world beyond the public one, the only one the child learns about in the mass media and other means of mass socializing.

Coons and Sugarman argue that the rules must be changed. The money the state raises for education should be redirected to the family. Families, not the experts, know best what children want and need most from schooling. Actually, Coons and Sugarman put the individual, not the family unit, at the center of their educational purposes. They follow the lead of John Stuart Mill in praising "Individuality, as One of the Elements of Well Being." They want "education for autonomy," education "to serve the best interests of the child" as defined by that child's family until the child can define it for him- or herself. As children mature, therefore, the choices respecting their educational needs and wants reflect the children's preferences more and the family's preferences less.

The authors are not, however, radical individualists. They recognize at the outset two necessary social purposes for education, namely, "to foster a consensus supporting the constitutional order" and "to achieve racial integration." Thus government must play a role in education. How can individual and family choice on the one hand be combined wisely with government influence on the other?

In *Education by Choice* the answer is a "regulated family choice" system funded by federal, state, and local monies. Under such a system the financial resources flow from the government directly to families. The parents of each child receive either a scholarship or a voucher. They are then free to choose any school that meets the state's educational requirements. Public schools will, of course, meet those requirements. So too will all other approved schools: nonprofit or profit-making, as well as church-related schools. Coons and Sugarman believe that such a system will facilitate the development of a wide variety of schools. The competition from nonpublic schools will force and expand variety within the public school system, both in styles of education—for example, traditional or open classroom—and in philosophies of

4

education—for example, progressive, Catholic, libertarian, or fundamentalist. A thousand flowers might bloom.

The state's requirements will ensure basic education in essential social skills and the survival of the constitutional order. Other requirements will promote social integration in several ways, and will threaten the loss of eligibility for noncompliant schools. Whatever rules the state establishes for racial integration, the result will in all likelihood be at least as good as or better than the present situation.

Coons and Sugarman add one more detail to the role played by the state under the system. They prefer a voucher program that ensures equality of access. This could be achieved by devising, in effect, a progressive funding plan. Low income families receive more voucher aid than families with a higher income. Since, in their preferred plan (they suggest several), all schools charge a tuition at least a bit higher than the value of the state vouchers, the poor family "adds on" less money to cover that tuition than the middle income family, and the middle income family adds less than the rich.

Although their book is detailed in its treatment of the issues that a free choice voucher system would raise, the authors intend only to give suggestions. They call for extensive experimentation and "a substantial trial." Yet they reject current school structures decisively and believe a pluralist educational system offers a far better prospect for both the child and society.

Their overall suggestions are akin to those of Berger and Neuhaus in that they want to shift some of the work of government to mediating structures—to families and nongovernment schools operated by voluntary associations. The presence of government will be reduced. To the extent that the government continues operating schools (and that will remain the reality in most places), the method of operation will depend less on remote expert administrators and more on the choice of parents and children. Choice means alternatives, and these alternatives will compel public schools to adapt their programs to the facts of a pluralist social order.

TOWARD A NEW PARADIGM

Berger and Neuhaus call for a new paradigm for the whole of American society. Coons and Sugarman offer a new paradigm for American education. We agree that both calls are much needed, and to the point, and timely. In colonial times American education reflected a pluralist approach to schooling. But from the Revolutionary era onward, American society became increasingly individualistic. During the past century, under the pressures of a highly industrialized society and imposing domestic and international crises, the nation has been gradually shifting toward a collectivist paradigm. Both studies by these four authors call for the revival of a pluralist paradigm, one reminiscent of earlier working relationships among society, the state, and the schools, although adapted to our times.

The word pluralism is firmly fixed in our American vocabulary. The reality of pluralism in our society is generally assumed. Nevertheless, since its independence the United States has not conducted its public affairs consistently within an authentic pluralist paradigm. We join these authors in this cause, even though our understanding of a pluralist social paradigm, grounded as it is in a different world-view, may differ from theirs.

In an essay entitled "Paradigms and Political Theories," Sheldon S. Wolin examines the idea that social decisions are shaped by a society's dominant "paradigm," and that a crisis in society calls for a change in paradigm.[3] Wolin adapts Thomas Kuhn's analysis of scientific revolutions[4] and applies it to the study of political change. Kuhn contended that science is dominated in each period of history by what he calls "normal science," by a specific conceptual model of the universe, a paradigm. Such a paradigm involves a theoretical view of the universe that not only embraces but also regulates all pertinent scientific investigation. The paradigm is thus a set of fundamental norms that give to the research of a period its legitimacy, for experimentation finds its point of reference in the original conceptual assumptions of the dominant paradigm.

Wolin proposes that we conceive of a given political society at any point "as a paradigm of an operative kind," much like Kuhn's scientific paradigm. Wolin first assumes that society is "a coherent whole in the sense of its customary political practices, institutions, laws, structure of authority, citizenship, and operative beliefs being organized and interrelated." He goes on to point out that "a politically organized society contains definite institutional arrangements, certain widely shared understandings regarding the location and use of political power, certain expectations about how authority ought to treat the members of society and about the claims that organized society can rightfully make upon its members." This shared set of values leads Wolin to a further conclusion: "In saying that the practices and beliefs of a society are organized and interrelated, that its members have certain expectations and share certain beliefs, one is saying that that society believes itself to be one thing rather than another. . . ." "This *ensemble* of practices and beliefs," he concludes, "may be said to form a paradigm in the sense that the society tries to carry on its political life in accordance with them."

This application of paradigm construction to political society can serve as a useful tool in our proposed analysis of social philosophies, such as individualism, collectivism, and pluralism, which represent fundamentally different views of society. From Wolin's comments it should be clear, however, that the paradigms he describes are more than simply differing theoretical constructs. The concept of a ruling paradigm points to the fact that a particular, deeply held view of social reality is translated into a structural understanding of social institutions and their relationship to each other. Individualist, collectivist, and pluralist views of reality, therefore, lead not only to different paradigms of society but also to different societies. Within each of these social paradigms, for example, one's understanding of the relationship between the state and the school is significantly different.

The Kuhn-Wolin insights also clarify what characterizes a fundamental social crisis. Kuhn argues that a scientific revolution occurs when one paradigm replaces another. This happens when the older paradigm proves incapable of dealing with the facts, when experiments and observations no longer fit the earlier conceptual scheme. The divergence between the prevailing paradigm and reality produces a "scientific crisis"; eventually the strain becomes so great that the older paradigm is repudiated by the scientific community. A new paradigm then becomes the basis for the new legitimate quests of science. This happened, for example, when the Copernican replaced the Ptolemaic cosmology.

Appealing to Kuhn, Wolin suggests that political paradigms are subject to strain and tension much like scientific paradigms. Challenges to the ruling paradigm may come from the outside, from foreign powers or ideologies, or from within, from new economic, social, or intellectual forces. The ruling political paradigm will either adjust to the challenges or it will be destroyed by them and replaced by a new paradigm. When this happens a revolution occurs, not only in the way people look at the world, but also in the way (given the new paradigm) they proceed in restructuring society.

In what follows we wish to make clear that while we find the Kuhn-Wolin ideas to be illuminating and helpful, we do not share all their presuppositions or conclusions. For instance, we do not agree with certain relativist and evolutionist assumptions implied in Kuhn's presentation. Furthermore, we think that Kuhn and Wolin fail to explain fully why paradigms break down and how new ones are created. Perhaps a better explanation of such processes can be found in a more avowedly religious view of life: a fundamental change in the way people look at the world represents a religious redirection of people's self-understanding, which in turn can lead to an attempt to reorder society. Despite these drawbacks, the Kuhn-Wolin analysis of the development of political theory in a period of crisis is useful in understanding the development of the social philosophies of individualism, collectivism, and pluralism.

Wolin himself suggests that the great political paradigms of the past are responses to a "crisis in belief" in a society:

> The intimate relation between crisis and theory is the result not only of the theorist's belief that the world is deeply flawed but of his strategic sense that crisis, and its usual accompaniments of institutional collapse and the breakdown of authority, affords an opportunity for a theory to reorder the world. This was the theme of Plato's *Republic*; of the last chapter of Machiavelli's *Prince* and the preface to Book II of the *Discorsi*; of Hobbes's *Leviathan*; and of virtually all that Marx wrote. In each case political crisis was not the product of the theorist's hyper-active imagination but of the actual state of affairs. . . . In each instance the theorist's response was not to offer a theory that would correspond to the facts, or "fit" them as snugly as the glove does the hand. Derangement in the world signified that the facts were skewed. A theory corresponding to a sick world would itself be a form of sickness. Instead, theories were offered as symbolic representations of what society would be like if it could be reordered.[5]

Any substantial change in society is the result of a crisis that the prevailing paradigm cannot withstand and that the existing leaders are incapable of solving. It is striking that new social philosophies develop only in a period of social crisis. Formal discussion of social philosophy usually takes place only when a society has arrived at a critical juncture in its history—either when it is about to disintegrate, when it is passing through an epochal phase of its history, or when a new society is coming into existence. When a society is developing "normally" the reigning social paradigm is taken for granted both by the masses and their leaders. It is only when a "crisis in belief" occurs in a society that fundamental questioning and discussion begin in a serious way. There are clear signs, we believe, that such a crisis is upon us.

WORLD-VIEWS AND SOCIAL PARADIGMS

The focus of this book is the American educational system. Clearly, however, we are concerned at the outset with a much broader concern: to understand the social philosophy or paradigm within which our society functions. For that paradigm serves to mold public policy in general and educational policy in particular.

Questions of educational reform, therefore, inevitably involve the fundamental structures of society, the role of the state in school operations, and the basic religious-philosophic presuppositions that are inescapably present in every public policy decision. Systems of law are never religiously neutral. They are always rooted in certain underlying principles. It is, therefore, of prime importance to examine carefully the vision of life that has shaped the prevailing American view of society, the state, and the schools.

Some might propose a more direct route into the matter of public justice and educational equity in American society. Why not deal at once with our contemporary situation? Is it not possible to get on with the present analysis without surveying competing social philosophies and their underlying faith commitments? In this book, however, we are proceeding on the assumption that the meaning of public policy in the field of education can be clarified best when seen within the framework of various social philosophies or paradigms. To bypass such fundamental reflection in favor of more instant solutions is to mistake the depth and duration of the issues we face and to reduce them to superficiality.

We therefore approach the issue at hand with this thesis: all proposals respecting society, the state, and the schools are rooted in and shaped by fundamental world-views. We believe that life as a whole is religion. Religious responses take on concrete shape in the way people structure their societies. The Dutch social theorist, Bob Goudzwaard, clarifies this point in his discussion of "three basic biblical rules which together explain man's relation to God and to his theoretical and practical pursuits":

> The first basic rule is that every man is serving god(s) in his life. This rule is known as Augustine's law of concentration. . . . The second basic rule is that every man is transformed into an image of his god. The choice of a god, of a real resting point in our lives, is not without consequences. . . . The third basic rule is that mankind creates and forms a structure of society in his own image. In the development of human civilization man forms, creates, and changes the structure of his society, and in doing so he portrays in his

work the intention of his own heart. He gives the structure of that society something of his own image and likeness.[6]

Echoing something of this thesis are authors of widely divergent perspectives who nevertheless concur in their acknowledgment that social paradigms rest upon deeply seated worldviews. Karl Hertz, for example, reminds us that "there is no Archimedian point of leverage in the social sciences." Objectivity can, therefore, never mean neutrality. It can only mean the ". . . recognition of one's own basic normative commitments."[7] Throughout this book, therefore, we shall make explicit our own assumptions and fundamental commitments as we attempt to uncover the structural and confessional assumptions and commitments undergirding other views.

TOWARD RENEWAL

Clarifying our presuppositions as we go, then, our study will trace the roots of the crisis of faith in our society's paradigms, and look toward the renewing force of a new organizing principle.

Basically, only three major social philosophies have shaped the history of our Western world. Collectivism, and later individualism, emerged as the two dominant social paradigms. Individualism makes the rights and liberties of individuals its ultimate concern; accordingly, it lacks any inherent social substance. Collectivism takes some social megastructure, such as the modern state, as the integrating norm for the entire social organism; it thus tends to undermine the rights of both individuals and plural associations. In practice, both collectivism and, paradoxically, individualism tend to bolster the power of a bureaucratic state. Pluralism, a third alternative, which arose in the wake of the Reformation, regards multiple associations, such as families, schools, the state, and churches, as the basic structuring principle for societal life. Pluralism, however, has generally not come to consistent expression.

Among American educators, individualism had William James as its leading spokesman, while collectivism had its leading advocate in William Torrey Harris. At the same time, however, there have been only muffled cries for a pluralist approach to education on the American scene. The clearest representatives of a pluralist vision stand in the reformational line of Calvin, Althusius, and Kuyper.

In American history, that line was paralleled by New England Puritanism, which honored pluralism in its recognition of the God-given rights of associations. With the rise of Enlightenment thought during the era of the Revolution, however, an individualist spirit gained ascendency in American legal thought and practice. As a result, only recently have our courts begun to follow the lead of other Western democracies in recognizing the public legal rights of associations in American society.

Originally, the American colonial educational system was pluralistic. Over the past two centuries, however, it has become increasingly monopolistic and autocratic under state control. Education in colonial America was free of the contemporary distinction between private-religious and public-secular in such matters as the legal standing and funding of all schools. But as the view of Enlightenment thinkers such as Thomas Jefferson and Horace Mann took hold, American education, originally shaped by more traditional religions, fell increasingly under the influence of a general civil religion based upon natural reason. This led during the nineteenth century to the full legal recognition and funding of only public schools.

At first the public schools were characterized by a deist or generally Protestant outlook. Eventually, however, this orientation was replaced by secular humanism. This world-view has been reinforced by recent Supreme Court interpretations of the nonestablishment clause of the Constitution. Though widely criticized as unhistorical, confusing, and inconsistent, this religious stance still holds. All the decisions taken by the justices during our times on questions of so-called church-state relations in the field of education reflect an uncritical acceptance of the private-religious and public-secular dichotomy. Both in theory and in practice, therefore, our present legal order discriminates against traditional religions, while at the same time it clearly expresses a bias in favor of secular humanism as the approved religion of our governmental educational system. This bias is confirmed by an examination of a sampling of curriculum materials approved and widely used in public schools.

The alternative to the individualist-collectivist convergence in American education is a pluralist view of society, the state, and the schools. Such a pluralist paradigm is workable, both in principle and in practice, with respect to the structures of society as well as the rights of various confessional groups within it. This is demonstrated by the educational policies of such democratic countries as England, Canada, Israel, Belgium, and the Netherlands.

Our case for pluralism, with liberty and justice for all, is an integral part of the Judeo-Christian tradition, rooted in the scriptures of the Old and New Testament. The Biblical message gives direction to public as well as private life. It points toward a pluralist way of life by calling for the recognition of a plurality of associations in society. Each sphere of human activity has its own identity, integrity, and right of existence. Yet together these various social institutions are to coordinate their interaction as partners in a pattern of social mutuality, thus contributing to the well-being of society as a whole.

In seeking to implement this case for pluralism we propose a number of strategies for constructive change. Renewal is made possible through any of three processes — by means of legislation, litigation, and constitutional amendment. Legislation might include considering a variety of plans, namely, income tax deductions for the cost of education, tax credits deducted directly from taxes due, or our preferred plan, tuition grants or vouchers made payable to the school of one's choice. Possible avenues of litigation include court action in the name of public justice envisioning equitable subsidy for non-state as well as state schools. A final alternative is to work for a constitutional amendment which would safeguard the rights of all schools as legally recognized associations in society. The conclusion therefore seems warranted that pluralism in society and in education is an idea whose time has come.

CHAPTER 2

THREE
ALTERNATIVE
SOCIAL PHILOSOPHIES

THE present sense of crisis in American society is deeper than bureaucratic red tape or white collar crime, more deep-seated than declining scholastic aptitude test scores, and more ominous than school vandalism. The crisis is one of structure and design. It concerns the way various institutions in society are organized and function. The time is ripe for the consideration of a new paradigm, a new way of looking at persistent problems, seeking needed renewal by means of structural change.

We have no desire in this book to join others at the wailing wall, issuing jeremiads against the sundry evils and injustices in society. Instead we offer a vision of hope, rooted in the Christian faith, but not limited to those who hold the Christian faith. In order to project clearly the contours of this vision of hope, we must compare and contrast it with other views of society, the state, and the schools. In so doing we will show what alternative social theories have been proposed and what they have produced, and thus, in advocating our own, also acknowledge the reality of the others.

Ways of analyzing and classifying society and social theories are legion. In our analysis we wish to identify what Leonard Boonin has called "the *categorical structures* of society rather than the features of *specific types* of existing societies." In an essay on "Man and Society: An Examination of Three Models" he outlines three basic structural models which he refers to as an "atomistic or individualistic" model, an "organic or holistic" model, and a "persons-in-relation" theory.[1] Although we use other labels, Boonin's identification of these views is very instructive. Of the first Boonin says:

> According to the atomistic view, society is merely a collection of individuals. What is real is the individuals who compose society. In metaphysical terms an atomist is a

> nominalist, i.e., one who denies the reality of abstractions and who believes that society is such an abstraction. . . . All that is real is such individuals and their states and properties.[2]

While this is neither his nor our full description of the first of these three views, it does speak to the ontological status of individuals, institutions, and society within the individualist paradigm.

In sharp contrast to his first model, Boonin depicts the second by saying:

> According to the organic-holistic model, . . . society is not a collection of individuals, but rather individuals are mere parts of society. What is real is society as a whole and members of society are only real in relation to this whole. In logical terms the relation of man to society is not that of a member to a class, but of a part to the whole.[3]

His description of the third, the persons-in-relation theory, is provocative, but inadequate for our purposes. Boonin holds that in this model

> what is real is neither the abstract individual of the atomistic model nor the concrete society of the organic model. . . . What is real is persons-in-relation. Society is a relational rather than a substantive concept. Society is a relation among persons bound together by roles which govern their interactions and which give rise to rights and obligations.[4]

While this description of the third model attempts to break the tension between the other two, it fails to argue the right of existence of a third entity, social institutions; it is simply a synthesis of the first two models.

Robert Horn's classification uses labels more like those we shall use. Horn also discovers three basic social philosophies, which he calls individualism, totalitarianism, and pluralism. He provides, moreover, an exposition of specific thinkers who are representative of these three.[5]

We are indebted to scholars such as these for their confirmation of our belief that justice can be done to the multiplicity of social theories by classifying them into three broad groups, which we have called individualism, collectivism, and pluralism. Each paradigm has its own view of reality. Each has developed its own set of principles in opposition to the others. All three have real standing in our Western world—sometimes competing with each other, sometimes overlapping, sometimes synthesized, sometimes emerging as mixed positions in theory as well as practice. Although we are aware that pluralism has been unable to gain as strong a foothold in our society as its two rival positions, it is our thesis that structural pluralism is our best hope for educational reform.

Robert Nisbet, a sociologist and the author of numerous books on social theory,[6] has stated succinctly our view of both the problem pluralism has faced in the past and the promise and potential it has for the future:

> It is the fate of pluralism that at no time in western philosophy has it ever seriously rivaled other forms of community in general appeal. The basic reason is not far to seek. As against the claims of unity, those of diversity and plurality must often seem an invitation to disorder, even anarchy. And the quest for the One is very old and sacred in the history of religion and philosophy alike. And yet . . . the attraction of the plural community . . . has been a strongly persistent feature of western culture. Living as we do in a world grown increasingly more centralized and collectivized, . . . it is possible to see in the plural community man's last best hope.[7]

As a first step we shall clarify the basic issues by identifying generically the meaning of individualism, collectivism, and pluralism, focusing on their contrasting views of society, the state, and the school. Our critique will clarify that form of pluralism we endorse as our vision of hope for the future.

GENERAL FEATURES

Individualism

View of society. Individualists, whether theistic or nontheistic, are at bottom committed to an atomistic view of society. For them the individual is the locus of authority and meaning in society. Only individuals can claim ontological status in society; that is, the fundamental unit of society is the individual. Social institutions are but ideas in our minds, names and concepts given to associations that are nothing more than an aggregate of self-determining individuals who join together because they share a common interest or purpose.

In a purely individualist social philosophy all social institutions have only a derived and therefore tentative contractual existence. Their authority and power over the individual must be carefully delimited. All forms of social institutions, from small units like the family to large ones like the state, are necessary, but they are regarded as nothing more than artificial, man-made entities and potential threats to the autonomy of the individual. For individualists a marriage, for example, is a contract between individuals who maintain their individuality, and the contract is binding only as long as the participants agree to it. Similarly, the family is merely an interacting framework for developing the rights and abilities of each family member. And business corporations are nothing more than artificial entities in which economic transactions take place among freely competing individuals.

View of the state. In a consistently individualist model, social institutions constitute man's secondary environment. Even the state is an artificial, contractual creation of free individuals acting together out of enlightened self-interest. The safeguarding of the inalienable rights of individuals is the chief function of government, which derives its powers from the consent of the governed. While this view accepts the inevitability of civil power being vested in a political order, the state remains a constant threat to the freedom of the individual. When the state no longer protects the rights of individuals, citizens have the fundamental right to abolish it and create a new one. The individualist stands for the dignity and worth and inalienable rights of each person. Eternal vigilance against state supremacy is therefore the watchword of the individualist. It is the price of true personal liberty.

View of the school. Consistent with this view of society and the role of the state in it, the ideal for individualism is a school that maximizes individual freedom for each learner in the school and maximizes the freedom of the parent in shaping that school. For individualists the locus of educational authority cannot be in the state or church, but in the individual parent or student as the consumer of educational services. Schools are thus to be founded through private initiative, and owned and operated by both profit and nonprofit organizations.

The state performs only an enabling function, and should be allowed only marginal intervention in shaping educational policy. State funding of education, the state's enabling function, is kept separate from operation and control of schools. This view, sometimes argued in terms of a free market economic theory, sometimes argued in terms of individual liberty, holds that the individual rights of parents and students come before the claims of the state in exercising control over education.

Within the school the curriculum should speak to the uniqueness of each learner. The development of individual gifts and potential has a higher priority than the development of common values and majoritarian views.

Collectivism

View of society. The obverse of individualism is collectivism. It advocates an organic, holistic view of society. The social collectivity — whether in the form of Tribe, universal Church, autocratic State, Class, political Party, utopian World Order, or some other social institution — is the primary reality. It has not merely artificial but actual ontological status. The one is more real than the many. Parts of a whole — say, citizens of the state — find their essence and meaning only within the framework of the whole. Moreover, the whole is more than the mere sum of its parts. It has a reality of its own, higher and more ultimate than that of its various elements. Meaningful human life cannot be reduced to individuals and subgroups, for universals possess a reality of existence beyond particulars. The autonomous, collective whole is normative for its subgroups and members.

Consistent with these philosophic premises, collectivists characteristically proclaim the solidarity of mankind, of people as a whole within such less than universal orders as the state, an association, or the political party. The deepest and most enduring reality in life is, however, the universal bond of brotherhood that incorporates a people into some megastructure of society. This totality structure gives the individual a corporate personality, a self beyond him- or herself. Basic rights therefore pertain solely to the controlling collectivity. Only in conformity to the collective will can people achieve unified and integrated lives. Such a social sense of belonging is of ultimate importance. Apart from their participation in society's collective purposes individuals are nothing. The collective whole is the end of all social and cultural activity; everything else is but a means to carry it out.

View of the state. For most modern collectivists the social collectivity takes on legally concrete form in the state. The state is politically omnipotent, sovereign. Its standards are absolute. Personalized in the government and its bureaucracy, the state's power can organize all other groups and individuals to fit into its all-encompassing life. Subgroups and individuals may be granted important powers and privileges by the governing authorities, but such grants are always conditional and designed to serve the final end of making the collective whole powerful and healthy. Thus, the collective state finally integrates all within the whole; all other social institutions are but means to carry out state ends.

View of the school. Consistent with its view of society and the state, the locus of educational authority is always one single large social institution. Historically, it has sometimes been the

Church and sometimes the State. Most concrete historical situations that are dominated by the collectivist mind reflect a conflict between these two entities as the rightful locus of educational authority, and the interaction between them proceeds under some doctrine of cooperation or separation between church and state.

Modern collectivism usually posits the state as that one centralized institution capable of creating community through schools. Thus the view emerges that schools are essentially a branch of government and are both owned and operated by the state. Only such schools are funded by the state. In this view other loci of educational authority may exist, but by sufferance and not by right.

The school curriculum is the means by which students are trained to better serve society as a whole and to develop a sense of community. Teachers are agents of the state, and not of parents, and are expected to help students fit themselves into their proper place in society. Thus, in serving well the needs of the state, the educational system is able also to serve well the needs of students.

Pluralism

View of society. The term pluralism, even more than the terms individualism and collectivism, is used in so many senses that a careful definition is essential for our purposes. Our generic definition of pluralism will contrast the clearest distinctions between this social philosophy and those we have just defined.

Pluralism is not simply a synthesis of, much less a compromise between, individualism and collectivism. It represents a third way of viewing the elements of society. Whereas the other two define the discrete individual or the collective whole as the locus of value and give higher ontological status to one or the other, pluralism holds that man is by nature a social creature. He therefore always stands in a plurality of social relationships. Thus he can never be reduced to either a mere atomistic individual or a mere integer in some social whole.

Accordingly, pluralism rejects the ultimacy of the individual standing apart from societal structures integral to his nature. It posits instead a persons-in-associations model as the framework within which man's individuality finds meaning. This view also denies that some large institution can lay claim to being the all-embracing social structure or the only one in which ultimate meaning is located. Pluralism holds instead that multiple social structures are real and meaningful. Societal entities, such as family, school, church, business corporations, and state, all have ontological standing. Sometimes called mediating structures, sometimes called societal spheres, these social realities exist alongside the state, and must be fully accorded their own rights of existence.

Various kinds of associations and institutions thus have standing before the law and have the right to protection. Their rights are analogous to, but not identical with, those accorded to individuals in the social philosophy of individualism. Structural pluralism, therefore, as the term implies, regards society as embracing a plurality of identities, a plurality of associations or institutions, each functioning in its own distinct sphere of influence. Concretely this means, for example, that worship belongs to the church, and not the state or business corporations; parenting belongs to the family, and not to the school or a labor association.

View of the state. The state in this view is neither the single all-embracing structure, having higher ontological status than any other social institution, as in collectivism; nor does it have a purely artificial, derived, and contractual status, as in individualism. It has its own distinct identity and sphere of influence. It is a state with a specifically limited scope, limited by and balanced by the rights of other social groupings and spheres. Its specific function is to promote public justice, to balance the rights and responsibilities of the other social spheres, to adjudicate differences between them as well as between individuals within them, and to promote and protect the rights of all of them. The state is the balance wheel which regulates and coordinates the work of the other wheels, ensuring a proper intermeshing of functions, and facilitating cooperation in partnership.

View of the school. Pluralism regards neither the family, the church, nor the state as the rightful locus of authority in education. That authority is vested in the school as an academic institution. The school is one of the multiple social structures that are all equally real and have ontological status; as an academic enterprise it has its own structural identity and sphere of authority. The school is not subsumed under the state, nor under the church or family, although it has working relationships with all three. The school serves neither state purposes, as in collectivism, nor purely personal or parental purposes, as in individualism, but is free to develop its own.

While parental authority is for the family and not the school, parents exercise choice in selecting the school that best fits their values. Similarly, ecclesiastical authority is for the church and not the school, but the church exercises its role in education by shaping its members' perceptions of life and learning. The state also has its own role, that of ensuring social justice and providing equal access to education for all. It must refrain from controlling the internal life of the school. In the name of justice and equity it may not discriminate in its funding policies to favor one educational philosophy over another.

Structural pluralism recognizes, therefore, one locus of educational authority, namely, the school, and assigns to the educational leaders within this academic sphere the responsibility for curricular programs and appropriate school policy, with the state cast into a supporting and enabling role.

CRITICAL REFLECTIONS

Three sets of images illustrate the social philosophies we have just sketched. Individualism is represented by a collection of atoms, with no social reality apart from their individual identity. Collectivism is a body, each part having no life and identity apart from the whole body, and the whole being more real than the sum of its parts. Pluralism is illustrated by a clock, in which the function of each wheel is equally real, while the whole is coordinated by a balance wheel.

It seems fair to say that all social models in the history of our Western world fit one or another of these three basic types. A fourth theory of society, offering a principled alternative to individualism, collectivism, and pluralism, has not yet emerged. There are many variations upon these three fundamental models, but such variations emerge primarily at the pragmatic level of public policy. There indeed we encounter a host of sometimes strange, sometimes creatively ingenious mixtures of these three paradigms. At bottom, however, these three exhaust all the available basic models.

Critique of Individualism

From a pluralist point of view, individualist social theory reflects a right insight gone wrong. Individualism does indeed embody an element of truth, for individual people do matter. Human rights are crucial. The individual is important, but he or she is not all-important. People are not their own religious starting-point, nor are they autonomous, a law unto themselves. Individual rights are not absolute and ultimate. There are norms that transcend the individual, to which he or she is subject, that define who he or she is. According to these norms, men and women are always in relationship to other men and women. These associations are intrinsic to their very being. From the very dawn of history human life is inextricably bound up in a web of relationships. A human is by definition a contextual being, a social creature. Individual human rights are therefore integrally related to the social order, the social environment within which we live out our lives.

Individualism makes one's sense of belonging to a community a theoretical problem for which the system provides no happy answer. Individualism begins by defining man as a being sufficient in himself. Only as an afterthought does it find ways to account for self-sufficient individuals being related to each other in communities. All such attempts turn out to be artificial, once social relationships are viewed as ancillary to man's real nature. Individualism simply ignores the fact that sociality and communality are structured into the creation of man's inner being.

Individualism therefore underestimates the associational character of human life within the creation order. At bottom it violates the solidarity of the social order and fails to acknowledge the radical unity of the human race. It atomizes people, disrupts true community, and fragmentizes society. As the Dutch philosopher, Herman Dooyeweerd, writes:

> According to the divine creation ordinances our temporal social order is not built up from atomistically construed autonomous individuals. The very birth of every child from the union of a set of parents is incompatible with an individualistic theory. [8]

Thus individualism represents a serious compromise of the Biblical view of reality. It is Christian in the sense that it takes man seriously, as Christianity does, viewing man as the image of God. But it is nonetheless a compromise. It takes individual man too seriously, ascribing to him an independence and autonomy which obscures his position of creaturely dependence. Individualism is therefore an impossible possibility: possible in that some tenaciously cling to it, but impossible in that as a social theory it cannot be implemented consistently. It lacks social substance. It belies man's deep-seated intuitive conviction that there is a fundamental unity to the human race and to human life. In the end individualism loses the very thing it is most concerned to protect: individual human rights within the public legal order. Personal justice can be properly protected only within an associational view of society. As Dooyeweerd says, only when the rights of individuals are theirs by virtue of their being members of a community or association and not as private persons can those rights be assured. [9]

Since individualism fails to recognize the importance of associational pluralism, it is not surprising that it regularly swings pendulum-style over to some form of collectivism and comes to expression with features of both social philosophies.

William James (1842–1910). Individualism is not simply a theoretical construct but one which is operative in American education. Its most prominent spokesman in the last century was William James. It is estimated that nine out of ten teachers studying psychology around the turn of the century read the works of James, especially his *Talks to Teachers*. He led the way in making empirical methods in psychology a matter of serious classroom consideration. His pupil-centered pedagogy was based upon a quietly assumed, largely nonarticulated individualist social philosophy. Invariably he appealed to the personal virtues, the heroic powers, the moral values of free individuals. His social comments, therefore, seldom moved beyond the maxim "live and let live."[10] This stance evokes Merle Curti's judgment that James's "psychological emphasis tended to make the school child-centered, rather than society-centered; and by doing so gave scientific support to individualism in American life at the expense of social values." By means of his theories of education James "made the American doctrine of 'rugged individualism' seem glorious, appropriate, and never to be forfeited."[11] Thus James captured the predominantly individualist social ideals of many Americans and gave them standing and respectability in education.

The key to both woe and weal in society, the state, and the schools, according to James, lies in the inner creative impulse of individual people. Human problems and solutions alike are rooted in the inner man, not in social structures or collective wholes. Social and political injustice, inequities in educational opportunity between the aristocratic elite and the urban poor, even severe privation among the working class—all this can be heroically endured, even romanticized, if only men display inner nobility of character. James's views generated little impetus toward reform of the public order. Social change comes only through the intellectual leadership of individuals. Highly gifted people must therefore be energized educationally to effect betterment in society. It is wrong either to deny or to suppress individual talent. The free exercise of one's private right of religion, free competition in the marketplace, the free interplay of ideas, with each person tolerant of the other: such a spirit of liberty creates the most favorable setting for the survival of the fittest and for social progress.

In James's view, there is no absolute truth. Truth is relative to individuals and situations. "Refusing to entertain the hypothesis of trans-empirical reality at all," James settles for what he calls a theistic and pluralistic (i.e., multi-particled) view of life and education.[12] He holds that "though one part of our experience may lean upon another part," nevertheless "experience as a whole is self-containing and leans on nothing."[13] Universals are illusory. There is, therefore, "no room for any grade or sort of truth outside of the framework of the pragmatic system, outside of that jungle of empirical workings and leadings, and their nearer or ulterior terminations, of which I seem to have written so unskillfully."[14]

At bottom James's highly developed educational philosophy, and his less highly developed theory of society, betrays a fundamental commitment to the ultimate value of the individual. He never calls this value into question, nor examines it critically; he forthrightly assumes and advocates it. He simply talks about "the common fact that here we are, a countless multitude of vessels of life, each of us pent in to peculiar difficulties, with which we must severally struggle by using whatever of fortitude and goodness we can summon up."[15]

James is, by his own confession, a "radical empiricist."[16] He stakes his philosophical claims, socially and educationally, upon the ultimate reality of concrete and tangible elements, that is, discrete particles and particulars. Wholes are but aggregates of parts. Universals are inductively understood from individual realities. According to Curti:

> With James radical empiricism stopped short of emphasizing the social whole, social institutions, and social justice, and concerned itself primarily with the role of the individual in the whole.[17]

Basic to James's empirical method is a view of reality which he calls pluralism. He argues that all world-views are either monist or pluralist. Since monism is untenable, he adopts as his starting-point pluralism, meaning little more than a view which is nonuniversal and noncollective. He speaks accordingly of a "pluralism of independent powers."[18] What James calls pluralism is actually equivalent to relativistic individualism. He describes it in this way: "Pluralism, accepting a universe unfinished, with doors and windows open to possibilities uncontrollable in advance, gives us even less religious certainty than monism, with its absolutely closed-in world." James's world-view reduced all reality to particular entities related to each other in very uncertain ways. Yet he holds that such individualism inspires a measure of hope. For "the world, it thinks, may be saved, on condition that its parts shall do their best." Yet, "as individual members of a pluralistic universe, we must recognize that, even though we do our best, the other factors also will have a voice in the result."[19]

True to his individualist commitment, James's "talks" on education are consistently couched in individualistic terms — "the teacher," "the pupil," "the individual," and "individual will."[20] If you think of students, says James, "as so many little systems of associating machinery, you will be astonished at the intimacy of insight into their operations and at the practicability of the results which you gain."[21] James nowhere speaks of education as an organic, social task. Education aims at individual adjustment to society, not at social transformation. It is child-centered, not society-centered; thus individualist, not collectivist, nor structurally pluralist. Training free individuals by helping them develop strong personal habits of virtue and morality is the best way to fit them for adaptation to their social environment. For James the goal of education is therefore "the organization of acquired habits on the part of the individual in such a way as to promote his personal well-being."[22] Thus, as Paul F. Boller puts it, "William James was a confirmed, . . . unreconstructed individualist; . . . and his philosophy of education as well as his metaphysics, epistemology, and ethics were highly individualistic."[23]

Critique of Collectivism

From a pluralist perspective, collectivism also represents a misdirected manifestation of social life. By all means, community is very important, as are human solidarity and enough sense of unity to allow society to function efficiently. But the whole, like the individual, can never itself be the all-important, all-enveloping standard for the rest of life. No human institution, however great or powerful, is the ultimate unit of society, whether the institution be the ancient city-state, the medieval church, or the modern state. Collectivism fails to honor the rightful distinction between what it takes to be the collective whole, whatever its institutional form, and the many different structures in society. It tends to make one institution a megastructure and to give it a messianic, trans-historical status, a status which the Judeo-Christian tradition reserves for the Kingdom of God alone. No earthly institution may thus be absolutized or divinized.

When collectivism is applied in practice it first blurs and eventually erases the line of demarcation between the state and society. Collectivism also obscures the identity and integrity of the many different social structures that coexist with the state. It eclipses true plurality by permitting one social institution to usurp the rightful authority of others. The end is often tyranny, however unintentional.

William T. Harris (1835–1908). The foundations of the American unified, common, and public school system as we know it today were laid around 1840 by Horace Mann. The second half of the nineteenth century witnessed a steady movement in the direction of its official establishment. One of its chief builders was Harris, a leading spokesman for collectivism in education, who led the way in designing the democratic ideals and monopolistic structure of the public school system. In 1906 James H. Canfield noted that Harris

> was quoted more frequently and with more approval by educational journals and by public-school teachers than any other American—not even excepting Horace Mann; and that he was one of the best loved as well as most widely known and influential educators in this or any country.[24]

A List of the Writings of William Torrey Harris, issued by Henry R. Evans in 1908, contains a phenomenal yet nonexhaustive register of four hundred seventy-nine published titles. Harris's influence reached its climax between 1899–1906 when he served as United States Commissioner of Education. Upon the death of Harris, a fellow educator offered this tribute: "Dr. William Torrey Harris holds a unique position in the history of American education. For nearly half a century he was mentor and intellectual guide for most of the men who within that period molded and shaped American education."[25]

Early in his teaching career Harris embraced the thought of the German philosopher Georg Hegel, whose *Philosophy of History* he claims to have read seventeen times. Harris exploited the conservative side of Hegel, and thus strengthened the typically American social attitudes of his countrymen. It was precisely the synthesis of conservative and revolutionary forces, both present in Hegel's dialectical view of history, that shaped Harris's view of society, the state, and the schools. Harris related the Christian religion both to Hegelian philosophy and to the traditional American beliefs in liberty, virtue, free enterprise, law and order, and future hope—all of which were rooted in what Harris assumed to be a common American commitment to theism, technological progress, and social Darwinism.

Harris believed that the structures of authority in the existing social order form a legitimate and necessary stage in the development of an ultimate world-spirit. Individual interests are subordinate to the good of the whole. The best way to achieve personal self-realization is by conforming to the divinely appointed world-order and by submitting to its established institutions. Ultimately all social classes will converge by being assimilated into the realizable rational destiny of all mankind. Christianity plays an instrumental role in forging this right relationship between individuals and the universal. Above all it can assist in the transmission of spiritual-cultural values, which is the central task of a unified system of education.

Harris's formative impact upon American public education is rooted in his devotion to Hegelian philosophy. He shares Hegel's idealism, ranking spiritual over material values; his evolutionary vision, evident in the idea of the unfolding progress of world-spirit; his dialectical method, believing that the historical process would eventually reconcile the residual anomalies in society; and his collectivism, the final absorption of every person into the cultural goals of a universal human civilization with America as its prototype. Harris therefore extols "the principle of the whole system"; he speaks of society as a "living organism" and the state as a "civil organism." In explaining such a concept of society Harris says that "the whole comes as a principle — the spirit that unites the details and makes them into an organism."[26] Thus, his Hegelian idealism allowed Harris as a representative social philosopher to confirm many Americans in their cherished ideals.

We find in Harris what is typical of much of Western history, a dialectical coalescence of individualist and collectivist motifs, with the latter emerging as dominant, thanks to a reliance on Hegelian social theory. Harris extols individual self-realization and the American tradition of individual freedom, but assimilates these ideals into an increasingly collectivist social order. He views this synthesis as the logical inheritance of a Roman state-centered society and an Anglo-Saxon individualism. The sweep of history lifts individuals upward to a higher plane of universal brotherhood. Signaling the great importance of history, Harris says that

> the school opens the windows of the soul that look out upon human history — upon the realm of the realized will of mankind. History is the biography not of individuals as individuals, but of institutions, the gigantic combinations of men, especially as nations. Each man in his isolated peculiarity is only a partial and imperfect realization of the humanity that is in him. He is mostly a possibility; he has realized but little of what is in him. But when he looks out upon his community, upon his nation, upon the entire race, through the window of history, he beholds his inner self reflected in a gigantic

reality. He learns to know his greater selves — those selves that are too great in all-sided completeness to be realized in a single individual life, and which, therefore, take on reality through individual combination, thus forming the great institutions of the race.[27]

True individuality can be realized only by subordination to the universal whole. Struggles between groups and classes are inevitable as mankind enters a new age; social, economic, and political conflicts are bound to arise. These antinomies lead, however, to new heights in the evolution of human civilization. Merle Curti puts it this way:

> As a Hegelian, he believed that the national state was the greatest of human institutions, necessary for civilization and for the realization of true individualism. Only through the state could the individual be free to absorb the benefits of civilization. Since the individual freely accepted the sovereignty of the state in order to secure true freedom, there could be no conflict between the interests of one and the other.[28]

The primary instrument in promoting this process of socialization is public education. Ignorance, most apparent among recent immigrants, blacks, and ghetto inhabitants, inhibits the progress of society. These groups must be brought into the mainstream of American life. With all their awkward diversities, they must be assimilated into the capitalist system, the civil religion of the American order. Education is the great elevator and unifier. The public school system trains children for the American state. It stabilizes the civil order in times of disorder. It inculcates democratic social values. It enables pupils to discover their identity and to realize their destiny collectively within the established social order. The public school system acts much like the social sciences, which work to homogenize the disparate elements of society. Though anomalies and inequities still stubbornly persist despite the great advances of the industrial revolution, the best way to remedy these imperfections is by means of universal public education.

Despite his system's complex internal dialectic, both Harris's theory and practice contributed strongly to the monopolizing trend in American education. His collectivism, drawing upon Hegelian thought, freed the individual from the peculiarities of his social group in order to assimilate him or her into the established public-legal-social order, with the public school as the chief agent of indoctrination.

Individualist-Collectivist Convergence

Collectivism and individualism have one thing in common: both tend to generate a society controlled from the top down. Collectivists arrive at this position smoothly and consistently by moving from their major ontological premise that only a universal social unit has ontological status to the social embodiment of that premise in an all-embracing megastructure. The individualist goes a different route, more indirect and circuitous. Individualists assume that society is made up of individuals who alone possess ontological status. In essence, therefore, the status of every institution in society is theoretically undercut, because all institutions are but the artificial creations of sovereign individuals. But the problem for the individual is that human beings are not self-sufficient. They need community and social institutions to meet many of their basic needs. As life becomes more complex even individualists are forced to look outside of themselves for help. While the state remains theoretically an artificial creation, it soon emerges from the artificial status it shares with every other institution to become pragmatically the most real institution in society. What therefore ontologically has no status is given a pragmatic primacy. This leaves individualists facing the same threats to their freedom as they face from a tyranny premised on the ontological primacy of a universal that manifests itself in an absolute state.

Around the turn of the century the Dutch statesman Abraham Kuyper noted that the common source of both modern individualism and collectivism is the Enlightenment philosophy of the French Revolution. He argued that the root principle of both traditions lies in the idea of "humanity emancipated from God and his established order. From this principle there develops not one line but two," namely liberal individualism and democratic socialism. The two are, however, at bottom one. For even socialism, "far from letting go of the individualistic starting-point . . . would rather found the social structure it wants to erect . . . on the sovereignty of the people, and thus on the individual will."[29]

Despite the fundamental, irreconcilable antithesis between individualism and collectivism in their views of ultimate reality, individualists are often forced pragmatically to join collectivists in accepting a megastructural view of the state. Principled individualists easily become pragmatic collectivists. This is true because individualism undercuts the ontological status of the many associations or institutions (other than the state) that meet so many of the daily needs of men and women. When these associations are weakened, people are pragmatically compelled to accept the state as the only agent capable of meeting their needs and creating some semblance of unity and order in society. Individualists may make this move reluctantly and with reservations. Collectivists do so unhesitatingly and without reservations. Nevertheless, the net effect on society, the state, and the schools is not much different. Individuals may still retain certain charter rights, but the final authority of the collectivist state is assured. In the end, individualists and collectivists become strange bedfellows, but bedfellows nonetheless. As one analyst put it:

> . . . they both presuppose society to be a system of interlocking institutions governed by the same principle of order and activity, . . . that is, both become interpretations that suppress the actual plurality, diversity, and contradiction among institutions and actions in the interests of providing a total rational account of human behavior. . . . Both theories become apologies for the most characteristic institution of the modern world: bureaucracy.[30]

Throughout the West individualists find themselves increasingly hard pressed by the persistent growth of social, economic, political, and educational institutions, which are rapidly taking on megastructural proportions. In the face of such disturbing developments individualists can do little more than bewail the trend of our times and attempt to defend certain basic human rights before the law. It is increasingly clear, however, that this is at best a holding action. There are even signs that the battle is being lost. So the conclusion must be faced: individual citizens, standing alone in their atomized existence, pose no lasting challenge to the growing power of social megastructures.

Nevertheless, our individualist-collectivist society resists pluralism, which seeks to recognize the structural rights of plural associations within the public-legal order. Such a recognition, it is feared, poses a serious threat to societal unity. The case is the same for confessional pluralism: granting official standing to the real religious differences among varying faith communities is viewed as divisive, a sectarian strategy, and a public menace. Therefore religion is made private and only cautiously accepted into public life. Either it is declared outright to be incompatible with consensus politics and disruptive of societal harmony — or its adherents are compelled to smuggle it into the public arena surreptitiously.[31]

Whether universalist institutions arise out of consistent collectivism or out of an individualism which evolves pragmatically into a contractual collectivism, mere tinkering with the system offers little promise for constructive change. Authentic reform calls for a more radical critique. As Dooyeweerd says, "The point is not to find a suitable middle road between individualism and collectivism, but to recognize the false root from which both spring forth."[32] Nothing short of fundamental reconstruction can reform the present individualist-collectivist convergence. It cannot be redirected from within simply by placing it, say, on a firmer footing or by creating more room for so-called mediating structures, or by infusing it with the higher morality of an earlier era in Western history. No consistently applied form of the individualist-collectivist coalition can really do full justice to the structural and confessional diversities inherent in contemporary society.

Increasingly in American society, both in its state and in its schools, we are being confronted by the effects of an ontological individualism that has evolved into a pragmatic collectivism. And this individualist-collectivist dilemma poses a number of vexing problems in education. Whose children are these who go to school, the family's or the state's? Can a consolidated, bureaucratic school system do justice to the prior rights of parents to make confessional decisions concerning the education of their children? In such a system, who exercises veto power, the citizen or the state? What standard shall shape the teaching-learning process, individual freedom or collective authority? What is the goal of education, personal self-realization or loyalty to the state? The responses to such questions about the schools will reflect basic assumptions about the role of the state in society. American individualism, now growing increasingly collectivist, leaves these questions hanging nebulously in the air. At best it offers ambiguous answers and takes ambivalent stands.

TOWARD PLURALISM

The Many Voices of Pluralism

Repeated calls for a more pluralist social order have arisen over the past century. It is noteworthy that such calls were being issued precisely at a time when the individualist-collectivist convergence was gaining a steadily firmer hold upon American society. The appeal of a pluralist community is as vigorous today as it had been in earlier decades, for many people sense that the individualist-collectivist synthesis is crumbling, unable to account for the persistent pluralist realities of daily experience. But there is no clear consensus among the continuing appeals for pluralism on what is meant by "pluralism."

A case in point is a study by the British scholar David Nicholls, entitled *Three Varieties of Pluralism*.[33] He opens his book with a quotation to the effect that "the concept of pluralism is ambiguous and contentious" since "one of the problems about the term 'pluralism' is the variety of connotations it possesses."[34] There is much difference, overlap, and contradiction in the use of the term pluralism. Nicholls's book therefore concentrates on "three principal uses of the term 'pluralism' by social and political theorists"—namely, the distinctive features of English, American, and colonial models of pluralism. Nicholls's analyses of the British and American versions of pluralism are particularly suited to our purposes.

Such English pluralists as J. N. Figgis, Harold Laski, G. D. H. Cole, and F. W. Maitland helped to shape a distinctive tradition of pluralist thinking that has been widely read in America since around the turn of this century. As a school of thought, their social philosophies appear to rest upon three basic tenets. First, they hold that human rights and freedoms are dependent upon a proper dispersion of power throughout society. Second, the reality of group personality embodied in social structures should be recognized in the public-legal order. Finally, as a corollary to these points, but reflecting the immediate political concern of English pluralists with the growing phenomenon of state absolutism, the notion of sovereignty vested exclusively in the state must be banished.

In America, according to Nicholls, pluralists appear "often to be justifying the political system as it actually operates in the United States." By pluralism Americans generally have in mind the interaction of freely competing interest groups, often operating through lobbies, each exerting pressure upon the state in support of its private cause, with the state acting as an amoral power broker to maintain equilibrium among these many causes. Associations abound, and Americans are great joiners. Associations are viewed, moreover, as vital to the check-and-balance process of political behavior. There are associations for capital and for labor, for manufacturers and for consumers, for churches, for teachers, for the environment, for almost every conceivable cause. Most of them are, however, single-issue organizations. Social groups of any level of complexity are merely collections of individuals, each of whom is defined by a complex of loyalties that modify each other. Politically, citizens act largely as an aggregate of private individuals, not in association. They generally vote their own set of private interests, not the common weal. Political power is therefore very decisive, tending to enthrone the principle that political might makes legal right.

31

Nicholls contends that pluralism is more satisfying than such individualism in that "a statement about a group cannot always be reduced to a series of statements about its members." He joins other English pluralists in preferring pluralism to collectivism, since groups "have an existence which does not derive from the state." Nicholls therefore concludes that "political liberty is more likely to survive in a genuine pluralist state than in other types of society."

Two American thinkers who understand pluralism as more than interest group liberalism are Robert MacIver and James Luther Adams. MacIver, a well-known sociologist,[35] advocates a "multi-group society" with a "limited or associational state" as the way to avoid the excesses of both nineteenth-century individualism and the burgeoning power of the collectivist state in the twentieth century. To preserve the rights and freedoms of the community and its associations, the state must be clearly distinguished from society. MacIver leans toward a kind of structural pluralism; he is critical of both individualism and collectivism:

> This individualist doctrine has been expressed in a great many different ways. All of them regard government as the enemy of liberty, even in those areas in which they recognize the need for government. While it has had some exponents in every age, it flourished greatly from the seventeenth to the nineteenth century, first in Western Europe and somewhat later in America. Over against it stands the doctrine of the all-embracing state — it is noteworthy that while the advocates of the first view usually speak of "government" the advocates of the second speak always of "the state." For them the state is the all-embracing unity to which we properly belong. It cannot "interfere" with our interests. If indeed we have any interests that the state disturbs, it is because we have not discovered our true interest. To that extent we are detached from the focus of our being, we have not found ourselves. Only in the state are we at one with ourselves and with our world.[36]

James Luther Adams also opposes both individualism and collectivism.[37] Like MacIver he looks to pluralism as an alternative social philosophy. As an ethicist he has been keenly interested in the history of Protestant social ethics, particularly in the theorists of voluntary associations from Johannes Althusius through Friedrich Julius Stahl and Otto Van Gierke to J. N. Figgis, F. W. Maitland, and E. Barker.

Adams contributed to the development of an associational interpretation of history. Since man is a social being, he forms groups. The different associations he forms in different periods of history, Adams believes, are a key to understanding the forms of power in a particular society.

Thus associations play a central role in Adams's social ethics. He begins with a doctrine of God as "a community-forming power." Man's response to God entails the formation of the many associations of life. These associations or institutions mediate spiritual reality and are indispensable elements of a free society. They are man's protection against atomistic individualism and collectivistic totalitarianism.

Both MacIver and Adams favor some form of pluralism. It is not clear, however, whether they do so at an ontological level or more practically at the level of public policy. And neither has brought his reflections on society and the state to bear significantly upon the issues of the schools.

During the past one hundred years, the formative period in the establishment of the nearly monopolistic public school system, credit is due primarily to the loyal opposition of Roman Catholic leaders for keeping the freedom of choice issue alive in American education. In their basically Thomist view, the state is not the sole locus of school authority. Multiple centers of authority must be recognized in the field of education. Accordingly, the educational rights of families and the church must also be upheld. This is what pluralism has generally come to mean in Roman Catholic circles. Pope Pius XI gave official formulation to this doctrine of multiple sources of school sponsorship in his 1936 encyclical on "Christian Education of Youth":

> Education is essentially a social and not merely individual activity. Now there are three necessary societies, distinct from one another and yet harmoniously combined by God, into which man is born: two, namely the family and civil society, belong to the natural order; the third, the Church, to the supernatural order. . . . Accordingly in the matter of education it is the right, or to speak more correctly, it is the duty of the State to protect in its legislation, the prior rights, already described, of the family as regards the Christian education of its offspring, and consequently also to respect the supernatural rights of the Church in this same realm of Christian education.[38]

Such a pronouncement rests upon a long and deep tradition. To that tradition Catholic educators can appeal effectively in defense of their understanding of the doctrine of educational pluralism over against the public policy consensus of the individualist-collectivist model, which locates school authority exclusively in the state.

Strong support for this doctrine also comes from outside the church. The United Nations, in Article 26 of its *Universal Declaration of Human Rights*, adopted in 1948, took the position that "parents have a prior right to choose the kind of education that shall be given to their children." The same article holds that "everyone has the right to education," and that "education shall be free, at least in the elementary and fundamental stages." The Catholic experience with American education, however, has been in stark contrast to the ideal spelled out in the United Nations *Declaration*. Keenly sensitive to this principle of freedom, Catholic educators stood up for parental rights in education as well as the church's right to operate in schools. More than any other group in American society they therefore resisted the majoritarian notion of a single locus of educational authority.

American Catholics drew further encouragement in recent years from the pronouncements of the Second Vatican Council. These documents speak forthrightly to the educational task of home, church, school, and state. The Council endorses the notion of pluralism in such language as this:

> The church gives high praise to those civil authorities and civil societies that show regard for the pluralistic character of modern society, and take into account the right of religious liberty, by helping families in such a way that in all schools the education of their children can be carried out according to the moral and religious convictions of each family.

The prior rights of parents in education are emphasized in these words:

> [For] parents, who have the first and inalienable duty and right to educate their children, should enjoy true freedom in their choice of schools. Consequently, public authority which has the obligation to oversee and defend the liberties of citizens, ought to see to it out of a concern for distributive justice, that public subsidies are allocated in such a way that, when selecting schools for their children, parents are genuinely free to follow their consciences.

The Council goes on to reassert the Thomist principle of sphere subsidiarity in relation to the state's role in education:

> Part of its [the state's] duty is to promote the education of the young in several ways: namely, by overseeing the duties

and rights of parents and of others who have a role in education, and by providing them with assistance; by implementing the principle of subsidiarity and completing the task of education, with attention to parental wishes, whenever the efforts of parents and of other groups are insufficient; and, moreover, by building its own schools and institutes, as the common good may demand.

The following excerpt appeals again to the traditional Roman Catholic principle of sphere subsidiarity to warn that a state monopoly in education means serious infringement upon basic human rights:

> But it must keep in mind the principle of subsidiarity, so that no kind of school monopoly arises. For such a monopoly would militate against the native rights of the human person, the development and spread of culture itself, the peaceful association of citizens, and the pluralism which exists today in very many societies.[39]

Leaning on this solid tradition, Roman Catholicism protested the collectivist monopoly of the governmental school system. It produced a respectable literature of dissent and maintained an alternative school system against overwhelming odds. It is rooted in an alternative view of society, the state, and the schools. Yet, this position leaves a number of questions unresolved regarding the respective roles of the home, the church, the state, and the school in the education of children. Each has rights. What, however, is the status of these respective rights and how do they relate to each other? Both in its ecclesiastical statements and its scholarly writings, Catholicism has identified the pluralism it describes with the concept of sphere subsidiarity.

When thus viewed within the classic Thomist tradition, the notion of sphere subsidiarity is at bottom a form of shared collectivism. Church and state are each viewed as collectivist institutions, each in its own sphere—the church in the sphere of the supernatural and the state in the sphere of the natural. True to the doctrine of the analogy of being, each of these "higher orders" has under it a series of "lower orders" over which it exercises jurisdiction. Thus in the realm of the natural the state has the right to operate secular schools, while in the realm of the supernatural the church has an equally legitimate right to operate religious schools. Thus this view of society, the state, and the schools is in fact little more than a shared collectivism, which divides the collectivist jurisdiction between the natural and the supernatural, the state and the church. Some families are free to send their children to public schools under state control, while others have a similar freedom with respect to nonpublic schools under church control. But the question remains whether the identity and integrity of the home, the school, and other social institutions can be maintained without rendering them subsidiary to either the church or the state.

This collectivist tendency in Roman Catholic views on education is evident in the writing of the philosopher Thomas Dubay. He argues that

> because the Catholic Church has received from God a direct commission to teach and because her function is a supernatural one, it follows that she is the primary and supreme educator of men. . . . [Further], it has been rightly remarked that the Catholic Church's right to educate is neither to be confused with nor derived from the right Catholic parents have over the education of their children. They are two distinct rights. It is thus perfectly true to say that Catholic schools exist as a result of two fundamental rights in education: the Church's divine commission to teach and the Catholic parents' rights to procure the religious formation of their offspring.[40]

Within Protestantism, the Calvinist tradition has also offered a version of structural pluralism. In contrast to the Catholic concept of sphere subsidiarity, the Calvinist tradition speaks of sphere sovereignty. This simply means that no sphere is subsumed under any other, but each operates with a sovereignty of its own. Perhaps this tradition is best expressed in H. Meeter's book *Basic Ideas of Calvinism*.[41]

The role assigned to the state is always crucial to any conception of society and its schools. Rejecting both state-absolutism and individualism, Meeter describes a theory in which a number of social boundaries are clearly delineated. One of these is expressed as follows:

> A third boundary limiting the State's authority lies in such natural spheres in society as the home, the school, the church, economic and social organizations, which do not owe their origin or mode of existence to the State, and have their own task entrusted to them by God. These are sovereign within their own boundaries. Only insofar as any of these should overstep its limits, or endanger the welfare of other spheres, or of individuals, or of the State, or insofar as by neglect of its duty should endanger the well-being of the State, has the State here a duty to perform. A case in point would occur when parents neglect the proper training

of their children, or when a husband tyrannizes over his wife, or one group in society tyrannizes over another group.[42]

Thus we have here an affirmation of the positive, but limited role of the state in society. Its basic task is to administer public justice evenhandedly among the various societal structures and faith communities. This task includes regulatory functions, coordinating and balancing the rights and freedoms of the various institutions and groups in society. It also includes protective functions, safeguarding the identity and integrity of each sphere in the pursuit of its own unique calling. In the face of injustice and inequity the state must act as umpire or referee to restore a just order. Normally, however, it may not interfere in the internal life of other spheres in society. It must serve an enabling role, facilitating the free and equitable development of each social sphere in partnership with others.

This Calvinist conception of pluralism implies a view of the school that is different from the Roman Catholic view. The school is a unique sphere in its own right, with an area of jurisdiction of its own. In offering examples of the application of this general principle, Meeter has this to say about the school as a distinct academic sphere:

> In a scientific* organization, as a school or university, no State can rightfully dictate the scientific conclusions to which such an institution must come. But the laws which are to be enforced are the laws inherent in the sphere itself, and the administration of the school naturally falls to those who are at the head of such a scientific organization as scientific leaders.[43]

Elsewhere Meeter makes it quite clear that such a position does not entail the individualist's rejection of a proper state role in education. Indeed, in its role as administrator of public justice the state can engage in "operating educational institutions for the sake of such citizens as would neglect the education of their children,"[44] even to the extent of breaking monopolies by direct subsidy to those in need of aid.

Meeter claims that this view of society, the state, and the schools can take its place with honor alongside other social philosophies. It has been so recognized by eminent scholars; Meeter appeals to the following statement by Ernst Troeltsch:

*The term "scientific" here is used not to denote either the method or content of the natural sciences, but to suggest a systematic body of thought and the scholarly work in it.

> Calvinism has balanced the two aspects of this antinomy
> [the relation between the individual and the community] in
> a very important and powerful manner. . . . Indeed, the
> great importance of the Calvinistic social theory does not
> consist merely in the fact that it is one great type of Christian
> social doctrine; its significance is due to the fact that it is one
> of the great types of sociological thought in general.[45]

In spite of such tributes to Calvinist social theory, it must be admitted that the advocates of a Calvinist view of pluralism have not been widely heard. Thus the impact of this understanding of structural and confessional pluralism on society, state, and school has been minimal.

One conclusion therefore forces itself upon us: a pluralist social paradigm has not been a strong contender on the American scene. For the last century America's vision of structural and confessional pluralism has suffered from a steady and now nearly total eclipse. The restoration of that vision will lead to a new advent of pluralism.

The Two Dimensions of Pluralism: Structural and Confessional

Pluralism has thus come to expression in many ways. The Calvinist notion of a pluralist social order sketched by Meeter, that which grows out of a relatively unknown but important Reformation tradition, is the expression we seek to explore in detail. It is important to bear in mind that this Calvinist pluralist tradition incorporates two basic dimensions: *structural* pluralism and *confessional* pluralism.

At bottom pluralism is anchored structurally in the ordered reality of creation. The world came into existence not as chaos, but as cosmos, a harmonious whole with a unified orientation and direction. Life is fundamentally of one piece. It has a unifying focus. Therefore our rich diversity of social tasks does not end in fragmentation. As life unfolds historically, taking on ever more complex and differentiated forms, this profound unity remains intact. Pluralism therefore envisions various spheres of social activity bound together in relationships of cooperation and partnership. The radically disruptive powers of evil are undeniably at work in the world, eroding human solidarity and social unity. But reconciliation is also a present reality. Redemption is for the restoration of creation, including a renewal of the social order.

The divinely ordained unity of the creation therefore carries with it an abiding normativity for societal life. This principle has been formulated in the idea of *sphere universality*. Created reality is not a seamless garment. It also discloses a rich diversity of cultural tasks, sets of human relationships, and spheres of social action. Dietrich Bonhoeffer drives this point home in his discussion of "the four mandates." He argues that

> the world is relative to Christ, no matter whether it knows it or not. This relativeness of the world to Christ assumes concrete form in certain mandates of God in the world. The Scriptures name four such mandates: labour, marriage, government, and church. . . . It is God's will that there shall be labour, marriage, government, and church in the world; and it is His will that all these, each in its own way, shall be through Christ, directed towards Christ, and in Christ. . . . This means that there can be no retreating from a "secular" into a "spiritual" sphere.[46]

We may quarrel with Bonhoeffer over the number of "mandates," but the point is that these God-given mandates are real, each claiming our active response in its own sphere of endeavor. As a single ray of light passing through a prism gets refracted into a multi-faceted rainbow of colors, so man's single calling opens up into a richly diversified spectrum of social callings. This range of callings, given with creation, develops historically, taking on contemporary shape and form in a diverse but harmonious group of social institutions. Each unit of the social structure performs its own unique function like the cogs of a clockwork, thus contributing to the unified operation of the timepiece as a whole, so that each social sphere has its own coexisting right of existence and reason for existence. No association lords it over another. Nor may one exercise its authority at the expense of another. Each has its own rightful area of jurisdiction. Each is entitled to full and equal standing before law. One is not reducible to another, nor may one assimilate another. Each claims its own inalienable, inviolable, nontransferable, and noninterchangeable rights and responsibilities. This is *structural* pluralism.

Our concept of pluralism also includes *confessional* pluralism. We live in a religiously splintered world, surrounded by a wide range of contrasting faith communities. Pluralism, as an alternative way of living together in society, seeks to reckon seriously with these very real philosophical differences. It seeks reforms by which the public legal rights as well as the private rights of all groups in society can be safeguarded within a common democratic order. Fundamental to this vision is the free exercise of religion in society, the state, and the schools, the universal right to equal protection under law, with justice and equity and liberty for all.

Although this pluralist view comes to its clearest expression here within a particular Christian tradition, it is not sectarian or parochial. It brings with it a cosmic perspective that embraces concerns common to all men. It disavows special pleading for the privileged status of established groups and vested interests. It is more truly cosmopolitan than either individualism or collectivism. Such pluralism not only recognizes the rightful diversity of various societal structures, but it also honors the religious heterogeneity of different faith communities within the public order. The rights that it affirms for one group in society it also insists upon for others.

This view of structural and confessional pluralism also acknowledges the fact that people who in principle hold to other perspectives often share some of these pluralist insights at a public policy level. Many who are basically individualist or collectivist in their outlooks nevertheless arrive at pluralist conclusions, prompted often by very practical considerations. We believe that this is so for a very fundamental reason, a reason rooted in the very nature of created reality. For, if this world is God's world, then the will of God for life in His world holds for all men and women. Then the impinging power of His transcendent norms for the way we live, and move, and have our being in society, the state, and the schools, will somehow find an echo in the way people, knowingly or unknowingly, respond to God's laws for human relationships.

A Reformation Tradition

At various times and places this pluralist vision for society has played a notable though generally rather subdued role in shaping the course of Western culture. It came to renewed expression during the Reformation era. Since then it has found its strongest support in the Calvinist tradition, particularly in the social philosophies of John Calvin himself, of Johannes Althusius, and of Abraham Kuyper.

Calvin's "Constructive Revolution."[47] The fundamental principle in Calvin's thought is the absolute authority of the Word of God. That Word speaks not merely to so-called sacred spiritual issues, understood in a narrowly spiritual way, but to life as a whole, including home, school, church, associations, the state, and all other institutions. Scripture serves as "spectacles" for "bleary-eyed men," enabling them to discern anew the bearing of the creation order upon the social order. In the Word we meet Christ "clothed with the gospel," as Calvin says, occupying center stage in the unfolding historical drama of redemption and standing at the crossroads of all human history. The Biblical message is therefore cosmic in scope. For redemption is the restoration of a fallen creation. The coming Kingdom is the all-embracing goal of history. All societal life, therefore, in its total extent and in all its parts, is religion in the sense of a coherent complex of ongoing responses, obedient and disobedient, to the overarching and undergirding power of divine revelation. The sovereign rule of God in Jesus Christ is therefore the unifying theme in Calvin's world-view.[48]

Given such convictions, Calvin found it impossible to accept uncritically the Constantinian-medieval pattern of the social order that his generation had inherited from fifteen hundred years of Western Christianity. It was a tradition that assumed the shared collectivity of church and state and that was deeply embedded in a synthesis of Christian and Aristotelian motifs, a synthesis that had been granted semi-official status on the basis of the grand social design set forth by Thomas Aquinas.

This Constantinian-Thomistic model was indeed hospitable to plural communities in society as adjuncts of church and state. Yet Calvin's holistic world-view led him to take issue with this long-standing paradigm of shared jurisdictions and the dualist beliefs and assumptions upon which it rested. The traditional pattern rent the religiously unified fabric of the social order. It compromised the integrity of the church and resulted in a secularized state. It canonized a dubious dichotomy, resulting in two orders of reality, one religious, the other secular.

In response, therefore, Calvin introduced a radical break with the old order: God's Word is no less normative for the state than for the church, though the nature of its claim is different for each institution.[49] Both are divinely ordained and therefore both are legitimately Christian spheres of service. Accordingly Calvin rebukes all negative attitudes toward the state. He decries all tendencies to withdraw from it. Concerning church and state, he says that these "two governments are not antithetical."[50] Every institution in society — home, academy, the marketplace, and industry, as well as the church and the state — offers an arena in which Christians fulfill their earthly callings.

Calvin's holistic view of society is partially compromised by his discussion of the "two kingdoms" and the "twofold jurisdiction." Calvin clearly offers a breakthrough toward a new view of society, justifying the claim of John T. McNeill, the American church historian, that "all modern western history would have been unrecognizably different without the perpetual play of Calvin's influence."[51] The foundation of a pluralist social theory certainly ranks high among his major contributions. However, the internal distinctions that Calvin makes within his holistic view of society still betray remnants of earlier scholastic patterns of thought. Even for Calvin, various social institutions are viewed as satellites clustered around the two leading social magnitudes, church and state. Thus the wholeness and inner integrity of his position are indeed partially compromised.

Basically, however, Calvin's social philosophy is not a reversion to the Constantinian-Thomist paradigm. It would be truer to Calvin's intent to interpret his references to "the two jurisdictions" as an intuitive reaching out toward what later came to be called the separation of church and state. In Calvin this idea means the separation of church and state as two social institutions, not — as in much of contemporary thought — the separation of a so-called public-secular from a private-religious order.[52] Thus he sowed seeds of social reformation, which, gradually germinating and ripening, bore their fruit in a later generation. Calvin grasped intuitively the idea that Althusius later set forth as associations-in-consociation, and that Kuyper still later elaborated under the concepts sphere sovereignty and sphere universality.[53]

The overall direction of Calvin's thinking is clear, however, pointing toward structural pluralism as the pattern for a just society. Confessional pluralism had not yet come to expression in his thinking or in that of his contemporaries. They were still living too much in the shadow of a society shaped by the ideal of an enforced universal Christendom. In fact, Calvin was sometimes guilty of violating the best even in his own conception of structural pluralism, as in the case of Servetus. The basic principles of a pluralist social order are, however, incipiently present in Calvin's thought. In that light we can understand his critique of an evil "everywhere dominant in Germany," where the state has "too much power in spiritual things." Similarly, Calvin criticizes the regime of Henry, King of England, because "they gave him supreme power in all things."[54]

Calvin's clearest statement of his basic principles on the social order occurs in two New Testament passages in his commentaries on the Bible. Commenting on Ephesians 5:21–6:9, where Paul admonishes his hearers to submit themselves mutually to each other within various life relationships, Calvin says:

> Paul comes now to the various groups; for besides the universal bond of subjection, some are more closely bound to each other, according to their respective callings. Society consists of groups, which are like yokes, in which there is a mutual obligation of parties. . . . So in society there are

six different classes, for each of which Paul lays down its peculiar duties.[55]

Calvin strikes a similar note in his lecture on I Peter 1:12– 17. There he focuses on this text: "Be ye subject for the Lord's sake to every ordinance of men." These words occasion the following comment:

> The verb KTIZEIN in Greek, from which KTISIS comes, means to form or construct a building. It corresponds to the word "ordinance," by which Peter reminds us that God the Maker of the world has not left the human race in a state of confusion, so that we live after the manner of beasts, but has given them, as it were, a building regularly formed, and divided into several compartments. It is called a human ordinance, not because it has been invented by men, but because it is a mode of living well-arranged and clearly ordered, appropriate to man.[56]

By carefully collating such concepts as "groups," "classes," "parties," "gifts," "callings," "yokes," "offices," and "compartments," each with its own God-given "bounds," "operations," "mutual obligations," "peculiar duties," and "ordinances," terms which Calvin uses here and in related passages, it is clear that he is opening the door to those structuring principles for a pluralist social order that were clarified and expanded by Althusius and Kuyper.

True to his view of the ordered unity and diversity among the structures of society, the life of the Geneva Academy, founded by Calvin in 1559, was interrelated in various ways with both the church and the state. But it was also able to maintain its own identity as a social institution within its own sphere of operations. The Dutch church historian, D. Nauta, notes the significance of the Academy in this sense:

> Naturally church and state must be understood here in keeping with Calvin's unique vision. This explains why at the founding of the Academy the absence of a papal bull and an imperial certificate was not even noticed. Geneva itself justified the right to establish the Academy. . . . With respect to the Academy the major emphasis fell upon the church, or rather the office of preaching. For ministers co-operated in the appointment of teachers and professors. The government was granted the right of confirmation. All instructors were also subject to ecclesiastical discipline. It would be inaccurate, however, to interpret this relationship as placing the Academy, and thereby science, under the

church. Church and school were meant to be two institutions standing side by side in society.[57]

Althusius's "Consociational Democracy." Johannes Althusius (1557–1638) belongs to the post- and counter-Reformation era. With modernity came the secular state, which was beginning to assume collectivist proportions, displacing the universal claims of the medieval church. Intense struggles erupted along church-state lines. Given the rapidly changing religious climate, there was little chance for the church ever to regain its former power. The immediate threat to a free and just society was the burgeoning power of an absolutist state. This was the challenge Althusius faced. In responding to it, Althusius stood virtually alone in offering a pluralist alternative. Robert Nisbet describes him as "one of the authentically great minds in the history of social theory and the true founder of the philosophy of plural community."[58] In sketching Althusius's ideas we draw upon his best-known book, *Politics*, published in 1614.[59]

According to Althusius, the sovereignty of God is the fundamental starting-point in rightly ordering the life of society. Absolute sovereignty belongs to God alone. This supreme, all-embracing sovereignty is rooted in God's work in creation, preservation, and redemption.

Earthly sovereignty, of whatever sort, is wholly dependent upon the sovereign God. By His almighty and beneficent will He establishes order in the world and confers upon each social structure its own measure of sovereignty. All earthly sovereignty is therefore derived sovereignty. It is not inherent in any office. It is never perpetual, universal, or above the law. It is always subservient to the will of God revealed in creation and in Scripture. Those endowed with it are responsible and answerable to God for their exercise of it. No ruler, administrator, or official of any rank wields unlimited authority. God retains His sovereign prerogatives as a charter right even in the act of bestowing certain sovereignties upon the various institutions in the social order.

Two comments are in order at this point. First, standing in the Reformation tradition, Althusius began to sense the significance of the Biblical doctrine of creation as the basis for a renewed understanding of God's good order for societal life. Second, Althusius redefined the traditional idea of sovereignty, the meaning of which had been reduced to political sovereignty. This older doctrine, lending support to the theory of the divine right of kings, granted rulers the authority to wield absolute power in society; it held that they are bound by no positive laws, that they stand-above the law, and that they acknowledge no earthly sovereignty alongside them. In redefining the idea of sovereignty, Althusius was led to take issue with all these deeply entrenched notions of political sovereignty.

God's sovereign rule in society, Althusius held, is direct. It is not mediated through either church or state. Neither church nor state is a collective whole of which other social institutions are parts. Each "association" exercises its own kind of sovereignty in keeping with its own unique nature. Regarding church and state, Althusius says that "each demands the whole man," but "according to the nature of each association." This holds also for all associations — families, guilds, schools, etc. Each has its own holy calling within the "symbiosis" (life together in society). One cannot legislate for the internal affairs of another. The ultimate goal of all, in their symbiotic unity, is God's glory and our neighbor's welfare.

In identifying the workings of the various "communities in community," Althusius distinguishes three basic kinds of social structures. First, there is the natural association of marriage and family, including the extended family and kinship clan. This is genuinely a social unit. The natural association is in a sense the model for all other associations. It holds an integral place and plays a significant role in the public legal order of the community as a whole. Next there are the collegial associations, which are vocationally oriented and voluntary in nature. These colleges include such social organizations as guilds of bakers and tailors, monasteries, unions of craftsmen and merchants, universities, parishes, mutual aid societies, social clubs, cultural organizations, etc. These associations also belong to and participate integrally in the life of the larger consociation.

Finally, there is the civil association, state government. Society, Althusius held, is not composed of an aggregate of abstract, atomized individuals who have no meaning or social status apart from their citizenship in the state. Their social identity is already established by their membership in the various natural and collegial associations. People participate in the symbiotic, consociational public community known as the state as members of these prior associations. Natural and collegial associations, not individual citizens, are the fundamental, functional building-blocks for the life of the state. The state as a public symbiosis rests upon the political sovereignty bestowed by God upon the people. They in turn exercise it communally in forming governments — local, regional, national — to serve the commonweal, the consociated well-being of the entire citizenry in all their life relationships.[60]

45

The state may therefore not exercise its authority at the expense of other associations. It may not negate, undermine, devour, or absorb them. Nor may it extend its powers to the internal affairs of other associations, for this would be an unwarranted intrusion upon their unique sovereignties. The very well-being of the political association depends upon a healthy and active plurality of natural and voluntary associations in society. Therefore no magistrate may act in his own right. He administers his office as a public servant, exercising the political sovereignty delegated to him consociationally by the body politic as it answers communally to its divine calling.

Accordingly, Althusius held that political sovereignty is never absolute, but always relative and limited, and that for four reasons. First, it is wholly dependent upon the divine world order. Second, the ruler is accountable to the political consociation. The powers of the state are limited, third, by the rights of other associations, and finally by its own divinely established internal law and order.

It is not surprising, then, that Althusius has been credited with providing the systematic climax of the reformational social thought of the sixteenth century, and with formulating the first clear statement of the complementary principle that in the later Calvinist tradition came to be known as sphere sovereignty and sphere universality.[61] Yet, from within the Calvinist perspective itself, it is possible to criticize the Althusian social philosophy on a number of points: (1) it betrays remnants of an earlier scholastic notion of hierarchy among social institutions; (2) legal norms are derived in part from theories of natural law; (3) a notion of popular sovereignty is present that leans toward a social contract theory of political authority; (4) theoretical precision is still lacking in delineating the structural and functional lines among the various associations in their consociational unity. Even granting all that, however, the contributions of Althusius to a pluralist social philosophy are considerable.[62]

Kuyper's "Sphere Sovereignty." A free church, a free school, and a free state within a free society: this formula for public policy captures Abraham Kuyper's (1837– 1920) vision of a just social order. In his time a commitment to the autonomy of human reason, embodied in free and independent individuals, a commitment developed by Enlightenment thought in the aftermath of the French Revolution, had led to the emergence of a collectivist state. All sectors of society, including church and school, had fallen under its control.

In the nineteenth-century Netherlands, however, a grassroots revival of classic Calvinism was beginning to stir among evangelical Christians. As preacher, journalist, educator, author, labor leader, elected representative, social reformer, and eventually Prime Minister of his country, Kuyper led a crusade to break the stranglehold of a secular state over the various institutions of society. He held that the natural line of demarcation between the authority of the state and that of the various spheres of society, established in the creation order, must be faithfully maintained if freedom and justice are to prevail. The rights of families, churches, schools, the press, and other associations must be defended against the encroachments of the modern state, for each social institution has its own God-given, inalienable reason for existence and right of existence. In the 1860's and '70's, therefore, Kuyper played a large role in organizing an alternative school movement. He argued the cause of public justice and educational equity for all, regardless of who should benefit by it, be they humanists, Roman Catholics, Jews, or Calvinists. This "school struggle" went on for half a century. Meanwhile, in 1880 he also led the way in founding a free Christian university in Amsterdam, one free of both church and state control.

Clearly, Kuyper was not an ivory-tower scholar. Throughout his career he thrust himself fully into the intensely spiritual struggles of his day. He sensed the deeply religious crises of Western civilization, standing then at the threshold of a post-Christian era. Superficial remedies were of no use where only a radical address to societal problems could help. Kuyper therefore emphasized the importance of facing up squarely to the conflicting "root-principles," the antithetical "life-principles" at work in modern society. He saw that Christianity rightly understood had historically "not merely pruned the branches and cleared the stem, but reached down to the very root of our human life."[63] In confronting fundamental issues, therefore, "if the battle is to be fought with honor and with a hope of victory, then principle must be arrayed against principle."[64]

Out of principle, therefore, Kuyper developed a pluralist alternative to both individualist and collectivist social philosophies. He opposed both of the prevailing theories—"that of Popular-sovereignty, as it has been antitheistically proclaimed in Paris in 1789; and that of State-sovereignty as it has of late been developed by the historico-pantheistic school of Germany. Both of these theories," he held, "are at heart identical,"[65] since both replace the sovereignty of God with some form of human sovereignty. Against the radical individualism of the Enlightenment Kuyper argued that "God might have created men as disconnected individuals; . . . but that was not the case. Man is created from man, and by virtue of his birth he is organically united with the whole race."[66] In individualism power "comes from the individual man to the many men; and in the many men, conceived as *the people*, there is thus hidden the deepest fountain of all sovereignty."[67] Though proclaimed in the name of freedom, individualism has not "resulted in anything else but the shackling of liberty in the irons of State-omnipotence."[68]

Kuyper was equally vigorous in his rejection of collectivism as a view of society, the state, and the schools. He recognized that, as a reaction to individualism, collectivism was mistaken in viewing society as "the sum total of the individuals"; yet it has "correctly seen that a people is no aggregate, but an organic whole."[69] He opposed collectivism just as vigorously, however, since it leads to the state becoming a law unto itself and reduces civil right to political might: "The State may never become an octopus which stifles the whole of life. It must occupy its own place, on its own root, among the other trees of the forest; and thus it must honor and maintain every form of life which grows independently in its own sacred autonomy."[70] It may therefore be said that Kuyper

> saw that both liberalism and socialism failed to comprehend the true nature of authority and freedom. Liberalism asserted the freedom of the individual, but failed to appreciate his involvement in social groups with their respective authority. On the other hand, socialism saw man as a community bound together by the authority of the State, but it failed to acknowledge the freedom of men in different spheres of life in society and nature, each operating under the immediate sovereignty of God, yet relatively independent of each other.[71]

At the heart of Kuyper's pluralist alternative lies the belief that man is not the measure of social reality, nor is any given social institution, whether it be the medieval church or the modern state. No social structure may lord it over another, for each sphere "has above it nothing but God."[72] The state and the social spheres "both have the same sacred obligation to maintain their God-given sovereign authority."[73] Any people, therefore, that abandons the rights of the family, the school, the university, or other associations to an absolutist state is inviting tyranny.

Appealing to the Biblical doctrine of creation order, Kuyper, relying on the pioneering work of Groen van Prinsterer (1801–1876),[74] elaborated the idea of sphere sovereignty as the basis of a Christian social philosophy. God's creating Word is the law for ordering our life relationships in all spheres of human endeavor. Each sphere has its own unique, inviolable, delegated authority. No sphere — not even those two great social institutions that tend to make imperialistic claims, the church and the state — may suppress or tyrannize or draw parasitically upon others. Each should act as a partner with all the others. In a just society there is no room for hierarchies of power and authority. Within each coordinate sphere man must exercise his divinely given office and calling, and men together must honor the rightful roles of each sphere in community life — just as each geared wheel in a clock performs its own function, and yet together with the others each contributes to the unified operation of the clock as a whole. In Kuyper's own words:

> Family, business, science, art, and so forth are all social spheres which do not owe their existence to the State, and do not derive the law of their life from the superiority of the state, but obey a higher authority within their own bosom, an authority which rules by the grace of God, just as the sovereignty of the State does.[75]

Impelled by this vision, Kuyper mobilized his beleaguered followers, mostly farm hands and poor laborers, and formed a common-cause coalition with kindred spirits in the Roman Catholic community. Acting jointly, the coalition launched a decades-long campaign against the prevailing notion that schools are by right state-controlled institutions and against the idea that education is a proper task of civil government. In the face of stubborn and overwhelming opposition from the establishment and charges of disloyalty and the disruption of national unity, despite repeated and crushing setbacks and defeats, the movement for public justice and equity in education gained momentum. Eventually the fundamental rightness of this position was accepted by all parties involved. Since about 1920, therefore, it has been the official public policy of the Netherlands to honor the prior right of family choice in education, to deal with all philosophies of education impartially, and to distribute revenues equitably to all schools, governmental and nongovernmental alike.[76] Kuyper's basic principles of structural and confessional pluralism in society, the state, and the schools were largely responsible for the success of this movement for justice and equity.

The tradition of pluralist social thought found its clearest expression in European countries during different eras in Western history. The work of Calvin, Althusius, and Kuyper demonstrates in addition, however, the real potential for a pluralist alternative to the contemporary convergence of individualist and collectivist traditions in our own society. More specifically, these pluralist views merit serious reconsideration as we rethink the current relationships in this country between society, the state, and the schools. Such a vision is not entirely alien to our American experience. To make this clear we turn now to the evolution of these ideas in American history.

CHAPTER 3

THE RIGHTS
OF ASSOCIATIONS
IN AMERICAN
THOUGHT
AND LAW

In Puritan New England, widely respected political thought maintained that associations had rights. By the time of the Revolution and throughout the nineteenth and well into the twentieth century, American political theory and law granted rights only to individuals. In American law today, both individuals and, in an ambiguous fashion, associations have rights.

At the outset we want to make clear that our use of the word *association* does *not* in any way imply an individualist understanding of the term, the mere coming together of individuals who share a common interest or purpose. In a nonindividualist social philosophy associations are such corporate social entities as the family, the church, the school, the business corporation, and the state. Associations or institutions are thus not simply the aggregate of individuals who make up the family, the church, the school, the corporation, and the state. The meaning of such groups is not exhausted by the meaning of the sum of their individual members. An association has meaning as an association. Institutions as such have ontological reality; they exist as corporate social entities.

Of course it is very true that the United States Supreme Court recognized the rights of the business corporation at an early date in our history. But it is our contention that while associations like a business corporation were sometimes acknowledged to have rights, such rights were limited, and they were granted either on the basis of the right of *individuals* to associate or on the assumption that associations were fictitious or artificial *persons*. Both arguments reflect an individualist view of rights, because associations or institutions like the family, the church, the school, the corporation, and the state were *not* acknowledged to have fundamental rights based upon their own structural identity and task in society. And it is in part precisely because the right of existence and reason for existence of such institutions has not been adequately recognized that public policy has often threatened or worked to the disadvantage of some associations in American society.

It is our contention that the Supreme Court is implicated in some of the public policy decisions that have undermined the structural integrity and task of associations in American society. The Supreme Court throughout most of its history has followed an individualist social philosophy rather than a pluralist view, which recognizes that a modern democratic society is made up of individuals in associations that ought to possess political rights as well as responsibilities. Why has the Court throughout much of its history shown a legal bias against the full recognition of the civil rights and liberties of associations? And what conclusions can be drawn from the fact that in the last several decades the Court has ambiguously begun to acknowledge and protect the civil rights of associations as well as individuals? Once the deep-seated historical and philosophical roots of the Supreme Court's individualist perspective are clear, it will be easier to understand why it has taken so many years for the Court to begin to reevaluate its position on the rights of associations.

FROM PLURALISM TO INDIVIDUALISM

The New England Puritan Mind

While America has been proudly individualist in political and social thought, the roots of individualism do not extend much beyond the middle of the eighteenth century. The late eighteenth- and nineteenth-century notion that associations were merely artificial persons was simply not current in the earlier world of New England Puritanism.* The language of New England Puritanism was filled rather with expressions asserting that the family, the church, and the commonwealth are real institutions created by God for human good. As Morgan writes:

> For each of the groups he [God] established a special order, consisting of the relationships which the members were sup-

*This is not to say that the concept of an association as an artificial person was an invention of the eighteenth century. The concept has a long history that stretches back to the time of Roman law. What is being suggested is that such a notion did not significantly influence early New England Puritanism.

posed to bear to one another; and respect for this order was the first thing he demanded in all societies, whether of family, church or state.[1]

While groups never exist independently of individuals, the "relationships" constitute a reality not possible between mere collections of individuals.

John Cotton (1584–1652), for example, clearly believed that God and not man created social institutions that were as real as man himself. Cotton's social philosophy rested on the belief that God's revelation was to give direction to man in every aspect of life in the world. Cotton, regarded by his contemporaries as one of the principal spokesman of New England Puritanism, made his position quite clear by noting his agreement with the English Puritan divine William Perkins (1558–1602). Perkins argued that the Word of God contained directives not only for theology but also for the sacred sciences of "ethicks, eoconomicks, politicks, church-government, prophecy, academy."[2] For these different spheres of life people were to study God's Word to discover how they should act as individuals in associations.

The different spheres of human inquiry corresponded roughly to different institutional structures in society. The Puritans believed that people were to form institutions according to God's will. For John Cotton this meant that God had prescribed rules for the right ordering not only "of private mans soule to everlasting blessedness with himselfe, but also for the right ordering of a mans family, yea, of the commonwealth too." The institutional life of society and the personal life of the individual were to reflect the fact that institutions and individuals were created and structured by God. In precise language Cotton pointed out that church and state were divine institutions, having separate structural identities. "*Gods institutions* (such as the government of church and commonwealth be) may be close and compact and co-ordinate one to another, and yet not confounded."[3] For Cotton both "the churches usurpation upon civill jurisdiction, *in ordine ad spiritualia*, and the commonwealths invasion upon ecclesiasticall administrations, *in ordine* to civill peace" must be avoided.[4]

While the New England Puritans continued the European tradition of one faith, one territory, they came to see that the structure of the state and the structure of the church must not be intertwined as they were in Europe. While both institutions must be controlled by the Saints, the structural identity and task of the different institutions should not be "confounded."

These and other Puritan convictions about the correct ordering of society were made into law by the General Court of Massachusetts in 1641. The Massachusetts *Body of Liberties* took a form that would later be referred to as a bill of rights. For our purposes it is important to emphasize that the *Body of Liberties* recognized the rights of individuals as well as the rights of associations or institutions.

In the *Body of Liberties* the General Court set forth the "liberties, immunities and priveledges" due to every individual, whether an inhabitant or a foreigner, and the "Rites, liberties and priveledges" concerning the church and the commonwealth.[5] The Puritan belief that man was created in the image of God and the understanding of the political rights of Englishmen led them to affirm constitutional guarantees for the civil rights of individuals. The modern reader easily comprehends Puritan laws guaranteeing that no man's life or honor, no man's wife or children, no man's goods or estates could be taken from him without due process of law. But the modern reader, steeped in an individualist tradition of liberal democracy, might find it difficult to understand the Puritan insistence that associations or institutions also have constitutional rights.

The Massachusetts *Body of Liberties*, for example, included a special section entitled "A Declaration of the Liberties the Lord Jesus hath given to the Churches." Among these liberties were guarantees that "Every Church hath full libertie to exercise all the ordinances of god, according to the rules of scripture," and "No injunctions are to be put upon any Church, Church officers or member in point of Doctrine, worship or Discipline, whether for substance or cercumstance besides the Institutions of the lord." Notice that these liberties were not simply the liberties of church members or even church officers. Rather, the church as a distinct structure of temporal reality could claim certain rights. The structural integrity of the church as institution was to be protected against unjust actions of either individuals or such other institutions as the state.

This did not mean, however, that the institutional church in New England was to be the all-encompassing structure of society. The church had to abide by the civil law of the Puritan Commonwealth. According to the *Body of Liberties*, the "Civil Authoritie hath power and libertie to see peace, ordinances and Rules of Christ observed in every church according to his word so it be done in a *Civill* and not in a *Ecclesiastical* way."[6] Church laws and civil laws were not to be confused. Each institution was responsible for its own sphere of life. This arrangement was not intended to be competitive or antagonistic; on the contrary, each institution was to perform its distinct task in cooperation with the others. According to the Cambridge Synod and Platform of 1646–1648:

> Church government stands in no opposition to civil govern-ment of common-wealths nor any intrencheth upon the au-thority of Civil magistrates in their jurisdictions . . . that they may both stand together and flourish, the one being helpful unto the other, in their distinct and due administration.[7]

The Puritans believed that the Bible was to direct the ac-tivities of the church, the commonwealth, and other God-ordained institutions. The original constitution of the New Haven Colony in 1639 made this quite clear. The first question in this document asked:

> Whether the scriptures do hold forth a perfect rule for the direction and government of all men in all duties which they are to perform to God and men, as well in families and commonwealth, as in matters of the church? This was as-sented unto by all, no man dissenting.[8]

In short, both in their world-view and in their laws the Puritans accorded rights not only to individual church members and citi-zens but also to institutions such as the church and the common-wealth in themselves.

The Puritans repeatedly used *prescribe* to refer to the sov-ereign actions of God. He had prescribed, for example, the insti-tutions of society, creating the structure of the family, the church, and the state for the good of people. The origin of these institu-tions and others was the sovereign act of God and not the creative act of human beings. It was totally appropriate, therefore, for John Cotton to refer to the institutions of church and common-wealth as "God's institutions." God alone was sovereign; His sov-ereign authority established social structures.

Directly related to the Puritan view of the prescribed insti-tutional structure of society was an understanding of "calling" and "office." William Perkins characterized calling as "a certain kind of life, ordained and imposed on man by God, for the common good."[9] The call was to the individual, but it was to serve in a social institution. God's calling to an individual to be a magistrate, for example, had meaning only insofar as the office of magistrate in the divinely ordained state served the commonwealth. The call-ing of a minister was to accept the office to preach the gospel in the church of God, and the calling of a father only had meaning as it related to an office in the family.

The interrelationship between a person's calling from God and the institutional life of a society can be seen quite explicitly in Perkins's understanding of the two ways God ordains callings. The first way is by "commanding and prescribing them particularly, as hee doth the most weightie callings in the family, Church, or commonwealth." But the concept of calling is not limited to these three institutions. For God's second way of ordaining callings is:

> by appointing and setting down certain lawes and commandements, generally; whereby we may easily gather, that he doth either approve, or not approove of them, though they bee not particularly prescribed in the word.[10]

Thus even though the calling to be a merchant or teacher is not mentioned in Scripture, these callings are also ordained by God.

This argument rests on Perkins's belief that the Word of God included directives not only for theology but for such "other sacred sciences" as "eoconomicks" and "academy." For Perkins and those he influenced, it was clear that God gave many "directives" and "callings" to people. God also provided social institutions in which callings and human needs were fulfilled. These institutions were not artificial creations of the sovereign will of people; in the deepest sense they were, as John Cotton declared, "God's Institutions." Obviously, an American individualist social philosophy and legal tradition has no real foundation in New England Puritanism.

While at first glance it might be assumed that the Puritan Congregational church and the commonwealth of Massachusetts Bay could be labeled democratic because local congregations chose their own ministers and citizens elected their own magistrates, Puritans were quite aware that their understanding of office and authority was not to be confused with a democratic or individualist view. In John Cotton's 1636 letter to Lord Say and Seal, he pointed out that God never ordained democracy "as a fitt government eyther for church or commonwealth."[11] Cotton stressed that a "government is not a democracy, if it be administered, not by the people, but by the governors . . . ," and for exactly the same reason he argued that church government "is justly denied . . . to be democratical, though the people chose their owne officers and rulers."[12]

The meaning of Cotton's remarks was clearly understood by Perry Miller. He points out that Cotton made clear that even though the people select individuals to fill offices in the church and commonwealth, the offices received their legitimacy and authority from God, not from the people. God, not the people, "prescribed" the offices needed in different social institutions. An important contrast between a Puritan and Enlightenment-democratic view of the state lies precisely in Miller's observation that from Cotton's perspective "even though the people did elect the person, the office was prescribed; they did not define its functions, nor was it responsible to the will or the whim of the electors."[13]

An essentially Puritan understanding of office, calling, and associations as divine institutions permeated the social philosophy of New England in the seventeenth century. But by the later eighteenth century an Enlightenment-democratic social philosophy dominated New England and most other sections of America. An understanding of some of the differences between a Puritan social philosophy and an Enlightenment-democratic perspective will help to clarify the historical and philosophical roots of the Supreme Court's individualist view of social reality.

The Enlightenment Mind

A new social philosophy or paradigm always emerges in response to a concrete historical situation. The crisis facing our society demands the emergence of such a new paradigm to meet the challenges of our day, just as the democratic-individualist paradigm of Enlightenment America replaced the more pluralist Puritan social order.

The context for the development of an Enlightenment social philosophy was the Revolutionary struggle between England and the colonies. After 1763 the colonists were confronted by a British Parliament that claimed absolute power and imposed burdens and controls that were believed to be intolerable. Whether in the form of taxes, control of trade, or the housing of British soldiers in private residences, British rule was seen as a repressive and arbitrary government. The theoretical problem posed was this: How could the colonies challenge the authority of the British Parliament? How could Parliament be called to task for specific acts? With what theory of government could colonial assemblies resist the authority of a sovereign British Parliament?

Colonial thinkers, increasingly committed to an Enlightenment perspective, were forced to develop a theory to justify rebellion and eventually revolution. The task took all of their creative energies because they were up against a view that Parliament was the locus of an absolute power that could not be questioned or challenged.

An example of a post-1688 British view of parliamentary

sovereignty manifested itself in the year of the British and colonial Stamp Act crisis (1765) when William Blackstone argued in his *Commentaries* "that there is and must be in all forms of government a supreme, irresistible, absolute, uncontrolled authority, in which the *jura summi imperii*, or the rights of sovereignty, reside." He also concluded that in England the sovereignty of the British Constitution was lodged in Parliament, the body whose actions "no power on earth can undo."[14]

One of the early protests against this view came from the pen of James Otis, a leading Boston lawyer and pamphleteer. He led the legal attack against Parliament's efforts to enforce the Navigation Acts, which were designed to control trade and to raise revenues. In *The Rights of The British Colonies Asserted and Proved* (1764) he set forth the view that common law took precedent over an act of Parliament.[15] To him a sovereign Parliament did not mean a Parliament with arbitrary power. He asserted that:

> To say Parliament is absolute and arbitrary is a contradiction. The Parliament cannot make 2 and 2, 5: omnipotency cannot do it. . . . The supreme power in a state is *jus dicere* only: *jus dare*, strictly speaking, belongs alone to God. . . . Parliaments are in all cases to *declare* what is for the good of the whole; but it is not the *declaration* of Parliament that makes it so. There must be in every instance a higher authority, GOD.[16]

Here is the anguish of a thinker attempting to defend the rights of the colonies against the claim that Parliament's legal powers were unlimited.

Suggestive as it was of older British conceptions regarding the limits of the power of the state, it was not convincing to those who believed that Parliament was sovereign and its legal powers were unlimited. For them Blackstone's statement, ". . . if Parliament will positively enact a thing to be done which is unreasonable, I know of no power that can control it," was far more convincing.[17]

Otis's argument sounded hollow because he did not challenge the fundamental assumptions upon which Parliamentary sovereignty rested. He was caught in a dilemma—attempting to limit the power of Parliament to the "law of nature and of God" while maintaining that no other temporal authority could challenge the sovereignty of Parliament if its actions were judged improper.

Otis never questioned the assumption that only Parliament could repeal its own acts. In the end, therefore, Otis's position amounted to a mere plea to a sovereign Parliament to recognize that its actions with respect to the colonies were unjust. Given his perspective, there was nothing the colonists could do until Parliament recognized the merits of their pleas for justice.

Enlightenment thinkers like John Adams, Benjamin Franklin, Thomas Jefferson, and others, could not accept the built-in limitation of Otis's position. They turned instead to Lockean individualism and carried it to the point where it could challenge the very foundation of parliamentary sovereignty. In their writings the specific debate over the prerogatives of the British Parliament soon became a full-scale discussion of whether or not any state has rights independent of the individuals resident in its territory. The British authorities pressed the claim that the colonies were subject to Parliament because they were merely artificial corporations receiving legal rights through charters granted by a sovereign Parliament; the Enlightenment thinkers turned this argument back on the British. They held that if their colonial governments were artificial creations, then every state, including the British Parliament, was merely an artificial creation of free and sovereign individuals. Once they came to this conclusion it was not difficult to demonstrate that in the name of individual sovereignty colonists were justified in taking up arms to resist England, and to proceed next to the creation of their own independent states. This was the genius of the Enlightenment mind.

At the heart of this new conception of politics, rooted in Lockean individualism, was the understanding that the people were the sovereign source of all political authority. Only the people could claim sovereign power because social reality was made up only of free and sovereign individuals who create artificial associations like the state.

A study of the early state constitutions, from the Pennsylvania Constitution of 1776 to the Massachusetts Constitution of 1780, indicates that the sovereignty of the people was indeed the foundational concept. The literature of the period is filled with the often repeated statement that the people are "the pure, original fountain of all legitimate authority."[18] Thus there emerged, in settled form, the political view of a social contract that was not a social contract between ruler and ruled, but rather a compact among the people themselves who created the state. Thomas Paine said it best: "To suppose that any government can be a party in compact with the whole people is to suppose it to have existence before it can have a right to exist."[19] He made it quite plain that government "has of itself no rights — They are altogether duties."[20]

In *The Age of Democratic Revolutions*, R. R. Palmer summarizes the significance of the individualist political theory basic to American political thought. He contends that the distinctive contribution of American Revolutionary theory was to develop a mechanism by which a sovereign people create a state. The mechanism of establishing a constitution and organs of government became known as the constitutional convention. "The constitutional convention in theory embodied the sovereignty of the people. The people chose it," according to Palmer, "not to govern, but to set up institutions of government." He continued:

> The convention, acting as the sovereign people, proceeded to draft a constitution and a declaration of rights. Certain "natural" or "inalienable" rights of the citizens were thus laid down at the same time as the powers of government. It was the constitution that created the powers of government, defined their scope, gave them legality, and balanced them one against another. The constitution was written and comprised in a single document. The constitution and accompanying declaration, drafted by the convention, must, in the developed theory, be ratified by the people. The convention thereupon disbanded and disappeared, lest its members have a vested interest in the offices they created. The constituent power went into abeyance, leaving the work of government to the authorities now constituted.[21]

By 1780 the people of Massachusetts created a constitution which fully embodied the dogma of popular sovereignty and was implemented through a constitutional convention that followed exactly the course of events outlined by Palmer.

Palmer also makes clear that "the idea that sovereignty lay with the people, and not with states or their governments, made possible in America a new kind of federal structure unknown in Europe." The American Revolutionary ideology led directly to "the new idea that, instead of the central government drawing its powers from the states, both central and state governments should draw their powers from the same source; the question was the limit between these two sets of derived powers." He concluded:

> The citizen, contrariwise, was simultaneously a citizen both of the United States and of his own state. He was the sovereign, not they. He chose to live under two constitutions, two sets of laws, two sets of courts and officials; theoretically, he had created them all, reserving to himself, under each set, certain liberties specified in declarations of rights.[22]

It was the American belief in popular sovereignty that so impressed Alexis de Tocqueville that he recorded that "any discussion of the political laws of the United States must begin with the dogma of the sovereignty of the people." It was this principle, Tocqueville observed, that was to be found "at the bottom of almost all human institutions" in the United States. It was "the creative principle of most of the English colonies in America" and in the Revolution "the dogma of the sovereignty of the people came out from the township and took possession of the [national] government; every class enlisted in its cause; the war was fought and victory obtained in its name; it became the law of laws." In America, Tocqueville concluded, "The people reign over the American political world as God rules over the universe. It is the cause and the end of all things; everything rises out of it and is absorbed back into it."[23]

American political thought was clearly based on an individualist social philosophy. The federal Constitution itself was designed to protect the rights of individuals. Some might argue that the failure to recognize the rights of associations as well as individuals was merely that the primary concern at the time was the safeguarding of individual rights; the fact that the rights of associations are not mentioned does not prove they were not taken seriously. Historians have observed that everywhere in the past we encounter things that remain unexplained only because they were completely self-understood in their time and, like all daily matters, were not thought necessary to write down.

While such an observation is sometimes valid, the evidence in this case suggests that, given the formative influence of an Enlightenment social philosophy and political mind, it is not surprising that the rights of associations were not recognized in the eighteenth century. To have recognized the independent rights of associations like the state would have been a radical challenge to the individualist assumptions of the Revolutionary ideology.

In the eighteenth century the principles of individualism and voluntarism structured the political-legal order in the United States. The stress on the individual dissolved the sense that associations or institutions have their own structural identity and rights. Soon every social institution was seen as nothing more than the free association of sovereign individuals. As Sidney Mead puts it, "All the lines of thinking of the eighteenth century converged on the idea of free, uncoerced, individual consent as the only proper basis for all man's organizations, civil and ecclesiastical."[24] The gospel of individualism triumphed, and there was little left of a Puritan social philosophy that recognized the multi-institutional as well as individual character of rights derived from a sovereign God.

Although Sidney Mead tends to see less contrast between the Puritan political philosophy and modern democracy than we have suggested, he does point out that the development of individualism undermined claims that civil rulers were God's representatives on earth. The development of individualism, according to Mead, meant that "this inversion in the conceptual order laid the foundation for modern democracy — the idea that sovereignty, the power of God for the creation of ordered communities, lies in 'the people' and is delegated by them to rulers responsible to them."[25] Notice two things in Mead's observation. First, in the Enlightenment perspective "the people" rather than God are the creators of "ordered communities" or associations like the state. Second, there is no room in an individualist perspective for the Puritan understanding of "office." Remember, in New England Puritanism a civil ruler is to be obeyed and respected by the people precisely because the person holds an office in a God-created institution. The civil ruler, in administering his magisterial office, is responsible first of all to God for the correct ordering of society. People elect their rulers, but the authority of magistrates comes from God and not the people. The Puritans believed that there are God-given norms for public justice that are binding upon the people.

The following diagrams summarize the contrast between a Puritan and Enlightenment political perspective.

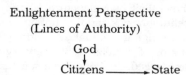

Puritan Perspective
(Lines of Authority)

The broken line indicates that while individuals are obviously necessary in the forming of particular states, God, not the people, is the Creator of the association or institution known as the state.

Enlightenment Perspective
(Lines of Authority)

God
↓
Citizens ⟶ State

In the Enlightenment perspective the lines of authority between citizens and the state are clear but the relationship of God to the state is ambiguous. For deist and liberal Christians God is more often than not merely the necessary hypothesis used to demonstrate that the political order is what reason made it. For evangelical Christians, gripped by an individualist spirit, the state is an artificial creation (deists and liberals agree) of individuals who are responsible to a sovereign God for their actions. In neither case, however, is God's sovereignty related *directly* to the state as one of the many God-created institutions in society. While there continued to be some individuals who believed that God was the Creator of "ordered communities" like the state, their position had little influence in shaping political thinking in the eighteenth century.

The belief that the people are the creators of "ordered communities," and that civil rulers are first of all responsible to the people, represented the great conceptual revolution of the eighteenth century. It came to maturity in the Revolutionary struggle with England and in the forming of state constitutions and eventually the federal Constitution. Increasingly the rights of such associations or institutions as the family, the church, and the state were replaced by an individualist perspective that recognized only the rights of individual family members, church members, and citizens. It is thus not surprising that such a firmly entrenched perspective came to guide and structure American law and the judicial reasoning of the United States Supreme Court.

THE RIGHTLESSNESS OF EARLY ASSOCIATIONS

The disjunction between political theory and applied law quickly became apparent, for the federal Constitution was out of touch with reality before the ink was dry. The fault was that the landscape of American life was filled with associations of great vitality and variety — but American legal thought and the Constitution at its drafting failed to recognize the rights and powers of associations.

The Constitution gave delegated powers to the federal government, left reserved powers with state governments, and, by adding the Bill of Rights, recognized the liberties and powers of individuals. The amended Constitution dealt with the sovereign individual and two "artificial" legal actors.

Sovereign individual

Artificial state government ⟍   ⟋ Artificial federal government

The individual is at the apex because the political orthodoxy expressed in the Preamble placed him there: "We the People of the United States, in Order to form a more perfect Union. . . ."

Throughout its history, the Supreme Court's decisions dealing with corporations or associations have demonstrated a legal bias favoring an individualist view of society. Because the Court assumed such a perspective, the legal freedom of and for associations or various institutions has proved difficult to establish clearly in American law. Just how hard can be shown by looking at the way in which corporations or associations were treated by judges who had to fit them into an individualist social philosophy and into the constitutional categories that emerged from such a perspective.

The Corporation and Constitutional Law

One prefatory comment is needed. In American law the corporation has not been narrowly defined. It has included business, charitable, fraternal, educational, and ecclesiastical institutions. It would be a mistake, therefore, to limit the concept of a corporation to business. To be sure, business corporations were soon to develop into a dominant feature of American life. If a business corporation won a right, that victory benefited other associations or institutions as well. Therefore, our attention can center at the outset on the business corporation, realizing that the legal definition of a corporation embraced other institutions as well.

Business corporations were not numerous in 1789, but Americans were familiar with them. Some early settlements were conducted as companies chartered by the Crown. In 1791 the Congress passed a law creating the Bank of the United States, an action that was to force the Supreme Court to decide landmark cases touching the meaning of the word "incorporation." One of those cases challenged the very existence of the bank; the case was decided in favor of the federal government's power to incorporate a bank.[26]

The question of the legal definition of an economic corporation was troublesome, for corporations caused problems that might end in law suits. Could corporations sue or be sued? Were not suits limited to persons? The Court decided that issue in 1809 respecting the Bank of the United States. Justice Marshall expressed the difficulty:

> That invisible, intangible, and artificial being, that mere legal entity, a corporation aggregate, is certainly not a citizen; and consequently cannot sue or be sued in the courts of the United States, unless the rights of the members, in this respect, can be exercised in their corporate name.[27]

As always, the great justice was equal to the challenge. He argued that while a corporation, not being a real entity like an individual, could not be involved in a suit, those who held stock in the corporation could be sued. So the suit against the corporation went on under the fiction that each stockholder was before the bar.

That legal fiction was too simplistic to last if a party wanted to sue a corporation in another state in a federal court. For as economic corporations grew, they had stockholders in all states, and the Supreme Court had earlier held that a person could not go into *federal* court if the adversary could be found within that person's home state. Only state courts were available for disputes between parties within a single state.[28] Since some stockholder of a large corporation was commonly found in each state, the "diversity jurisdiction" of the federal courts was useless. A litigant against corporations could not use the federal courts, though many litigants preferred federal trials.

Faced with this problem, the Supreme Court in 1844 changed its fiction. It still asserted that a corporation was confined to the state of its incorporation, regardless where its members lived. Noting the unnaturalness of the thing, the court said,

> . . . a corporation created by and doing business in a particular State, is to be deemed to all intents and purposes as a person, although an artificial person, an inhabitant of the same State, for the purposes of its incorporation, capable of being treated as a citizen of that State, as much as a natural person.[29]

That fiction lasted only ten years, for in 1854 the high court created a new and still-enduring fiction. It held that for purposes of suits in federal courts, all stockholders are citizens of the state of incorporation.[30]

Clearly, the economic corporation did not fit the individualist categories of law inherited from Britain and refined by an Enlightenment ideology. Not being a person, it had a nebulous legal existence in spite of having been created by sovereign individuals and recognized by law. The Supreme Court's opinions on corporate law have been marked by what Arthur Selwyn Murray has called a "poverty of theory."[31]

The "poverty of theory" was masked for a time by the fact that when jurists committed to an individualist social philosophy ran into such societal entities as the business corporation, they were clever enough not to admit that something was wrong with their theoretical model. The anomaly was handled within the individualist paradigm by simply defining a business corporation as an artificial person.*

A legal theory that inadequately defined business corporations did not much hinder their vigor, for there was a societal bias in favor of their day-to-day functioning. In 1819, the same year the Court found the Bank of the United States to be of legitimate parentage, it also found that another association had constitutional protection against a state that wanted to restructure its board of trustees. The state was New Hampshire. The "association" was Dartmouth College, which operated under a charter granted by a British monarch before 1776. The Chief Justice, in the Court's majority opinion, found the ancient British charter was a still-effective "contract" — and states, said the Constitution, could not impair "the obligation of contracts."[32] One implication was that corporate charters then being granted by state governments limited state powers respecting those corporations forever. But Justice Marshall conceded that states might reserve the power to "amend, alter and repeal" such instruments.[33] His concession to state power was not lost on the states. Articles of incorporation were, thereafter, commonly qualified to protect the general interest.[34] But corporations had put their fictitious legal foot in the Constitution's "obligation of contract" door and in a variety of cases their qualified rights against the states were assured. But note well: the legal right of Dartmouth College was not recognized because it was an educational corporation that had rights as an independent academic entity. Rather, it was protected by law only because it could claim the status of an economic corporation, that is, an artificial person having property rights.

In the nineteenth century, attorneys for economic corporations did not rest easily with this and similar decisions. Justices like Marshall were mortal, states were fickle, and the "obligation of contracts" clause was, given state power to "amend, alter and repeal," a weak reed. Happily for those attorneys, the Fourteenth Amendment was added to the Constitution, protecting former slaves as "persons." A "person" was any person once the word

---

*This kind of semantic juggling reminds one of the widely publicized incidents in the 1979 ceremonial tour of Queen Elizabeth through the strict Moslem countries bordering the Persian Gulf. Moslem law prohibits women from socializing with men in public. Its stricture was honored on the Queen's visit to Saudi Arabia by declaring her "an honorary man." This legal fiction announced, it is reported that the duties of King Khalid, who was the Queen's host, no longer clashed with those of King Khalid the devout Moslem. In retrospect, American jurists had only a little more difficulty defining economic corporations as individuals than Moslem jurists had in defining Queen Elizabeth as a man.

was written down; by legal reasoning the corporation was found to be an "artificial person" meriting some — not full — Fourteenth Amendment protections in the *Granger* cases.[35] From that day to this, artificial corporate "persons" have been supremely confident that they possess the sundry rights of economic liberty, due process of law, and the equal protection of the laws in good, if qualified, measure.

But while the Fourteenth Amendment's words were a Magna Carta for corporations, these agencies still operated under limitations inapplicable to real persons. Corporations remained "artificial." Thus, while given economic protections, they were not ". . . endowed with the inalienable rights of a natural person."[36]

The distinction made a difference. In *Pierce* v. *Society of Sisters* (1925) the Supreme Court struck down an Oregon law requiring that children attend only public schools for state-mandated education. The nub of the Society of Sisters' constitutional defense, the court found, rested *not* in freedom of religion or in the school's right to exist as an institution dedicated to the education of children according to the religious values of the parents. While the unanimous opinion written by Justice McReynolds paid incidental homage to rights of parents, the Sisters carried their claim because they were a corporation with property rights under the Fourteenth Amendment. Their religious and educational endeavor had to be treated as economic to give them constitutional protection. "Appellees are corporations, and therefore, it is said, they cannot claim . . . the liberty which the Fourteenth Amendment guarantees. Accepted in the proper sense, this is true."[37] Put bluntly, a religious academic institution had property rights but not religious or other civil rights.

That difference long lurked in the shadows of the American law of free expression. In *Hague* v. *C.I.O.* (1939) a local labor union, a nationally incorporated labor organization, and individual union members filed a suit against the state of New Jersey. They claimed, under the Fourteenth Amendment, the First Amendment's rights of freedom of assembly, speech, and freedom of expression. They had been denied freedom to hold meetings in a public place under a local ordinance. In vindicating the rights of only the *individual* union members, the Supreme Court said:

> Natural persons, and they alone, are entitled to the privileges and immunities which Section 1 of the Fourteenth Amendment secures for "citizens of the United States." Only the individual respondents may, therefore, maintain this suit.[38]

Thus, associations or corporations, whether business, educational, or one of the many kinds of institutions which often acted as if they were lord of the manor in the United States, did not have full run of the house. They were like individual members of the family, in some respects, but did not share their fundamental freedoms because their separate, unique identities and political rights were not recognized.

The story in the case of churches has been vastly different from that of other corporations — up to a point. The cup of power and liberty of churches — local and denominational — runneth over. No other association is more autonomous and less subject to that common qualification, "excepting for reasonable regulation," as long as the discussion centers on what courts understand as religious activity and internal church government.

The legal explanation for the church's relative autonomy, as it has developed in judicial opinion, is found in the twin religion clauses of the First Amendment. No other association can point to such a starting-point in its quest for freedom. The legal basis for the liberty of churches is distinct from that of other corporations and associations, so that analogies between them are misleading. But the inherent difficulties of the legal status of the church as a social institution are at least as disturbing as the difficulties other associations have in earning that status.

Churches get involved with law suits for many reasons. One of the most common is this: the bitter internal conflicts among the members of some church require that disputed property claims be resolved. The losers in a dispute among God's people appeal to Caesar's judges to certify that, though they lost by church rules, the property is still theirs.

Since 1872, however, the Supreme Court has consistently insisted that the First Amendment's twin religion clauses mean that courts cannot enter into disputes (1) over theological doctrine, (2) over church organization, or (3) over normal church operation.[39] Such disputes must be settled within the churches' local or broader organizations by the churches' own recognized written or unwritten rules or by religiously neutral principles of corporate law. The courts can intervene only to ensure that there has not been fraud or that the winners in the conflict are not ousted from the property by threat or force. The courts will attempt only to make sure that law and order is maintained when combatants fight for spoils. But courts do so in accordance with church procedure.

This means that in a congregational church, the majority will of the members controls if it constitutes a majority at a properly called business meeting. In an hierarchical church, the highest official — say, the bishop — speaks the finally authoritative word. In a presbyterian style church, the highest representative body, such as the Synod, controls. No disgruntled group, however true to its church's original creed, can use creedal faithfulness in a government court to overturn the "heretical" church's own due process decisions.

In *Watson* v. *Jones* (1872) the Supreme Court summarized its view of the church as the "wholly other":

> In this country the full and free right to entertain any religious belief, to practice any religious principle, and to teach any religious doctrine which does not violate the laws of morality and property, and which does not infringe personal rights, is conceded to all. The law knows no heresy, and is committed to the support of no dogma, the establishment of no sect. . . . All who unite themselves to such a body . . . [the denomination] do so with the implied consent to [its] government, and are bound to submit to it. But it would be a vain consent and would lead to the total subversion of such religious bodies, if anyone aggrieved by one of their decisions could appeal to the secular courts and have [those decisions] reversed.[40]

This opinion indicates that federal constitutional law does not give legal recognition to the right of the church in a way analogous to the rights of other associations and corporations. Rather, American law denies that government holds normal jurisdiction over the church. The church is viewed for most purposes as an unknown before the law, beyond the reach of regular court action. Therefore the church's cup of liberty in what the court defines as religious matters does indeed run over, for that cup represents a very special, sacred vineyard beyond the borders of American law. That border encompasses only matters that the law says belong to the secular domain. The church as a religious association or corporation, especially in the nonsecular, specifically religious dimension of its life, is the "wholly other."

The court thus operates with a long-standing commitment to the secular-religious dichotomy.[41] Granted that perspective, the court is obligated to draw a line of demarcation between the religiously "wholly other" and the secular and to define where one begins and the other ends. A central thesis of this book calls the validity of this distinction into question.

All corporations and associations, the church included, have found only an ambiguous place in American legal thought and practice. Until recently, none of them was recognized as possessing firm legal reality. Some had to pass under the pretense of being fictitious persons. Ecclesiastical corporations, as religious associations, were declared to be legal aliens. True, many different kinds of institutions were able to operate in American society. But none was able to do so as a social structure with its own unique legal integrity.

THE RIGHTS OF ASSOCIATIONS IN RECENT YEARS

The First Step: Freedom for Associations

The facts of life have the power in the long run to sabotage constitutional notions that contradict them and to force a realistic adjustment of society's rules. In a society that boasted of freedom and in which all sorts of associations were active, the Supreme Court inevitably found that these associations had to have a legally defensible existence of their own and rights that suited their needs. This development is still in progress.

While we have already noted that economic corporations had won some rights as "persons" in the nineteenth century and churches in the same era had won autonomy in the court-defined spiritual sphere, freedom of and for association was not spelled out clearly by the Supreme Court until a series of landmark cases between 1958 and 1963.[42]

Freedom of association (the phrase does not appear in the Bill of Rights) as a freedom of the First and Fourteenth Amendment was first announced by the Supreme Court in *NAACP* v. *Alabama* (1958).[43] But the announcement reflected the Court's uncertainty. In its decision the Court did not jump boldly to the position that associations *as associations* had rights. The NAACP had urged that it, as an association, was ". . . constitutionally entitled to resist official inquiry (by Alabama) into its membership lists."[44] The cautious Justice Harlan, speaking for the Court, chose to accept the case as one argued by the NAACP on behalf of its individual members, thus continuing earlier precedents which recognized only individuals as having rights.

But the justice had a fleeting second thought. In passing he noted:

> The reasonable likelihood that the Association itself through diminished financial support and membership may be adversely affected if production (of the membership lists) is compelled, is a further factor pointing towards our holding that petitioner has standing to complain of the production order on behalf of its members.

Although his opinion focused on the individual, Justice Harlan argued that the effectiveness of free expression would be enhanced by group effort and that it was, therefore, "beyond debate that freedom to engage in association for the advancement of beliefs and ideas is an inseparable aspect of the 'liberty' assured by the Due Process Clause of the Fourteenth Amendment."[45]

Following that case, the NAACP, harassed by the laws of several southern states, won a series of decisions that widened the scope of free association and that finally defined in legal terms the activities of the association as a group, not just the efforts of the association to defend its members' individual rights. The climax of this series of cases came in *NAACP* v. *Button* (1963).

In that case Justice Brennan ruled on behalf of the Supreme Court that: "We think [the NAACP] may assert . . . [the] right [to associate] *on its own behalf*, because, though a corporation, it is directly engaged in those activities, claimed to be constitutionally protected, which the statute would curtail." Pointedly, he added, "We hold that the activities *of the NAACP*, its affiliates, and legal staff shown on this record are modes of expression and association protected by the First and Fourteenth Amendment." And ". . . there is no longer any doubt that the First and Fourteenth Amendments protect certain forms of orderly *group activity*."[46]

By 1963, freedom of association was, at long last, freedom *for* association. The Supreme Court continues to use "of," but the implication of its opinions has been that freedom *of* association, which could be merely a sort of right to assemble for individuals, covers freedom *for* associations to act in a wide variety of ways.

Why was this victory for freedom of and for association won by the NAACP? There are many reasons related to the issue itself, the climate of opinion, and the nature of the Warren Court. But one key reason is this: over the years the Supreme Court, in a hit or miss way, and without using the category "freedom of association," had written passages in its opinions favoring some liberty for some associations. That is, in facing the concrete demands of a wide range of associations in a free society the Court had responded by developing all the precedent necessary for interpreting "freedom of association" in a manner that meant freedom of and for association. In the NAACP cases it took the final logical step.

From First Step to the Present

Since the Supreme Court first announced rights of and for associations in the NAACP cases, further decisions have added to these rights, increased the variety of institutions that have successfully asserted them, and restated the case law of group rights in ways that have explicated the concept more sharply. Such progress continues to be evident, even in some very recent cases. Both the "liberal" Warren Court and the "conservative" Burger Court have followed the precedent of the NAACP opinions.

New rights for association. The "right of privacy" appears nowhere in the Bill of Rights or in the Constitution. It is a concept that was constructed out of certain implications in those documents. The right of privacy was asserted in *Griswold* v. *Connecticut* (1965), which struck down a state law forbidding giving information about contraception to married couples. The core of the decision concerned the association of marriage, securing its right of privacy from unreasonable state interference. Justice Douglas wrote eloquently for the majority:

> We deal with a right of privacy older than the Bill of Rights — older than our political parties, older than our school system. Marriage is a coming together for better or worse, hopefully enduring and intimate to the degree of being sacred. It is an association that promotes a way of life, not causes; a harmony in living, not political faiths; a bi-lateral loyalty, not commercial or social projects. Yet it is an association for as noble a purpose as any involved in our prior decisions.[47]

Douglas specifically referred to political parties and schools because he had earlier said that these associations also enjoyed areas of autonomy under law. The entire opinion was built on the assumption that associations other than the state had a life of their own that required ample elbow room for their best development.

Another more recently established right is freedom of commercial advertising. This liberty was articulated in a case argued by a newspaper editor, but the secondary beneficiary in the dispute was an association that advertised in his paper to make its counseling services known.[48] The precedent was shortly applied in the case of an incorporated association of citizens that wanted to publish prices that pharmacies charged for commonly prescribed drugs. The victory of the citizens association ensured that the new liberty of advertising would not be the liberty of editors or the media only.[49]

This freedom of commercial advertising served as a basis for announcing the freedom of corporate political advertising a few years later. At that time the justices weighed the free expression rights of business corporations against both a state interest in fair political campaigns and individual stockholders' interests in the use of corporate funds for purposes they might not approve.

The case was *First National Bank of Boston* v. *Bellotti* (1978). The decision held unconstitutional under the freedoms of the First and Fourteenth Amendments a Massachusetts law that forbade corporate expenditures for advertising related to referendum campaigns on issues not directly affecting the corporation. The opinion of the Court, written by Justice Powell, explicitly repudiated the *Pierce* case cited above, which limited the rights of corporations to property rights, saying, "the Court has not identified a separate source for [free speech] rights when it has been asserted by corporations." The Court expressly rejected the idea that only corporations involved in publication or broadcasting had free expression rights. Furthermore, it refused to protect the individual stockholders of the corporation who might disagree with the ideas that corporation's advertising expressed.[50] Individual right could not be used to overturn the decision of the corporation.

New associations that won rights. Another association that won rights in case law following the NAACP cases was the political party. It had always been subject to substantial state controls, for it served as part of the election process and machinery of all states. While its members' right to be associated with it had been protected earlier, giving it some status that hinted at its freedom, an unequivocal statement of its own rights as an association cannot be found in Supreme Court opinions until 1975. Then, in *Cousins* v. *Wigoda*, Justice Brennan's majority opinion stated:

> The National Democratic Party *and* its adherents enjoy a constitutionally protected right of political association. There can no longer be any doubt that freedom to associate with others for the *common* advancement of political beliefs and ideas is a form of "orderly group activity" protected by the First and Fourteenth Amendments.[51]

Lest it seem that this decision still smacks of a party right built partially on individual members' rights, a later case involved a political party as an organization that claimed a First Amendment liberty of free expression against the restrictive decision of T.V. networks—a restriction approved by the Federal Communications Commission. Though the Supreme Court decided in favor of the networks and the FCC, in *Columbia Broadcasting System* v. *Democratic National Committee* (1973) all the justices *assumed* the political party's committee had a perfect right to express its collective ideas and had standing in court to defend that right.[52] Note that the chief antagonists in this battle, each asserting a claim of freedom of the press, were private corporations.

Enhancement of rights of associations. Occasionally, cases and opinions aid the cause of liberty by doing an exceptionally effective job of summarizing earlier precedents that support it. Freedom of nonprofit associations was forcefully announced again by majority and minority judges alike in *Moose Lodge* v. *Irvis*, in 1972. The majority of six judges in that case agreed that the lodge, in spite of its possession of a state liquor license, remained a private association. Being private, it could discriminate against minority races in its liquor service. The minority held that the possession of a state liquor license made the lodge's liquor sale a public matter. Therefore, the association could not discriminate in the sale of alcoholic beverages. But dissenting Justice Douglas wanted to clarify the law respecting private associations. Except where they were involved in closely regulated matters such as liquor sales, they were free of state interference. He applied his concept of privacy to such groups, saying:

> My view of the First Amendment and the related guarantees of the Bill of Rights is that they create a zone of privacy which precludes government from interfering with private clubs or groups. The associational rights which our system honors permit all white, all black, all brown, and all yellow clubs to be formed. They also permit all Catholic, all Jewish, or all agnostic clubs to be established. Government may not tell a man or woman who his or her associates must be. The individual can be as selective as he desires. So the fact that the Moose Lodge allows only Caucasians to join or come as guests is constitutionally irrelevant, as is the decision of the Black Muslims to admit to their services only members of their race.[53]

While this is minority dicta, it represents the Court's position rather well and no majority judge contradicted the statement.

Another reinforcement of the rights of associations came in a case that pitted the "natural family" against a foster family. The latter was attempting to retain custody of a child that New York had officially placed in its care. In doing so, it claimed the same due process rights that a "natural family" could assert when a child was removed from its custody. The unanimous decision in *Smith* v. *Organization of Foster Families* (1977) favored New York's less demanding due process protection of the foster family.[54] In it the Court summarized in a detailed way the law of family rights. The decision merits analysis for its conclusion that a family is an association protected from state power. There is " 'freedom of personal choice' " respecting it in several ways.[55] The state cannot restrict one's choice of a marriage partner;[56] nor can its rules respecting mandatory maternity leaves from state employment unduly burden the decision to have children;[57] nor can it indirectly limit a married couple's freedom by restricting information sources concerning contraception.[58]

The last two cases cited imply that "freedom of personal choice" does not adequately describe the basis of the rights of the family. Beyond personal freedom exists a " 'private realm of family life which the state cannot enter.' "[59]

The privacy and autonomy of the family include parental power " 'to conceive and raise one's children.' "[60] The freedom respecting the raising of children is broadly defined.

> "It is cardinal with us that the custody, care and nurture of the child reside first in the parents, whose primary function and freedom include preparation for obligations the state can neither supply nor hinder."[61]

Also, the family is free to create for itself a special "way of life," even if that means it must be given qualified exception from state compulsory school attendance laws.[62]

What is the family? It is more than the nuclear family, for it includes children and their guardian aunt, and children and their uncles, aunts, or grandmothers.[63] In sum:

> Ours is by no means a tradition limited to respect for the bonds uniting the members of the nuclear family. [The] . . . Constitution prevents . . . [a local government] from standardizing its children and its adults by forcing all to live in certain narrowly defined family patterns.[64]

Is the foster family a family? Yes, in a qualified way. Foster families are more than a collection of unrelated individuals, and, as the *Smith* majority argued, such families are not mere utilitarian creations of the state, for they merit certain procedural rights, which will be described below. Further, a family can exist although the parents are never legally married.[65]

Most of this discussion has concerned the substantive rights of the family—i.e., the rights to do certain things or to enjoy a given condition or way of life. But, as noted, families have procedural rights as well—i.e., rights to the protection of a regularized process of law. Thus, a state action that results in removal of a child from his or her biological parents would have to involve the most "rigorous" standards of due process—a full-blown judicial hearing having the demanding level of protections associated with a criminal trial. The foster family also is entitled to due process of law, but it can expect a lesser level of procedural rights — one appropriate to the "special nature" of the foster relationship.[66]

What once had been rather scattered cases related to family rights were here organized into a forceful statement of that institution's liberty in law. The *Smith* case opinion buttresses each earlier opinion by showing how each was part of a comprehensive legal development.

The NAACP cases have lived up to the promise that many hoped they offered. Freedom of and for associations has grown in case law. The Supreme Court has chosen its path decisively and is still clearly defining it at the time of this writing. The freedom for association principle, however, remains to be actively applied to the school as an association.

IMPLICATIONS FOR LEGAL THOUGHT AND PRACTICE

The highest of American courts has now repeatedly used the phrase freedom *of* association in contexts implying freedom *for* association. Its justices have at last begun creating a legal justification for this broad right. That justification often begins with the right of the individual to join with others to expand his or her influence, but it also now concedes that associations *as* associations are entitled to zones of privacy for their unhindered operation and that they have their own unique interests. These interests may even run counter to some of the interests of their members and of the government.

Since the NAACP cases first began, the scholarly legal bibliography on freedom of association has become long.[67] Most of the scholarship strongly defends the rights of associations. One notable exception is the writing of Thomas I. Emerson, a great champion of freedom in general. He argues that freedom of and for association is necessary and should be protected by constitutional law, but that such protection can be accomplished adequately under more traditionally used freedoms of the Bill of Rights, such as freedom of expression and assembly.

He pointedly warns that the kinds of associations and their diverse functions in society are staggeringly numerous. The principles required to separate their needed freedoms from the proper power the state has over them will be impossible to devise. Thus freedom of association will become meaningless, lost in a maze of regulation and circumscription.[68]

There are, however, rejoinders to Emerson's argument. First, even if his individualist reading of the new legal category were the only way to interpret it, one could answer Emerson's basic concern by pointing out that other phrases in the Constitution—due process of law, for example—are also so broad that they seem meaningless on their face. But legislation and case laws have given such constitutional guarantees a developed form and utility. The same is probably true for an individualist interpretation of the freedom of association; as precedents mount, its meaning is refined into a more precise definition. Just such a process has begun to delineate the limits of the term in cases that have rejected the claim. For example, in *United States* v. *Nixon* the Court did not accept the argument that freedom of association for the President and his staff in the White House Office gave them protection from judicial use of the infamous White House tapes in a criminal proceeding.[69]

A second and more fundamental criticism of Emerson's position is that he fails to recognize that the new legal category of freedom of and for associations has come to mean more than simply the right of individuals to associate. The Court has now recognized that associations as associations have rights. It is difficult to know what will be the future legal and political implications of the development. There is a reasonable chance that this legal category may be used in new and creative ways to protect the rights of some of the basic institutions in society. Certainly such development will take time and mistakes will be made along the way. The errors made in the name of other Constitutional guarantees have been many and sometimes awesome. Yet it has been wise for the Supreme Court to continue the search for new legal categories which more adequately correspond to social reality.

It is important to notice that the constitutions of a great many countries recognize the rights of societal structures such as the family, school, and church (or combinations thereof) side by side with the rights of individuals. For instance, Ireland's Constitution states that:

> The State recognizes the Family as the natural primary and fundamental unit group of Society, and as a moral institution possessing inalienable and imprescriptable rights, antecedent and superior to all positive law.[70]

Furthermore, nations such as Malaysia, Ireland, and the Netherlands give both legal recognition and financial aid to private schools. A good example is the Dutch Constitution:

> In these regulations the freedom of private education concerning the choice of means of instruction and appointment of teachers shall particularly be respected.

> Private general elementary education fulfilling conditions to be imposed by law shall be defrayed from public funds according to the same standards as public education.
>
> The education upon which private general secondary education and preparatory University education shall be granted contributions from public funds shall be fixed by law.[71]

Recognition is also given in numerous constitutions to the rights of denominations and other avowedly religious institutions. In many cases the rights of associations are granted explicit legal status in provisions such as:

> The State shall protect associations, corporate bodies, societies and communities that have as their purpose the better fulfillment of the aims of human beings and shall promote the organization of co-operatives and other institutions devoted to the improvement of the public economy.[72]

Lastly, the United Nations Declaration of Human Rights announces, "Everyone has the right to freedom of . . . association," and, concerning family rights, "Parents have a prior right to choose the kind of education that shall be given to their children."[73]

If we take seriously the belief that associations are necessary for the healthy life of both individuals and society, as more and more nations around the world are acknowledging, it is important that we recognize that an individualist social philosophy does not provide adequate grounds upon which to defend the rights of associations. One of the tasks that remains is to develop greater clarity regarding the ontology of associations so that the rights of individuals in relationship to the rights of different associations can be balanced.[74] Such reflection will clarify legal language, which will in turn lead to new insights regarding constitutional law. A pluralist understanding of associations and the rights of and for associations must be accepted in a free society, if its freedom is to be well served.

CHAPTER 4

THE POLITICAL AND CONSTITUTIONAL STRUGGLE OVER SCHOOL FUNDING

UNFORTUNATELY, much of the history of the nineteenth-century school struggle is not widely known. Few people realize, for example, that a clean line of separation between private and public schools, a line that so divides schools that it is assumed wrong for public funds to support nongovernment primary and secondary schools, is a very modern development. Bernard Bailyn puts it this way:

> The modern conception of public education, the very idea of a clean line of separation between "private" and "public," was unknown before the end of the eighteenth century. Its origins are part of a complex story, involving changes in the role of the state as well as in the general institutional character of society. It is elaborately woven into the fabric of early modern history.[1]

Today the distinction between private and public schools has become ingrained in our contemporary understanding of education. It manifests itself in every Supreme Court decision relating to public funding for nongovernment schools.

Several questions can be asked in reference to the modern distinctions between secular public schools and religious private schools: one, *why* did the supposedly clean line of separation develop; two, *how* did it develop; and finally, *what* have been the legal implications of this development? In order to answer these and other questions it is necessary to turn to the "complex story" that Bailyn says lies behind such modern notions as the absolute distinction between public and private schools.*

---

*Much of the material used to tell the "complex story" in this chapter is taken from a yet to be published manuscript written by Professors Rockne McCarthy, James Skillen, and William Harper entitled *Dis-*

IN COLONIAL AMERICA

In colonial America no clean line separated public from private schools and no distinctions were made between secular and religious schools. On this latter point it is important to emphasize that in its manifestation of a unified world-view, seventeenth-century New England was nearer the medieval than the modern world. The assumption, for example, that a fundamental unity existed between faith and reason was a characteristic feature of both medieval and American colonial thought.

A common assumption throughout colonial New England was that the central purpose of human life, including education, was to promote the Christian faith and to advance the Christian life. Religious schools, therefore, were to play an important role in society. The notion that it is desirable and possible to separate religion from education, to make religion an entirely private matter by confining it to personal beliefs and to family and church matters, is a modern assumption that did not shape the educational theory of the early settlers.

In colonial America, there was therefore little concern to differentiate sharply public from private schools. While the terms public and private were used, no clean line of demarcation separated the two kinds of institutions in several important respects. For example, more often than not both public and private schools consciously taught from a religious perspective and both received public funds to support their academic work.

It was common practice in colonial America for public funds to go to private schools in the form of land grants and taxes. The justification for this practice was that private schools were providing a public service to the community. The fact that private schools were owned and managed by individuals, religious groups, or churches did not disqualify them from being considered "public" institutions when it came to such matters as funding. This was the case, for example, in Massachusetts. That state was the last of the original states to adopt a constitution. When it finally did so in 1780 its constitution reflected the seventeenth-century pattern of public support for both public and private schools. The constitution clearly stated that ". . . the duty of legislators and magistrates, in all future periods of this Commonwealth, is to cherish the interests of literature and the sciences," and "to encourage

establishment a Second Time: Public Justice for American Schools. The research and writing of the manuscript were funded by the Association for Public Justice Education Fund. We are grateful to the authors and the Association for the use of this material.

private societies and public institutions" in the promotion of agriculture, sciences, commerce, the trades, and the arts.[2]

In Massachusetts, as elsewhere, both "private societies and public institutions" were encouraged in their educational enterprise by means of the use of public funds. One of the most important of the "private societies" was the academy. Academies were private institutions with their own boards of trustees. But their funding was not limited to private support. Because the academy's role in secondary education was widely accepted as serving a public interest, many states like Massachusetts actively encouraged their growth and development through grants of land and money.

While the distinction between public and private schools was relevant in matters of ownership and management, it was irrelevant in such matters as funding. Thus "public" implied the performance of broad social functions. It was not limited to public or private control or to distinctions between secular and religious education. In colonial America there was no clean line of separation between public and private schools.

IN THE EIGHTEENTH CENTURY

A clear distinction between public and private schools emerged in the last half of the eighteenth century. Why and how it did so are questions that, as Bailyn points out, involve changes in the general institutional character of society. More particularly, these were changes in the role of the state with respect to several of the nonpolitical associations or institutions in society; they were the result in large part of both the religious-philosophical and political developments of the American Revolutionary era.

Thomas Jefferson made a major contribution to the development of Enlightenment ideology and to changes in the institutional structure of the society. He influenced national decisions in Philadelphia as well as local decisions in his home state of Virginia where he served as a member of the legislature. In 1779 he introduced several bills that, taken together, provide important insights into his religious-philosophical perspective and the way in which that perspective guided his vision for a new institutional order in society.

Jefferson's "Bill for Religious Freedom" was designed to disestablish the Anglican Church in Virginia. In colonial America most of the original colonies continued the European practice of establishing state churches. In Massachusetts, for example, the salaries of only Congregational ministers were paid from public funds. In Virginia the Anglican Church enjoyed this special status.

During and after the Revolutionary struggle there was a growing conviction that it was unjust to tax every citizen for the support of a particular church. Jefferson led the protest in Virginia, and when his bill passed, Virginia became the first state to disestablish a church.

Jefferson's work to disestablish the Anglican Church was related to his efforts to establish a system of public primary and secondary schools in Virginia. His educational plans were outlined in a "Bill for the More General Diffusion of Knowledge." Referring to this and similar bills introduced into the Virginia legislature in 1779, Jefferson said in his autobiography:

> I consider four of these bills, passed or reported, as forming a system by which every fibre would be eradicated of ancient or future aristocracy; and a foundation laid for a government truly republican. . . . The restoration of the rights of conscience relieved the people from taxation for the support of a religion not theirs; for the establishment was truly of the religion of the rich, the dissenting sects being entirely composed of the less wealthy people, and these, by the bill for a general education, would be qualified to understand their rights, to maintain them, and to exercise with intelligence their part in self-government. . . .[3] *

In Jefferson's mind public schools were to play a central role in the process of establishing republican principles in America. Before the break-up of the medieval world the Roman Catholic Church played a central role in establishing common principles and values in society. With the demise of the medieval church, citizens became divided among rival religions. In an age when competing churches represented sectarian battles among citizens, some people came to see the possibility of using public education as a means of erasing the sectarian battle lines and once again creating a society based on common principles and values. In the vision of Thomas Jefferson, for example, sectarian churches were to be disestablished and replaced by a public school establishment. One of the goals of the new establishment would be the spread of a public (as in *republic*an) faith throughout society.

The distinction between public and private religion was at the heart of Jefferson's thought. In his Enlightenment rationalism,

*Justice Rutledge, in a dissenting opinion in the 1947 *Everson* decision, noted that the first enacted portion of Jefferson's Code "was the statute barring entailments. Primogeniture soon followed. Much longer the author was to wait for enactment of the Bill for Religious Freedom; and not until after his death was the corollary bill to be accepted in prin-

public religion referred to what he assumed to be a universal morality, while private religion described the sectarian beliefs of such groups as the Presbyterians, Baptists, and Methodists. The sectarians, Jefferson concluded, were unenlightened individuals who did not comprehend the universal truths of religion. Since Jefferson assumed that the stability of society demanded the acceptance of a common morality, the presence of sectarianism represented a constant threat to the public order. The remaining unenlightened sectarians were allotted their place in society as long as they accepted the fact that they were sectarians and were therefore to keep their religious beliefs outside of the public-legal order.

This privatization of religion was not forced upon people. The revival movement known as the Great Awakening was one of the forces that produced a form of religious individualism in which people freely accepted the argument that religion was limited to an individual's personal communion with God and such private spheres of life as the family and the church. The Christian community thereby accepted a dualist view of life in which a so-called secular realm existed alongside a religious realm. This division of life into two separate spheres conveniently matched Jefferson's distinction between private sectarian and public nonsectarian morality.

While Jefferson argued that sectarian religion must be privatized lest it disrupt society, he maintained that society must be undergirded by a common, nonsectarian morality. This public morality was essentially a rational view of life which Jefferson assumed everyone could accept because he believed its truthfulness was self-evident. Jefferson identified this public morality with the very principles of republicanism. And in his mind one of the primary purposes of public schools was to spread Enlightenment-republican principles throughout society.

Jefferson's distinction between a public nonsectarian religion and a private sectarian religion was not as self-evident as it was self-serving. Jefferson's religion was universal and self-evident only to those individuals who agreed with his religious assumptions. To those who did not agree, his religion was simply a form of Deism, which represented only one of the many sectarian religions competing for dominance in society.

---

ciple which he considered most important of all, namely, to provide for common education at public expense. However, he linked this with disestablishment as corollary prime parts in a system of basic freedoms." Everson v. Board of Education, 330 U.S. 1 (1947).

Jefferson's definition of his religion as common and universal and all other religions as sectarian and parochial was self-
serving because the distinction allowed his religion to lay claim to
the public life of the country. All other religions were relegated
to the private sphere of individual conscience, family, and church
life. Jefferson's Enlightenment view of the nature of religion and
the limits of religious freedom eventually came to dominate the
nineteenth-century school conflict.

In our second chapter we noted that principled individualists easily become pragmatic collectivists. We see this tendency in
Jefferson's thought—a fundamental tension between his theoretical commitment to individualism and a pragmatic bent toward
collectivism. This tension is particularly evident when it comes to
public education. On the one hand Jefferson believed that individuals must constantly guard against surrendering their freedom
to the state and that an educated citizenry was the best and most
effective curb on government. On the other hand he willingly
gave to the government the power to educate citizens in a given
perspective. The fusion of these beliefs created a fundamental
tension that is illustrated in Jefferson's dealings with the University of Virginia.

Jefferson was instrumental in founding the university as an
institution supported with public monies and administered by
public authorities. The university was to manifest the spirit of the
man who "swore eternal hostility to tyranny over the minds of
men." And yet, when it came time to hire the faculty, Jefferson
wrote to James Madison about the need to find an advocate of
their understanding of republicanism to teach law. It became evident that the legal perspective of Jefferson's and Madison's fellow Virginian, Federalist Chief Justice John Marshall, was not
welcome at the University of Virginia. The university was to be
a bastion of so-called orthodox republicanism. In Jefferson's letter
to Madison he declared that:

> It is in our seminary that the vestal flame is to be kept alive;
> from thence it is to spread anew over our own and the sister
> States. If we are true and vigilant in our trust, within a
> dozen or twenty years a majority of our own legislature will
> be from one school, and many disciples will have carried its
> doctrine home with them to their several states, and will
> have leavened the whole mass.[4]

Jefferson's evangelistic rhetoric was matched by his ardent
censorship of the books students were permitted to read as texts.
This action was to ensure that no ideas were taught at the uni-

versity which were not compatible with his understanding of political orthodoxy. In typically rationalistic fashion Jefferson considered theological heresies to be irrelevant. But this was not the case with political heresies:

> There is one branch in which we are the best judges, in which heresies may not be taught, of so interesting a character to our own State, and to the United States, as to make it a duty in us to lay down the principles which are to be taught. It is that of government. . . . It is our duty to guard against the dissemination of such [Federalist] principles among our youth, and the diffusion of that poison, by a previous prescription of the texts to be followed in their discourses.[5]

Jefferson's thought, therefore, revealed a tension between his theoretical commitment to individualism and his pragmatic bent toward collectivism. This was more than just a quirk in Jefferson's personality. We have argued elsewhere in this book that such a tension is a fundamental problem inherent in an individualist social philosophy. Consistent individualism inevitably leads to anarchy. Thus the individualist must take some action to guarantee order in society. More often than not the state emerges from its "artificial status" to become in practice the most real and most powerful institution in society. Jefferson did not take a direct route to the state. He turned instead to the school as the primary institution to guarantee the order and freedom he desired in society. In Jefferson's thought the school gave up its autonomy to the state and became little more than a department of the state. And Jefferson saw nothing wrong with indoctrinating students into a philosophy of government as long as it corresponded to his understanding of orthodoxy.

It is to the credit of Benjamin Rush, a Philadelphia doctor and close friend of Jefferson, that at least once he saw that Jefferson's program was but another form of sectarianism. "We only change the names of our vices and follies in different periods of time," he wrote. "Religious bigotry has yielded to political intolerance. The man who used to hate his neighbor for being a Churchman or a Quaker now hates him with equal cordiality for being a Tory."[6] After the Revolutionary War Rush could have replaced the name Tory with Federalist or Republican and the meaning would not have changed.

Even though Rush was deeply committed to individual freedom and saw the danger of political intolerance, he followed the same route into pragmatic collectivism that Jefferson followed. Rush shared the concern of the ruling Anglo-Saxon elite that the social and political stability of Pennsylvania was being threatened by the increasing movement of foreign immigrants into the state. He turned to public schools as an ideal instrument for Americanizing the new arrivals. He unabashedly predicted that "our schools of learning, by producing one general and uniform system of education, will render the mass of the people more homogeneous and thereby fit them more easily for uniform and peaceable government."[7] He even went on to make clear that he considered it possible and desirable "to convert men into republican machines. This must be done," Rush argued, "if we expect them to perform their parts properly in the great machine of the government of the state."[8] And continuing the mechanistic analogy, Rush concluded that "the will of the people must be fitted to each other by means of education before they can be made to produce regularity and unison in government."[9]

In the thought of Jefferson we clearly see the beginnings of the religious-philosophical argument that there should be a clean line of separation between public nonsectarian and private sectarian institutions. And in Jefferson, but even more clearly in Rush, we see the beginnings of the political argument that public schools are a perfect mechanism for securing a stable political and social order. But the plans of Jefferson, Rush, and others to establish a system of public schools to inculcate Enlightenment-republican values and beliefs did not emerge in their lifetime. That is the story of early nineteenth-century developments to which we now turn.

IN THE NINETEENTH CENTURY

It was not until the first half of the nineteenth century that a legal attempt was made to draw a "clean line of separation" between public and private schools. The development was directly related to the outworking of Jeffersonian assumptions regarding nonsectarian and sectarian religion and the belief in the importance of a system of public schools to ensure the stability and welfare of the republic. Clear evidence of these two assumptions can be found, for example, in the work of Horace Mann (1796–1859).

In Massachusetts, a state where academies and other non-government institutions received public funds, Mann worked hard for the establishment of a system of public schools that alone received state funds. He was successful in that he convinced enough people that a system of public schools which championed a supposedly nonsectarian religion was essential to the well-being of the social, economic, and political order of the state. Public funds should not be permitted to go to academies or denominational schools because, Mann argued, public monies must be restricted to schools run and administered by the state and schools where a nonsectarian form of religion was taught. In his mind "the Religion of Heaven should be taught to children, while the creeds of men should be postponed until their Minds were sufficiently matured to weigh Evidence and Arguments."[10] Mann was himself a Unitarian, and his nonsectarian ("Religion of Heaven") and sectarian ("creeds of men") categories matched Jefferson's deistic distinction between religion defined as a public or common moral code and religion as a private promotion of sectarian dogmas and beliefs. What Jefferson was not able to accomplish for public education in Virginia in the 1780's and '90's, Mann was able to accomplish in Massachusetts in the 1830's and '40's. Massachusetts became the first state in the Union to establish a monopolistic governmental funding policy for schools.

There is little doubt that there was a pressing need in Massachusetts and elsewhere for the creation of more schools to meet the educational needs of a growing population. Expanding educational opportunities, however, did not have to be synonymous with the elimination of public funds to nongovernment schools and thus the establishment of a monopolistic funding policy. The fact that this happened is more a demonstration of the power of a majoritarian ideology than of the indisputable normativity of the policy.

The same monopolistic, governmental funding policy for schools that emerged in Massachusetts also occurred in New York City, and the same two Jeffersonian assumptions regarding religion and politics underlay the New York policy. Although the history in the New York situation is complex, the records are clear that the clean line of separation between public and private schools rested upon the assumed distinction between nonsectarian and sectarian religion. For example, in New York City at the turn of the nineteenth century, public funds from New York State's "permanent school fund" were used to support church schools as well as several charitable organizations that provided free education for needy children. The allotment to the denominational and charitable institutions was divided in proportion to the number of students given free education and was only to be used to pay teachers' salaries.[11]

In 1805, however, the New York State legislature chartered the New York Free School Society. The legislature in 1807 granted the Society what became known as the "peculiar privilege" of receiving public funds to pay teachers' salaries *and* to construct and equip its school building. None of the other groups shared in the construction and equipment funds.

The favored status of the New York Free School Society was soon challenged by Baptists when they requested and received from the state legislators funds for school equipment and construction costs as well as for teachers' salaries. The Free School Society's response was to attack both the integrity of the Baptist school organization and the legitimacy of *any* public money going to support what it labelled "sectarian" education. The curricula of the Baptist and the Society's schools were substantially the same, and yet the Free School Society argued that its religious instruction was nonsectarian. The issue was suddenly being argued on different grounds. It was no longer simply a question of Baptist participation in public funding for buildings and equipment, but rather the Society's contention that funding even for teachers' salaries in sectarian schools was illegitimate. "It is totally incompatible with our republican institutions," the Society argued, "and a dangerous precedent" to allow any portion of the public money to be spent "by the clergy or church trustees for the support of *sectarian* education."[12]

Although New York Secretary of State John Van Ness Yates supported the Baptist position and urged the New York legislature to extend the "peculiar privilege" to all schools, his advice was rejected. The legislature decided instead to turn over the controversial issue of designating recipients of school funds in New York City to the city's Common Council. The next year, on the advice of its legal committee, the Council rejected the Baptist request and ruled that no public money could thereafter go to "sectarian" schools.[13] The Council accepted the Society's distinction between private and public schools and between sectarian and nonsectarian education. The following year, as if to reinforce the claim that it alone represented "nonsectarian," "public" education, the Free School Society changed its name to the New York *Public* School Society. Its property and buildings were turned over to the city, and the Mayor and Recorder were re-appointed as *ex-officio* members of the Board. The Society then received from the city a perpetual lease of the property and buildings and what amounted to legal recognition that only its nonsectarian version of education would thereafter receive public support.

This is an early example of why and how a legal distinction emerged between public and private schools. In the Baptist–Public School Society struggle, however, there was not yet a clean line of separation between public and private schools. Despite the fact that the Society changed its name, turned over its property and buildings to the city, and accepted public money, it remained a private philanthropic organization run by a self-perpetuating board of trustees.

The final and complete separation occurred as a result of a second controversy, this time between the Public School Society and the Catholic schools in New York City. By 1839 the Public School Society operated eighty-six schools, with an average total attendance of some 12,000 students. In that year, the Roman Catholic Church operated seven Catholic Free Schools in the city, "open to all children, without discrimination," with more than 5,000 students in attendance.[14] It was not surprising, therefore, that Catholics began pressing the city's Common Council for a proportional share of the school fund.

Once again the whole question came before the Law Committee to decide on the constitutionality of the request. The report of the committee is important because it is a clear indication of the future direction of the legal debate surrounding education. The report concluded that Catholic schools were not entitled to public funds because they were not "common" or public schools. A common school was defined as one open to all in which "those branches of education, and those only, ought to be taught, which tend to prepare a child for the ordinary business of life."[15] The report continued by arguing that, "if religion be taught in a school, it strips it of one of the characteristics of a common school, as all *religious* and *sectarian* studies have a direct reference to a future state, and *are not necessary* to prepare a child for the mechanical or any other business."[16] Such a judgment about the relevancy of religion to everyday life was itself clearly a religious judgment, though a judgment made on supposedly neutral, nonreligious grounds. The Law Committee's report moved beyond the usual sectarian-nonsectarian distinction and argued for a distinction between religious and nonreligious studies. It is important to emphasize this change, for here we find a very early legal example of a new use of the old distinction in a clearly political struggle between two different groups over the question of public funding of schools. This distinction clearly involved the acknowledgment of supposedly neutral, nonreligious, "secular" matters in education.

In this political-legal struggle the Jeffersonian distinction between sectarian and nonsectarian religion was being replaced by the modern religious-secular distinction. The report of the Law Committee reflected this development. The political character of the decision is clear from the fact that the Law Committee decided that public funds could continue to go to the schools of the Public School Society even though they were run by a private board of trustees and reflected a Protestant world and life view complete with readings from the King James Bible. What was at stake was the political issue of whether or not minorities had a right to public educational funds and the religious issue concerning the nature of religion—whether or not life could be divided between a non-religious or "secular" sphere and a religious sphere. The two issues were interrelated because the public-private distinction rested on the secular-religious distinction. Just as the old Jeffersonian distinction between sectarian and nonsectarian was not as self-evident as it was self-serving, the secular and religious distinction was a self-serving definition used by Protestants to exclude Catholics from participating in the common school fund.

From the Catholic perspective these definitions seemed to be politically motivated, and religiously and philosophically biased. Bishop Hughes pointed out that one of the stated goals of the Public School Society was the "early religious instruction" of children.[17] He went on to point out the obvious bias against Catholics in this "early religious instruction," and insisted that no correction of the bias could be possible *without giving just ground for exception to other denominations.*[18] In this comment Hughes clearly set forth the fundamental dilemma created by every effort to maintain a majoritarian, monopolistic, public school system in a religiously pluralist society. He pointed out that it was impossible for one group of Christians to teach the "essentials of religion" without offending the beliefs of some other group, because there would always be differences among Christians as to what the essentials of religion should be. And if it were assumed that religion could be eliminated from education, then students would be left "to the advantage of infidelity."[19] The fundamental dilemma of a monopolistic, governmental funding policy for schools was plain. Since some people believed that education would always be religious (that is, that it could never be neutral) in some form, whether Protestant, Catholic, secular (the "advantage of infidelity"), or in some other way, a funding policy which favored one group's perspective over another was fundamentally unjust. Hughes made his point well, but few really heard what he was saying.

One who did was the New York Secretary of State, John C. Spencer. Acting in his capacity as *ex-officio* superintendent of public schools, he submitted in 1841 an official report to the state senate, which was then embroiled in the New York City educational struggle. Spencer began by examining the Catholic claim that justice demanded they receive a proportional share of public funds for their schools:

> It can scarcely be necessary to say that the founders of these schools, and those who wish to establish others, have absolute rights to the benefits of a common burthen; and that

any system which deprives them of their just share in the application of a common and public fund must be justified, if at all, by a necessity which demands the sacrifice of individual rights, for the accomplishment of a social benefit of paramount importance. It is presumed no such necessity can be urged in the present instance.[20]

The Secretary of State's response to those who opposed use of public funds for sectarian purposes was similar to that of Bishop Hughes. Spencer replied that all instruction is in some ways sectarian: "No books can be found, no reading lessons can be selected, which do not contain more or less of some principles of religious faith, either directly avowed, or indirectly assumed."[21] He applied this point directly to the activities of the Public School Society:

Even the moderate degree of religious instruction which the Public School Society imparts, must therefore be sectarian; that is, it must favor one set of opinions in opposition to another, or others; and it is believed that this always will be the result, in any course of education that the wit of man can devise.[22]

Spencer, like Bishop Hughes, closed his argument by pointing out that it is impossible to avoid sectarianism by abolishing religious instruction altogether: "On the contrary, it would be in itself sectarian; because it would be consonant to the views of a peculiar class, and opposed to the opinions of other classes."[23]

Spencer, as a scholar, went to the heart of the matter by pointing out that calling something secular, and meaning by that nonreligious, was a statement that was meaningful only within a dualist view of life — a division of life into two separate spheres of existence, one religious, the other secular or nonreligious. To those who did not share this dualist view of life, who believed that religion was central to every aspect of life, the argument was not self-evident. The question that Spencer faced was how to do justice to these two opposing views in the allocation of public funds to schools. He concluded that justice demanded an evenhanded distribution of public funds to all schools, regardless of their perspective on education.

Spencer could not convince the legislators. In the face of the growing anti-Catholic sentiment of the Nativist movement, any hope that a Protestant majority would approve educational funds going to the Catholic minority was out of the question. The best that could be accomplished was for the city to take over the schools of the Public School Society and place them under the supervision of an elected Board of Education and State Superintendent of public schools. The city's action formalized a clean line of separation between public and private schools. In the end, the public school movement in New York City transformed the city's pluralistic funding policy into a monopolistic funding policy similar to that in Massachusetts and to the policies that were developing in other parts of the country.

An understanding of this transformation helps answer the questions of why and how a clean line of separation between public and private schools developed in the first half of the nineteenth century. The separation became as deeply rooted in American law as did the presumed secular-religious dichotomy upon which it was based. Throughout its recent history, the Supreme Court has handled school funding cases in a way that reflects these nineteenth-century presumptions.

SUPREME COURT DECISIONS ON SCHOOLS

A nine-judge United States Supreme Court with members appointed at different times for an indeterminate tenure by presidents of different political parties and persuasions, and approved by an independent Senate of one hundred proudly autonomous members, is not likely to display legal unity, let alone philosophic unity. To the extent that the Supreme Court shapes law on a given subject, we are not governed by a single, logical body of rules. We are governed by rules that are eclectic. This eclecticism results not merely from differences between judges. It also results from the issues presented to the Court and the context in which they finally reach the Court. An education case before the Court today may turn on fine distinctions. Next year a related case may turn on some broad policy issue. The next such case may not be brought to the Court for several years; perhaps it will be raised during the disruptive time of war. Our high court, then, by its very nature and by the structure of the judicial system is not designed to produce a neat legal or philosophic unity.

But while that point ought never to be forgotten, there are also powerful systemic pressures that give much consistency and coherence to judicial action and to our law. Supreme Court justices are a peculiar elite, chosen in part because they reflect most of the expectations of the American political establishment. They are all members of the American bar, educated in remarkably similar law schools, guided by their practicing colleagues in the mysteries of an esoteric profession, which is unified in part by materials printed by a surprisingly few legal publishing houses. One of the norms of the legal establishment is the rule of *stare decises* — that is, commitment to the polestar of settled precedent. And if it turns out (as it always does) that there are two or more polestars on an issue, the experts have laid down rules, sometimes honored, on how to choose between them.

American law, then, is not a capricious amalgam. It reflects the long-standing assumptions and biases of our society. The Supreme Court's opinions on school cases grow out of the prevailing legal construct that governs judicial reasoning. The nineteenth-century settlement of the public-private school conflict has its present-day counterpart, for when the Supreme Court became involved in the debate over public funding of schools in the twentieth century, it inherited the nineteenth-century definitions and uncritically accepted them as self-evident truths.

The Supreme Court's Construct Governing School Funding

The Court begins all opinions on the constitutionality of government aid to nongovernment schools with the First Amendment's few words that there shall be "no law respecting an establishment of religion, or prohibiting the free exercise thereof. . . ." A huge body of legal interpretation has been developed on that slender foundation. In the past decade alone the Supreme Court has handled fourteen major cases that took up the issue of the constitutionality of state and federal aid to nongovernment schools. Some of those cases were broken down into as many as six subissues on which the justices voted separately. Thus the justices have voted on twenty-five issues in the fourteen cases. In all of these decisions the Court has repeatedly agreed on a single assumption that it has consistently used to judge the propriety of an aid law.

This single assumption comes to expression in the three-part test as set forth most recently in the 1977 *Wolman* v. *Walter* decision. It reads:

> In order to pass muster, a statute must have a secular legislative purpose, must have a principal or primary effect that neither advances nor inhibits religion, and must not foster an excessive government entanglement with religion.[24]

This test reflects in large measure the public-private and secular-religious legal construct that emerged out of the nineteenth-century school battle. This construct has been permanently enshrined in Supreme Court cases dealing with schools ever since the famous *Everson* decision in 1947.

The *Everson* case dealt with the constitutionality of a New Jersey statute that allowed local school districts to reimburse parents for the transportation of children to and from all schools except those run for profit. The appellant challenged the law in part on the ground that the statute authorized reimbursement to parents of children attending religious schools, and was, therefore, an unconstitutional establishment of religion.

Justice Black, in the majority opinion, took care to point out that the First Amendment had, to use Jefferson's words, erected "a wall of separation between Church and State." He emphasized that the wall of separation could not be narrowly defined to exclude only state support to churches. According to the justice the "establishment of religion" clause must be broadly interpreted to prohibit either a state or the Federal Government from passing laws which "aid one religion, aid all religions, or prefer one religion over another."[25] He then added: "No tax in any amount, large or small, can be levied to support any religious activities or institutions, whatever they may be called, or whatever form they may adopt to teach or practice religion."[26]

After making this pronouncement, however, Black attempted to show that the New Jersey law did not break the wall of separation because it did "no more than provide a general program to help parents get their children, regardless of their religion, safely and expeditiously to and from accredited schools."[27] The juxtaposition of the argument that the Constitution demands a high wall of separation between church and state and the argument that it is nevertheless constitutionally permissible to use state funds to pay the transportation cost of students attending religious schools led Justice Jackson, in his dissenting opinion, to declare: "The case which comes to mind quite irresistibly as a most fitting precedent is that of Julia who, according to Byron, while whispering 'I will ne'er consent,' — consented."[28]

While Jackson's consternation was shared by the other dissenting justices, in our opinion there is a far more fundamental problem which runs through both the majority and minority opinions. Our consternation is that justices on both sides accepted uncritically the public-private and secular-religious distinctions. The majority decided on the basis of the secular– public welfare argument that the New Jersey law was constitutional. The minority decided on the basis of the religious– private function argument that the law was unconstitutional. Justice Rutledge put the options this way:

> To say that New Jersey's appropriation and her use of the power of taxation for raising the funds appropriated are not for public purposes but are for private ends, is to say that they are for the support of religion and religious teaching.

Conversely, to say that they are for public purposes is to say that they are not for religious ones.[29]

This public-private and secular-religious dichotomy has been used to interpret the establishment and free exercise clauses of the First Amendment in every case dealing with government funding for schools. We know of no clear example in which a justice has fundamentally questioned the legitimacy of the dichotomy. The closest a justice has come to this can be found in Jackson's dissenting opinion in the *Everson* case. The following passage has merit because in it Jackson accurately describes the premise upon which the public school movement developed in the nineteenth century; Jackson asks two important questions:

> It [the public school] is a relatively recent development dating from about 1840. It is organized on the premise that secular education can be isolated from all religious teaching so that the school can inculcate all needed temporal knowledge and also maintain a strict and lofty neutrality as to religion. The assumption is that after the individual has been instructed in worldly wisdom he will be better fitted to choose his religion. Whether such a disjunction is possible, and if possible whether it is wise, are questions I need not try to answer.[30]

Since the secular-religious disjunction was central to the development of the public school movement, why did Jackson not see the need to answer his own questions regarding the possibility and wisdom of such a disjunction? Perhaps Jackson believed that for purposes of law the questions had already been answered by the First Amendment. If this was the case the issue of whether or not the secular-religious disjunction was possible, let alone wise, was not pursued by Jackson because this very dichotomy serves as the theoretical model that guided his judicial interpretation of the First Amendment. There was no need to question the legitimacy of the disjunction, once the secular-religious dichotomy was regarded as established in law by the First Amendment. Legally, therefore, it is considered a self-evident truth.

The construct controlling the Court's interpretation of the First Amendment as applied to questions of government funding of schools is the public-private and secular-religious disjunction. But obviously the justices disagree on where to draw the line. Majority and minority opinions on this issue are built upon differing legal standards. Some admit that drawing the line is based upon the justices' own predilections, while others insist there is a clear constitutional standard.

The first position is reflected in Justice Jackson's concurring opinion in the *McCollum* case, decided one year after *Everson*. Jackson pointed out that "the task of separating the secular from the religious in education is one of magnitude, intricacy, and delicacy."[31] It is not too difficult to determine when a creed or a catechism is being taught or when ceremonial acts are occurring in schools. But how is it possible to monitor the teaching of a "secular" subject from a "religious" viewpoint: "How can one draw the line to safeguard against the teaching of history, for example, from a religious viewpoint"? Jackson puts the dilemma in this way: "But how one can teach, with satisfaction or even with justice to all faiths, such subjects as the story of the Reformation, the Inquisition, or even the New England effort to found 'a Church without a Bishop and a State without a King' is more than I know."[32]

The dilemma led Jackson to observe that "when instruction turns to proselyting and imparting knowledge becomes evangelism is, except in the crudest cases, a subtle inquiry."[33] At best, therefore, Jackson believed that justices must admit that the drawing of a line between the secular and the religious "is a matter on which we can find no law but our own prepossessions."[34]

This admission of personal biases or predilections in the drawing of the secular-religious line was not acceptable to Justice Douglas. In the 1952 *Zorach* case he went out of his way to reject Jackson's argument. Douglas held that decisions must rest firmly on a constitutional standard, and that standard is the separation of church and state.[35]

It is important to recognize that Douglas's clarity concerning a constitutional standard was based upon the assumption that the secular-religious disjunction was coterminous with the phrase separation of state (secular) and church (religious). But is it the case that a church is a solely religious institution and that it is therefore illegitimate to refer to it as a secular institution? Is it the case that a state is solely a secular institution and that it is therefore illegitimate to refer to it as a religious institution? The answer to these questions depends upon certain presuppositions or "prepossessions." If a person's definitions presuppose a dualistic view of life, the separation of life into a religious and a nonreligious or secular sphere, then the identification of church with religion and state with secular is a meaningful position. But if one holds to a nondualistic, holistic view of life, such an identification does not correspond with that person's view of reality. From this perspective, secular simply means of or pertaining to this world. Then all institutions—families, schools, churches—no matter how religious, must also be viewed as secular institutions.

This latter perspective rests on the assumption that religion is not a thing in itself. Religion is always intrinsic to the life of an individual or to the identity of an institution. It is impossible, from this perspective, to separate religion from life, to call one individual or institution religious and another secular in the sense of nonreligious.

Our society encompasses a variety of fundamentally different views of reality. Justice Douglas accepted as self-evident a dualist view of life, thus uncritically assuming that a secular-religious disjunction must be equated with a constitutional understanding of the separation of church and state. The assumed disjunction itself has become the constitutional standard used to judge all questions of government funding of schools.

Jackson's statement about "prepossessions" was limited to the difficulty of where to draw the secular-religious disjunction in education. Neither Jackson nor Douglas questioned the assumption that such a line can legitimately be drawn. To date, no justice in any school case has moved beyond the debate of where such a line should be drawn to the question of whether or not the First Amendment requires a secular-religious line to be drawn at all. And the justices' attempts to apply the secular-religious separation have themselves resulted in divided legal reasoning.

One Test But Several Meanings

Since 1947 the Supreme Court has in practice used the secular-religious disjunction to set the minimum meaning of "separation of church and state." Writing on this matter actually began in *Bradfield* v. *Roberts* (1899).[36] In this case the Court held that no constitutional establishment of religion was created when the federal government contracted with the Catholic Sisters of Charity who operated Providence Hospital in Washington, D. C., for the care of poor patients. The government even paid for the construction of a building on hospital grounds. A taxpayer claimed that this was an establishment of religion, since the payments aided a religious body. The Court disagreed, saying that the hospital corporation, chartered by Congress for the secular purposes of healing the sick, carried out this secular function properly. It made no difference that the Sisters were all of the Catholic faith or under the administration of the Catholic church. The faith of persons acquiring such a secular corporate charter was constitutionally of no concern to the government.

If healing the sick in a secular, though religiously controlled corporation, is a secular matter, is educating the young in a church-related school that meets the secular educational needs and requirements of the state also a secular matter? The answer is both "Yes" and "No" according to the Supreme Court. It is "Yes" at the college level of education, and "No" at the pre-college level. Why the difference?

The college–pre-college line. In three separate cases in the 1970's the Supreme Court decided that federal and state aid to church-related colleges was constitutional because these colleges were performing secular functions in a relatively secular way. In no case did the Court find otherwise. Since many state aids to church-related elementary and secondary education have been declared unconstitutional, the Court felt compelled to explain the difference between the two educational levels.

The task first fell to Chief Justice Burger, in *Tilton* v. *Richardson* (1971).[37] In upholding a federal program that gave grants to accredited, church-related colleges for construction of buildings designated for only secular uses, the Chief Justice explained why college education had a more secular dimension than pre-college education:

> College students are less impressionable and less susceptible to religious indoctrination. . . . College . . . courses tend to limit the opportunities for sectarian influence by virtue of their own internal disciplines. Many church-related colleges . . . are characterized by a high degree of academic freedom and seek to evoke free and critical responses from their students.[38] *

Further, the schools at issue admitted students and hired faculty not of their religious faiths, did not require attendance at religious services, and taught required nonsectarian religion courses according to academic and professional standards. No attempt, the schools had shown, was made to indoctrinate students or to proselytize. Indeed, at two of the Catholic schools involved, Jewish rabbis taught required theology courses.

In later cases in which state governments assisted church-related colleges in floating bonds for construction of secular facilities[39] and gave noncategorical grants for secular instruction to such colleges,[40] Justices Powell and Blackmun respectively re-

---

*Daniel Patrick Moynihan points out that the Chief Justice's statement concerning the relative impressionability of college and pre-college students is an example of an assertion by the Court that is not supported by social science research. Moynihan, "Social Science and the Courts," *The Public Interest*, No. 54 (Winter, 1979), pp. 12– 31.

peated in their own way the Chief Justice's differentiation. In all three cases there were strongly worded dissents from three or four judges who thought that either the colleges were too religious to qualify for aid or that the degree of their religiosity merited further judicial study. But a line is a line, and church-related hospitals and colleges are secular by the grace of these decisions, while church-related elementary and secondary schools are not. When the Supreme Court looks at these pre-college schools it sees agencies that are too religious to receive state aid.

In striking down a Rhode Island law that gave limited financial assistance to teachers of secular subjects in church-related schools, Chief Justice Burger wrote for the majority that:

> On the basis of these findings the District Court concluded that the parochial schools constituted "an integral part of the religious mission of the Catholic Church." The various characteristics of the schools make them "a powerful vehicle for transmitting the Catholic faith to the next generation." This process of inculcating religious doctrine is, of course, enhanced by the impressionable age of the pupils, in primary schools particularly. In short, parochial schools involve substantial religious activity and purpose.[41]

Likewise Justice Stewart, in deciding for a majority of six that the loan of secular instructional materials that could conceivably be diverted to religious purposes was unconstitutional, said:

> Even though earmarked for secular purposes, when it flows to an institution in which religion is so pervasive that a substantial portion of its functions are subsumed in the religious mission, state aid has the impermissible primary effect of advancing religion.[42]

Indeed, all justices treat church-related elementary and secondary schools as if they have a more religious dimension than church-related colleges. While justices such as Brennan, Marshall, and Stevens concede that some church-related colleges may be treated as secular,[43] they make no such concession for lower-level schools.

The direct-indirect line. For two of the justices another distinction is important. Until 1980, Justices Burger and Rehnquist rejected direct aid to church-related elementary and secondary schools, even if it supports only a secular program. In *Levitt* v. *Committee* and *Committee* v. *Nyquist* (1973) the Chief Justice spoke his mind on the matter of direct aid.[44] The former case involved state payments for testing and required record-keeping. The part of the latter case to which the Chief Justice objected involved state payment to church-related schools for costs of regular maintenance and repair of buildings. In his single opinion, which treated both programs, Burger found the state laws to be fatally flawed. They gave "direct money grants" to the schools. The schools' use of these grants might relate to the religious aspects of their total efforts, producing a constitutionally forbidden religious effect on the students. Thus these legislative efforts failed to pass the three-part test referred to earlier in this chapter.

The Chief Justice argued vigorously, nevertheless, that indirect aid to nonpublic schools was perfectly sound. In other parts of *Committee* v. *Nyquist* and in *Sloan* v. *Lemon*[45] he voted to uphold programs that did all the following: gave state tuition reimbursements to poor parents who paid private school tuitions, awarded graduated tax benefits to other parents incurring the same expense, and provided state funding to an independent Parent Reimbursement Authority that passed the money on to those who paid such tuitions. Though these programs involved far more money than that involved in programs he voted against, Chief Justice Burger found them constitutionally proper, because they only indirectly benefited these schools. He argued that legal precedents back to 1947, at least, clearly indicated that "government aid to individuals generally stands on an entirely different footing from direct aid to religious institutions."[46] The G.I. bill had shown this. But this argument impressed only Justices Rehnquist and White. Five others thought the indirect aid program made those who benefited from them mere "conduits," passing on state dollars to church-related agencies.

The five-judge majority in part of *Wolman* v. *Walter* (1977) stressed the improper directness of state aid as it struck down an Ohio program that paid church-related schools for the bus transportation needed for field trips to secular sites.[47] Presumably, had the state reimbursed students who had been required by their schools to pay to go on the field trips, the payment would have been allowed. The presumption is legally sound, for in another part of *Wolman* v. *Walter* and in *Meek* v. *Pittenger* (1975) the Supreme Court by 6–3 majorities approved two almost identical programs that lent secular textbooks to students in nonpublic schools.[48] These loans were made directly to the students. Therefore, the indirect benefit to the school was constitutionally immaterial.

The direct-indirect distinction was somewhat blurred in a 1980 decision, *Committee* v. *Regan* (63 L Ed 2d 94 [1980]), which by the narrow margin of 5–4 permitted strictly audited, direct state payments to private schools for state-mandated record keeping and state-mandated testing similar to that required in public schools. Although Justice White's majority opinion said that nothing constitutionally new was being approved by the decision, these were in fact direct payments, unlike the indirect aid in earlier programs that won approval; the minority opinion of Justice Blackmun made much of this point. Perhaps one can say that direct state payments to nonpublic schools are acceptable if they support only audited, state-mandated programs of a "mechanically secular" nature.

Of course, since some indirect aid programs stand — for example, textbook loans — while others fall — for example, tuition reimbursements — this standard of the constitutionality of a program is not determinative in itself. A further standard was needed.

The administrative-political entanglement line. Entanglement as a test in church-state decisions arose first in a tax case, not an education case.[49] Upholding a New York property tax law that was challenged because it gave exemption to churches, the Chief Justice, speaking for a seven-judge majority, noted that a central purpose of the establishment clause was to eliminate strife between church and state. With the facts of Western history as background, the founding fathers, he argued, had wisely drafted the First Amendment to reduce as much as possible that interaction between the two institutions that created religio-political strife. He concluded that tax exemption, compared to taxation, reduced strife-causing entanglement.

The Chief Justice applied this analysis to educational aid laws in *Lemon* v. *Kurtzman* and *Earley* v. *Dicenso* in 1971.[50] The former involved Pennsylvania payments to nonpublic schools for teaching specified secular subjects. The latter, as noted above, concerned Rhode Island salary supplements to poorly paid teachers of secular subjects in church-related schools. Burger, besides objecting to the direct payments, as already noted, found that to ensure the secularity of both programs the states would have to monitor them closely — so closely that there would be an excessive degree of church-state entanglement. Legal precedent as spelled out in his tax opinion forbade this, even for this judge, sympathetic to the cause of nongovernment schools.

This forbidden entanglement, it seemed clear, was primarily a matter of the administrative reviews the programs would require. State inspection would have to be rather demanding. But the Chief Justice added a further comment about entanglement in these cases that was to haunt him in later ones. Entanglement, he stated, could be broader than administrative inspections; it could also be a matter of disputes in state politics. Partisans for aid to church-related schools might square off against opponents of that aid in elections and in legislatures. The entanglements Burger feared could be both administrative and political.

This position caused the Chief Justice difficulty with six of his brethren. With the potential for two kinds of excessive entanglement, the justices had an easy time finding or imagining some of it whatever form of aid was before them. Justice Stewart found "excessive entanglement" even in the administration of that part of the Pennsylvania programs reviewed in *Meek* v. *Pittenger* that provided public employees for remedial and accelerated instruction, guidance counseling and testing, and speech and hearing services in private schools. Though only public employees were used, the entanglement would result because, he thought, the state would have to make certain that in the atmosphere of the religious school even the state's employees did not "inculcate religion."[51] Blackmun took essentially the same stance regarding payment for field trips at issue in *Wolman* v. *Walter*.[52] Powell buttressed his opinion, striking down the tax benefits of *Committee* v. *Nyquist*, by referring to the "grave potential of entanglement in the broader sense of continuing political strife."[53] Brennan held that all three programs at issue in *Meek* had to be stricken because of the "broader base of entanglement" between church and state occasioned by the political divisiveness of such substantially funded programs.[54]

Yet Burger thought that Stewart's suggestion in *Meek* was "extravagant." Rehnquist decided, moreover, that the justices had created a trap for themselves. In order for the state to ensure that its programs created no primary effect that was religious, it had to supervise its aid programs with such care that entanglement necessarily resulted. Was not, therefore, the Court's use of the entanglement test "a promise to the ear to be broken to the hope, a teasing illusion like a munificent bequest in a pauper's will?"[55] Clearly, their understanding of the entanglement test provided more heated intra-court exchange than any of the others.

A more basic judgment might be that such heated intra-court exchange reveals that even fellow justices sense that the majority Court is here reaching desperately for some added criterion to strike down what their basic bias or "prepossession" requires, rather than articulating a clear third test of constitutionality. Court analyst William Ball has observed that on "the political division along religious lines" the Court has "detoured into hitherto unknown, if not forbidden, constitutional territory."[56] He points out that here religion is not only declared to be a purely private matter, but that any possible intrusion into public life is politically divisive, and therefore automatically unconstitutional.

The entanglement test represents the full fruition of the Enlightenment mind, and it is expressed by the highest court in the land. In the name of constitutionality the entanglement test forbids even the possibility that religious beliefs may enter the public arena and cause "political strife." Pressed to articulate an ever finer line between the religious and the secular, the private and the public, the Supreme Court has clarified itself into exposing its basic bias. It has driven a theistic world-view, and the schools that express it, into the wilderness, far from the public arena where only that which is "secular" may enter. Now, however, the Court's consensus seems to be crumbling in the face of social realities; there is hope for the future.

Divided Three Ways

The evolution of legal precedent on the issue of school funding has produced a persistent voting pattern in the Supreme Court of three equal blocs, which have been labeled and described by Richard E. Morgan.[57] The nature of these blocs illustrates how a Court, united on the basic construct that the secular and religious can be distinguished, still must struggle mightily to achieve unity in the face of the realities of the day-to-day workings of society.

The accommodationists. Chief Justice Burger and Justices White and Rehnquist are the most willing to approve laws that benefit church-related education. Called the accommodationists, since 1971 (see Table I, p. 104) they have voted together to uphold twenty of twenty-five separate state and federal efforts to give such benefits. They have been divided only two times. The most significant of their united votes were those upholding the following aid programs: state tuition reimbursements to poor parents who paid nonpublic school tuitions,[58] state tax deductions for such tuitions,[59] and state indirect tuition reimbursements to parents who sent their children to private schools.[60] All these were dissenting votes. The accommodationist bloc has been in the minority thirteen of the twenty-five times.

The super-separationists. Justices Brennan, Marshall, and Stevens[61] insist upon the most consistent application of the secular-religious dichotomy and therefore the most complete or strict separation of church and state respecting aid to nonpublic schools. Counting another super-separationist, Justice Douglas, whom Stevens replaced, they have been united twenty-two times as they voted to strike down various aspects of aid laws since 1971, and divided only three times. They voted with the majority in thirteen of the twenty-five church-state issues (see Table I). The most revealing of their united votes were those opposing state laws providing secular textbooks for students of private schools[62] and all state and federal aid programs that assisted church-related colleges.[63]

The moderate separationists. Justices Stewart, Powell, and Blackmun are the middle bloc of the divided court. Two or three of them have been with the majority on all twenty-five votes under analysis. Justice Blackmun has never dissented, the only justice who has always been in the majority on school funding decisions. They have been united twenty times to uphold, among other things, the textbook and college aid programs that the super-separationists rejected. They joined with the super-separationists thirteen times to strike down, among other things, the tuition reimbursements and tax benefits that the accommodationists approved. Their votes really control the Court's decisions on school funding, so their "score" shown in Table I is the same as the "score" of the entire court. Therefore, their opinions merit the closest attention.

The importance of the disagreements among the justices is clearly shown in tabular form.

TABLE I:
Voting of Supreme Court on Aid to
Nongovernment Education in Cases from 1971 to 1980[64]

	Times Bloc Upheld Constitutionality of Aid Measure	Times Bloc Opposed Constitutionality of Aid Measure	Times Bloc was Split
The Accommodationist Bloc	20	5	2
The Moderate Separationist Bloc	12	13	5
The Super-Separationist Bloc	3	22	3
Voting of Court Majority	12	13	

The persistent division shows that the Court has found no useful test, single or multiple, by which to interpret the establishment clause, even though it accepts unanimously the disjunction between the secular and the religious.

The Meaning of the Division

In its twistings and turnings through the labyrinthine maze of cases before it for the past thirty years, the Supreme Court has produced its version of the dividing line between the constitutionally permissible and the prohibited forms of aid to nongovernment schools. The present status of the whole confused issue is this:

Aid for Nongovernment Schools

Permissible Aid*	*Prohibited Aid*
1. loans of secular, approved textbooks to students	1. teaching secular subjects
2. bus transportation	2. maintenance of school buildings
3. administration of standardized tests	3. salary supplements for teachers of secular subjects
4. administration of diagnostic tests for those with learning problems	4. development and administration of tests
5. therapeutic services to those with learning problems	5. reimbursement of tuition to low income parents
6. direct payment for state-mandated record keeping and testing, subject to audit.	6. state income tax allowances for tuition
	7. professional services of counseling, testing, and remedial education
	8. instructional materials (maps, projectors, etc.)
	9. loan of instructional materials (except secular textbooks)
	10. field trips to secular sites

The length of the lists reveals that on balance the Supreme Court has hindered more than helped educational pluralism. The Court has itself been a major stumbling block to the development of a strong pluralist elementary and secondary school system in the nation. It has found constitutionally permissible only those forms of aid that are peripheral to the main academic task of the school as school. Moreover, the amounts of money involved are minimal, if not minuscule.

*Not included in the list are those federal funds funneled through the Elementary and Secondary Education Act since 1966, which include permanent loan of library books and some instructional equipments to schools which qualify because of the presence of educationally deprived students. A special "by-pass" feature of this federal legislation enables this aid to flow directly to nongovernment schools in those states whose constitutions prohibit such aid through state means.

The divisions within the Court on these matters reveal an unstable Court, a Court divided increasingly against itself on the application of the dividing line between the secular and the religious. Some hope remains that a change in the membership of the Court produces further change in the kinds of aid that are permissible. However, no substantial change is likely until the fundamental bias of the Court is acknowledged and a pluralistic structure of government funding for schools replaces the existing monopolistic structure.

Such a development would require a change in the interpretation of the establishment clause. Unless that fundamental change occurs, some funding of educational pluralism at the elementary and secondary levels will remain an option, but an option that is not much realized. Nongovernmental schools in the context of present American society are a possibility only for those who can afford the additional expense. For the rich, the expense presents no great problem. But for the vast majority of Americans, the problem is very real. For the poor there is no choice. They are caught in the public school establishment because the Court has denied almost all governmental funding for nongovernment education.

Curiously, the establishment clause that was meant to help maximize religious freedom and choice has become the prime stumbling block in the path of educational pluralism and the free choice of schools that pluralism makes possible. This is not because the establishment clause prohibits funding for nongovernmental schools in some ultimate way; the funding of church-related colleges shows that such funding is indeed possible. The obstruction is a public-private and secular-religious disjunction that is so deeply embedded in the American consciousness and the judicial reasoning of the Supreme Court that it is difficult to see our way clear of that false distinction.

CHAPTER 5

CONFESSIONAL PLURALISM AND SCHOOL FUNDING

HOW can a society committed to religious freedom deal, equitably and justly, with all those schools whose existence arises directly and consciously out of some religious commitment, whether those schools are organized under the auspices of the church or by parents' groups? Can such schools be only tolerated but not encouraged? Can they exist by sufferance only but not by right? Can they be excluded from a fair share of the taxes that society allocates for educating its citizens?

As long as the artificial secular-religious distinction dominates both judicial reasoning and public attitudes, full equality between public and nonpublic schools will remain effectively blocked. In point of fact, however, the public schools, far from being religiously neutral, do endorse and exhibit religion, the religion of naturalistic humanism. Were the Supreme Court to recognize the evidence presented here, the legal system would find itself in a quandary. If the Court has ruled consistently that public money may not aid religion, and if it can be shown that public schools teach a real and legally defined religion, then the courts must abandon the secular-religious distinction and decide either to fund no schools, or to fund all schools. This potential judicial dilemma is, in part, of the Court's own making, and is the product of a society that has so accepted the privatizing of religion that it does not see in what sense all education is religious, that all schools, and not just those announcing it, have a religious outlook.

THE SECULAR-RELIGIOUS LINE: A DEAD END

After thirty years of effort, it has become increasingly apparent that to distinguish between the secular and the religious in nongovernmental education is an exercise in futility. The courts have rightly found that the school committed to promoting a theistic world-and-life view does not separate out the religious and secular aspects of that world-view. Such schools in fact deliberately seek to integrate all aspects of the school program into a holistic vision in which all aspects of life and learning are understood theistically. While not all such schools exhibit such integration with equal success, the commitment to it is what makes these schools distinctive.

It has taken the courts thirty years, since the *Everson* bus case in 1947, to discover what such schools knew all along, namely, that such a division between secular and religious is a legal fiction, formalized by the courts to settle specific cases, but not fitting the educational reality of such schools. The legal fiction has survived only because the cases which confronted the courts earlier, such as bus rides for nonpublic school students, were clearly separated from the school day. Once the precedent was set, subsequent courts have labored at following it, and in the process have drawn an increasingly finer line between that which is secular and that which is religious.

The *Wolman* case in 1977, exactly thirty years after *Everson*, shows the arbitrariness of such a line to even the most disinterested spectator. In *Wolman*, tax aid for wall maps and charts in nonpublic schools became impermissible as did aid for field trips. But a public subsidy for secular textbooks was permissible, whereas a subsidy to provide overhead projectors for classroom instruction was not. Those familiar with classroom instruction will recognize that the key factor in the use of any materials is the teacher, and that secular textbooks can be turned to "religious" ends with as great ease as "religious" comments can be made on a field trip.

The Court itself was sharply split on the matter of field trips, with five justices finding them impermissible, and four finding them permissible within the bounds of the establishment clause. Justice Powell noted in a separate but concurring opinion that the decision resulted in "a loss of some analytical tidiness." Justice Blackmun in the majority opinion was even led to admit that the wall of separation had in the course of recent cases come to be expressed as a "blurred, indistinct, and variable barrier depending on all the circumstances of a particular relationship."[1]

Such split decisions, complete with public admissions of the arbitrariness of the line between the secular and religious dimensions of education, represent the judicial mind at the end of its tether. Thus the time is ripe to call into question the legitimacy of the secular-religious distinction itself. While the courts have faced the problem of the dividing line in nonpublic schools, they have not faced the same question concerning public schools. If the same evidence were examined and if the same reasoning were applied to public schools, it would be found that they too reflect an interpenetration of secular and "religious" elements and that they in fact reflect a religious world-view. The funding of public schools violates the establishment clause as much as the funding of nonpublic schools.

PUBLIC SCHOOLS AND RELIGION

The courts have not faced the right question until now, because in the cases before them religion has been defined in a very limited way. It is therefore necessary to define the term with more precision and in a way that more truly reflects educational realities. Philip Phenix provides a helpful identification of the three qualities of religion that have relevance for the school. Phenix describes these three qualities as (1) cultic, (2) cultural pattern, and (3) ultimate commitment.[2]

The cultic aspect of religion is its set of ritual practices, such as prayers, the singing of hymns, or the recitation of creeds. The cultural pattern of religion denotes the establishment of religious organizations, with their attendant beliefs and their expression in a social dimension. The cultic character of religion has been thoroughly litigated, such that prayers and Bible reading in the public schools have been found to violate the establishment clause. The cultural pattern quality of religion has been less litigated, but has resulted in what is called the objective study of religion: the study of religious poetry, art, and music, or the study of the beliefs of organized religion as objective, historical phenomena.[3] Religious poetry may be studied only if it is treated objectively, i.e., as a feature of the culture, but not as a belief to be accepted. Similarly, the position of organized religion on slavery during the Civil War, or the Roman Catholic position on abortion in the sixties, may be included in the curriculum, but may only be treated as one of many views.

The third quality of religion, religion as an ultimate commitment, cuts more to the heart of the educational question than either of the first two. The heart commitment quality of religion, according to Phenix, describes what Paul Tillich called the area of "ultimate concern" and what Erich Fromm called "life's orientation." At this level, religion is those ultimate sanctions beyond which there is no appeal, which give meaning and direction to the life of the holder, and which give birth to the cultic and cultural pattern aspects of religion. For example, the ritual of prayer or the celebration of Christmas as the birth of Christ makes sense only if there is a commitment-level belief in a Being who can hear prayers and who sent his Son.

Religion as Life Orientation

It is religion's quality of ultimate commitment, of a fundamental life orientation, that stands in need of legal definition. Public controversy and litigation have focused almost exclusively on the first two, in some ways more visible, aspects of religion, blinding us to the deeper problem in the public schools, namely, the problem of religion as ultimate commitment. Educational philosophers and scholars almost unanimously agree with Phenix that the gaining of a total view of life, a perspective, is an essential and inescapable ingredient in an educational program.[4] Some refer to this as value education; some, such as the Educational Policies Commission of the National Education Association, refer to it as the teaching of moral and spiritual values.[5] The Commission explicitly argues for the necessity of providing sanctions for the behaviors recommended by teachers, whether of promptness, honesty, or racial tolerance. This is surely part of the function of religion defined by Phenix as the commitment aspect. All but those who accept the conventional wisdom that the public school is neutral toward religion realize that some life orientation is inescapably present in the process of studying geography, literature, and history. In this commitment sense of the term, all education is intrinsically religious.

The religious nature of all education was recognized in the past. An understanding of religion as life orientation, and not just as a manifestation of its cultic practices and institutional expression, is evidenced in the words of The Northwest Ordinance of 1787: "Religion, morality, and knowledge being necessary to good government and the happiness of mankind, schools and the means of education shall forever be encouraged." These words not only make an explicit connection between religion and morality; they also remind us of the inevitable expression of religion in schools and education throughout the colonial period and the nineteenth century.

The Myth of Neutrality

As we have shown in the previous chapter, the idea of a public school that is neutral toward religion is a product of the last one hundred years. It has been made plausible by defining religion as consisting of only its first two qualities. Thus, public schools are assumed to achieve neutrality by removing all cultic practices:

they avoid favoring the Protestant or Catholic versions of the Bible by reading from neither. Since Catholics and Protestants have different versions of the Lord's Prayer, and because Jews cannot support either version, neutrality is assumed by eliminating the prayer. All officially sanctioned prayers, such as the Regents' Prayer, are similarly dropped because atheist children cannot be asked to support any prayer, no matter how nonsectarian its content.

Similarly, religious neutrality in public schools is presumed when the cultural pattern meaning of religion is "neutralized" by treating religious art, music, and literature objectively, that is, by describing their existence and by not evaluating the views expressed in them. Organized religion's views on social questions are treated as yet another cultural phenomenon, not as beliefs that could provide guidelines for behavior.

It may be argued, and often has been, that elimination of cultic practices is far from neutral, but rather teaches the irrelevance and uselessness of such practices. It may also be argued that treating religions and their insights objectively also actually teaches their nonnormativity. Both approaches may thus imply that the cultic and cultural forms of religious expression have no direct bearing on the really important questions of life and learning. They may have personal meaning and validity for those who accept them, but they are not normative for any aspect of the public school educational enterprise.

Valid as these observations about the nonneutrality of public education are, they do not strike at the root of the matter. Whether or not the elimination of the first two aspects of religion contributes to the supposed neutrality of public education, the question remains whether the public school can be neutral toward the third aspect.

The problem posed by a serious consideration of religion as a life orientation is this: by what "faith," i.e., value system, can the public school proceed in decision making, whether about racial integration or homogeneous grouping, and with what "faith" or life orientation shall teachers work in providing sanctions for conduct expected in the classroom? How can this be done in a common school in a society where there are multiple faiths, theistic, nontheistic, and agnostic, by which free men have chosen to live? It is at this level of religion that the myth of neutrality needs to be exposed.

A sense of what "neutral" values have been used in the past may be found in the report of the Educational Policies Commission on *Moral and Spiritual Values in Public Schools*. In the context of an illustration concerning stealing, the Commission advocated appeals to civil law, property rights, group approval, and personal integrity as appropriate sanctions. The Commission, while acknowledging the "powerful sanctions of religious creeds and doctrines," concludes that "they may not be explicitly invoked in the public school classroom."[6] This is nonneutrality with a vengeance.

There is abundant evidence that public schools, having abandoned their rootage in the traditional theistic religions, have replaced them with a new religion, the religion of naturalistic humanism. The accumulation of such evidence highlights the emerging constitutional quandary, and leads to the conclusion that only by funding all schools can the state be impartial toward all religions as they are expressed in education.

HUMANISM AS A RELIGION

For a number of years church historians and sociologists of religion have described the American phenomenon known as *civil* religion, a generic term used to identify the overarching commitments of a society that shape public policy and even institutional behavior. It is what Will Herberg calls the American Way of Life. He notes that while the *professed* faith of many Americans is some form of theism, the *operative* faith, that which governs their day-to-day decisions, is of a different sort.[7] It is not simply a common denominator religion, a synthesis of elements common to numerous religions. While it "has no creedal formulation, it nevertheless has its symbols and its rituals, its holidays and its liturgy, its saints and its sancta."[8] It competes with traditional religions for the ultimate loyalty of the American people.

The generic term civil religion has also been defined in other ways. Church historian Martin Marty has summarized five different meanings of the term.[9] They range all the way from "religious nationalism" and "Protestant civic piety" to "the democratic faith," as in Gunnar Myrdal's *American Creed* or John Dewey's *A Common Faith*. The term has also been used to stand for a universal religion that stands in judgment over particular religions, as well as for the kind of folk religion of the American Way of Life that Will Herberg describes.

What civil religion, as it has been understood by sociologists up to now, lacks is a clear creedal formulation that facilitates an empirical study of its presence in the public school. This is not to say that both the defenders of the public school and those who charge that it promulgates a "new" religion are not in agreement that any school system at bottom is religious in nature. Richard

Neuhaus, among others, has shown that the defenders of the public school admit that the public school is an expression of a religious vision. As an example he quotes Sidney Mead, an American religious historian, to the effect that:

> . . . of necessity the state in its public-education system is and always has been teaching religion. It does so because the well-being of the nation and state demands this foundation of shared beliefs. . . . In this sense the public-school system of the United States *is* its established church.[10]

Neuhaus has called this "religion of secularism" the "bootleg religion" of the public school.[11]

The observation that the public schools have moved slowly, but inexorably, from a commitment to a nonsectarian Protestantism to a life orientation that is in conflict with theism may be found in all sorts of literature: that of strident journalism as well as of sober scholarship, that of polemic pamphleteering as well as reasoned reaction.[12] Many names have been given to this ideology; the labels come from philosophy (pragmatism, positivism) and from political philosophy (democratism, secular democracy). Since our concern is with identifying the religio-ethical bias of the public schools, we shall simply use the term humanism.

Its Legal Recognition

Traditionally, religion has been legally defined in terms of those creeds that are held by organized churches and that subscribe to some form of theism. Such is no longer the case. The judicial system has been challenged by a number of nontheists who claim for their views the rights and privileges previously accorded only to theists. A brief survey of these cases should establish the generalization that a wide variety of secular and humanist belief systems have been legally recognized as religions, even though they lack creedal statement as a reference.

In 1961 the U.S. Supreme Court handled a case in which a Maryland notary public had been disqualified from office because he refused to declare his belief in the existence of God. The Court ruled in favor of allowing him to be a notary public. In ruling on the case the Court stated:

> We repeat and again reaffirm that neither a State nor the Federal Government can constitutionally force a person "to profess a belief in any religion." Neither can they constitutionally pass laws or impose requirements which aid all religions as against non-believers, and neither can they aid

those religions based on a belief in the existence of God as against those religions founded on different beliefs.[13]

The Court left no doubt about what it meant by those religions founded on different beliefs. A footnote added: "Among religions in this country which do not teach what would generally be considered a belief in the existence of God are Buddhism, Taoism, Ethical Culture, Secular Humanism, and others." The addition of Ethical Culture and Secular Humanism as systems of beliefs that have legal standing as religions is particularly relevant to the assertion that humanism is a religion.

This strikingly different and broader definition had some precedents in cases decided by state Supreme Courts. In 1957 the Washington Ethical Society and the Fellowship of Humanity were plaintiffs in Washington, D.C., and in the California courts seeking recovery of property taxes on the grounds that their property was used for religious worship, though they did not profess belief in a supreme being, God, or gods. In ruling that such a corporation's property was entitled to exemption from city and county property taxes, the California court, in *Fellowship of Humanity* v. *County of Alameda*, made it quite clear that it recognized such corporations as religious bodies. The argument for this conclusion was that a contrary decision

> would exclude all Taoist China and in the western world all believers in Comte's religion of humanism in which humanity is exalted to the throne occupied by a supreme being in monotheistic religions.[14]

The opinion in that California case referred to the judgment of a scholar of religion:

> A new definition of religion itself is already emerging. . . . The idea of religion without God is shocking to Christians, Jews, Mohammedans, but Buddha and Confucius long ago founded non-theistic religions, and some modern Unitarian Humanists insist that the idea of God is a positive hindrance to the progress of real religion. . . . An inclusive definition, then, must recognize both varieties of religion, theistic and non-theistic.[15]

Two other more recent cases concern the basis for conscientious objector exemption from the draft. In both *Seeger* v. *United States* in 1965 and *Welsh* v. *United States* in 1970, the Court held that belief in God or the grounding of beliefs about war in a specific theistic creed were not required for conscientious objector status. In the *Seeger* case the Court held that a purely personal ethical creed was adequate ground for exemption because such was "a sincere and meaningful belief which occupies in the life of the possessor a place parallel to that filled by the God of those admittedly qualifying for the exemption."[16]

One recent case in 1977 should suffice to show that programs in public schools have come under judicial scrutiny. In a course entitled "Science of Creative Intelligence," with a textbook by the same name, Transcendental Meditation had been offered as an elective in five New Jersey high schools until challenged by a group of parents. Both the Federal District Court in Newark[17] and the U.S. 3rd Circuit Court of Appeals held that Transcendental Meditation is a religion and that its introduction in public schools violates the establishment clause of the First Amendment. An Appellate Court judge noted that the case presented a

> novel and important question that may not be disposed of on the basis of past precedent. . . . This is the first appellate court decision, to my knowledge, that has concluded that a set of ideas constitutes a religion over the objection and protestations of secularity by those espousing those ideas.[18]

The U.S. Supreme Court refused to hear the case on appeal, thus allowing the lower decision to stand.

These cases make it clear that since 1961 the courts have radically broadened the meaning of the term "religion" to include several nontheistic, naturalistic value systems. In order to be recognized as a religion for the purposes of law such value systems need not include commitment to a Supreme Being, need not be expressive of an institutionalized church, and need not, although they may, embrace ritual practices. The public school curriculum itself, with its textbooks, may be said to be teaching religion under this broadened definition, and should be declared by the Court to be in violation of the establishment clause.

Its Humanist Emphasis

The secular religion of humanism is a pervasive force in public education; the literature on the subject is vast,[19] and the doctrine is professed not only by opponents of the public school but also by its defenders. Leo Pfeffer, a longtime counsel in court cases dealing with different phases of religion and education, has described the "triumphs of secular humanism" in resolving both the question of religion in public education[20] and governmental aid to religious schools.[21] In the section on aid to what he calls parochial schools he observes that church-related colleges have become increasingly nonsectarian and even secular, and thus

. . . in this arena, it is not Protestantism, Catholicism, or Judaism which will emerge the victor, but secular humanism, a cultural force which in many respects is stronger in the United States than any of the major religious groups or any alliance among them.[22]

This "cultural force" has been given many names, each label focusing on a different quality of the value system it describes, yet none detailing a clear set of tenets, or describing a creedal formulation. The noun *humanism* is common to many of these descriptions, but since the term has been used in so many periods and settings, it must be made clear which variety of humanism is under analysis in this study. There are, for example, the Renaissance humanism of Erasmus, the literary humanism of Alexander Pope, and the religious humanism of the American Unitarian Association.[23] Two recently reprinted documents help to define for our purposes a specific, contemporary American humanist system of values.

Its Creedal Formulation

Humanist Manifesto I (1933) and *Humanist Manifesto II* (1973), which originally appeared in periodicals published by the American Humanist Association,[24] were published jointly in 1976.[25] Both documents were signed by noted scholars in the fields of education, theology, philosophy, and other disciplines. Together, the documents constitute the creedal statements of naturalistic humanism, and they make explicit the contrast between that doctrine and any theistic belief.

That the manifestos describe a religious creed is readily apparent. The first of the fifteen theses of *Manifesto I* affirms, "Religious humanists regard the universe as self-existing and not created."[20] This assertion is in marked contrast to the first article of the Apostles' Creed: "I believe in God the Father, Almighty, Maker of heaven and earth." Sprinkled throughout *Manifesto II* are a number of similar assertions, which prove that it, too, is regarded as an alternative and rival religion, not just as an ethical code of conduct.

In order to demonstrate that the manifestos are indeed religious affirmations, we have collated the two rather extensive documents and reduced them to a series of seven "doctrines" that constitute the heart of the creed of humanism. We have not arranged them in any order of priority, nor do they follow a sequence used in the manifestos themselves. Our summary is simply intended to provide a point of reference in the analysis that follows, and to make it apparent that humanism is not simply a social, political, or economic creed, but an expression of ultimate, religious commitments regarding the nature and destiny of man.

*Summary of a Humanist Creed**

1. Humanism holds to an evolutionary explanation of both human rights and development.

Manifesto I, second thesis:
> Humanism believes that man is a part of nature, and that he has emerged as a result of a continuous process.

Manifesto II, second thesis:
> Modern science discredits such historic concepts as the "ghost in the machine" and the "separable soul." Rather, science affirms that the human species is an emergence from natural evolutionary forces. As far as we know, the total personality is a function of the biological organism transacting in a social and cultural context.

2. Humanism believes that the scientific method is applicable to all areas of human concern, and is the only valid means of determining truth.

Manifesto I, fifth thesis:
> Religion must formulate its hopes and plans in the light of the scientific spirit and method.

Manifesto II, Preface:
> We need to extend the uses of scientific method, not renounce them.

Manifesto II, first thesis:
> The controlled use of scientific methods, which have transformed the natural and social sciences since the Renaissance, must be extended further in the solution of human problems.

3. Humanism affirms cultural relativism, the belief that values are grounded only in a given culture and have no transcultural normativity.

Manifesto I, fifth thesis:
> Humanism asserts that the nature of the universe depicted by modern science makes unacceptable any supernatural or cosmic guarantees of human values.

---

*While this summary from *Humanist Manifesto I* (1933) and *Humanist Manifesto II* (1973) is the work of the Center, a remarkably similar list of six "tenets" of humanism has been identified by John Whitehead and John Conlan, "The Establishment of the Religion of Secular Humanism and its First Amendment Implications," *Texas Tech Law Review*, 10 (1978).

Manifesto II, third thesis:

> We affirm that moral values derive their source from human experience. Ethics is autonomous and situational, needing no theological or ideological sanction. Ethics stems from human need and interest.

4. Humanism affirms an anthropocentric and naturalistic view of life.

Manifesto I, eighth thesis:

> Religious humanism considers the complete realization of human personality to be the end of man's life and seeks its development and fulfillment in the here and now.

Manifesto I, tenth thesis:

> It follows that there will be no uniquely religious emotions and attitudes of the kind hitherto associated with belief in the supernatural.

Manifesto I, fifteenth thesis:

> Man is at last becoming aware that he alone is responsible for the realization of the world of his dreams, that he has within himself the power for its achievement.

Manifesto II, first thesis:

> We find insufficient evidence for belief in the existence of a supernatural; it is either meaningless or irrelevant to the question of the survival and fulfillment of the human race. As non-theists we begin with humans, not God, nature, not deity. But we can discover no divine purpose or providence for the human species. While there is much we do not know, humans are responsible for what we are or will become. No deity will save us; we must save ourselves.

5. Humanism affirms an ethic of individualism, one in which personal values take precedence over community standards for behavior.

Manifesto II, fifth thesis:

> The preciousness and dignity of the individual person is a central humanist value. . . . We believe in maximum individual autonomy consonant with social responsibility.

Manifesto II, sixth thesis:

> While we do not approve of exploitive, denigrating forms of sexual expression, neither do we wish to prohibit, by law or social sanction, sexual behavior between consenting adults. . . . Short of harming others or compelling them to do likewise, individuals should be permitted to pursue their life styles as they desire.

Manifesto II, seventh thesis:

> To enhance freedom and dignity the individual must experience a full range of civil liberties in all societies. . . . It also includes a recognition of an individual's right to die with dignity, euthanasia, and the right to suicide.

6.   Humanism affirms cultural determinism, the belief that values in a given society are largely determined by environmental circumstances.

Manifesto I, fourth thesis:

> Humanism recognizes that man's religious culture and civilization, as clearly depicted by anthropology and history, are the product of a gradual development due to his interaction with his natural environment and with his social heritage. The individual born into a particular culture is largely molded to that culture.

7.   Humanism believes in the innate goodness and perfectibility of the human species.

Humanist Manifesto I, fifteenth thesis:

> We assert that humanism will: (a) affirm life rather than deny it; (b) seek to elicit possibilities of life, not flee from it; and (c) endeavor to establish the conditions of a satisfactory life for all, not merely for the few. By this positive morale and intention humanism will be guided, and from this perspective and alignment the techniques and efforts of humanism will flow. . . . Man is at last becoming aware that he alone is responsible for the realization of the world of his dreams, that he has within himself the power for its achievement. He must set intelligence and will to the task.

Humanist Manifesto II, Preface:

> But views that merely reject theism are not equivalent to humanism. They lack commitment to the positive belief in the possibilities of human progress and the values central to it. . . . The humanist outlook will tap the creativity of each human being and provide the vision and courage for us to work together. This outlook emphasizes the role human beings can play in their own spheres of action.

Humanists themselves regard their views as a religion. Corliss Lamont, signer of both manifestos, admits that humanism has many features that we associate with religion, including its being "an integrated and inclusive way of life" and "a supreme commitment."[27] The renowned educational philosopher John Dewey, signer of *Manifesto I*, and once president of the American Humanist Association, held that this faith was really the faith of the American people. In his book appropriately named *A Common Faith*, he ended his description of its characteristics with the assertion:

> Here we have all the elements for a religious faith that shall not be confined to sect, class, or race. Such a faith has always been implicitly the common faith of mankind. It remains to make it explicit and militant.[28]

This seems to be a clear statement of Dewey's intention to make schools the instrument of such a vision.

None of the foregoing, however, constitutes empirical and systematic evidence that theism in public schools has been replaced by some form of humanism. For that we turn to evidence of humanism's direct effect on the classroom environment and instruction by the dual means of elimination and affirmation.

PUBLIC SCHOOLS AND HUMANIST RELIGION

It is a truism in education that the outcome of education can be shaped as much by what is excluded as by what is included. Schools are inevitably engaged in choosing between what to teach and what to ignore, and the pattern of such decisions conveys a message. It is that underlying message that we seek to expose here.

Inculcation by Elimination

There is mounting evidence that in obvious as well as subtle ways, sometimes by deliberate intention and often only unconsciously, the public school environment has been divested of various forms of theistic thought and practice. Some of the evidence is well known and requires no documentation. Some is less well known and will require more than the general charge that something called humanism is rapidly gaining the field by eliminating its chief competitor, theism. A series of Supreme Court cases, in which the plaintiffs have usually been nontheists, has resulted in the exclusion from the school environment of a great many theistic thoughts and practices. The Lord's Prayer and Bible reading as opening exercises or as homeroom activities have been eliminated, after being widely practiced for many years, and being mandated by law in some states. A nonsectarian prayer has also been barred, if it is composed or led by school officials. Even moments of meditation, in which each student is free to compose his own prayer or meditation, are a matter of legal controversy in some states. Religious instruction under released time provisions has been struck down, except where it is held off school premises. Graduation ceremonies or services in churches led by clergy, distribution of Bibles on school premises, singing of songs with a theistic content in school programs: all these are presently being challenged in many school districts. It can be reliably predicted that some of these, too, will be banned. The celebration of Christmas, seen by many as "the season to be jolly," is for many public school teachers the season to be wary because of the fine line between teaching *about* religion and the teaching *of* religion at Christmas. For those wishing guidance on these matters the conventional wisdom has been summarized by the Commission on Religion in the Public Schools under the auspices of the Association of School Administrators.[29] No one is sure what the next steps toward eliminating theism from the public school will be.

It might be argued that theistic rituals and practices can be eliminated without removing theism as an outlook or perspective from the classroom, for they are instances of the "cultic" aspect of religion we have referred to earlier. Nevertheless, their presence had clearly marked for the students the life orientation within which the public school operated. Their absence creates a vacuum into which something must flow.

The Educational Policies Commission of the National Educational Association has pushed the elimination of theism from the classroom one step beyond what the courts have required. In *Moral and Spiritual Values in Public Schools*, the Commission asserted that the providing of sanctions for behavior and belief is a necessary ingredient of classroom instruction. This providing of sanctions is certainly part of the function of religion defined by Phenix as "ultimate commitment" and has been one of the ways in which theism has been used in the public school in the past. The Commission, while acknowledging the "powerful sanctions of religious creeds and doctrines," concludes that "they may not be explicitly invoked in the public school classroom."[30] Other sanctions are accepted as legitimate. When both theistic practices and theistic sanctions are banned, a doubly strong vacuum is created.

Another form of the inculcation of humanism through the elimination of theism occurs in the matter of textbook content. One comparative study of two junior high literature anthologies published by the same company twenty-five years apart revealed that the editors had, perhaps unconsciously, reduced significantly the number of references to theistic thought and practice in the characters in stories, and in poems and essays. In this limited sampling it appeared that in the forties there were three times as many lines devoted to theistic expression as in the sixties.[31]

Another study of textbooks in Missouri came to a similar conclusion about the decline of attention given to traditional theism in those texts under analysis. One significant conclusion noted:

> The closer we get in textbook descriptions of present day life and literature the fewer theistic references there are. There is a noticeable tapering-off of religious references in the modern period. Thus an alert student may feel that the textbook dealing with today's problems no longer cites religion as a molding force in society.[32]

We cite but one more example of how the treatment of theism in textbooks has changed. Kanawha County, West Virginia, was the site of a textbook controversy in the early seventies. The details have been thoroughly treated in numerous sources.[33] Two analysts, working independently of each other, concluded that at bottom the conflict was ideological and that it was between traditional theism and some form of humanism. George Hillocks, a University of Chicago professor of education and an expert in language arts, did an analysis of the language arts textbooks that precipitated the controversy. Part of his analysis revealed that only seven of forty-six poems in a given text dealt with matters in the Christian tradition, and only six of the thirty-eight prose selections mentioned Christians or Christian beliefs explicitly.[34] In addition, he noted that all six of the prose selections were "pejorative of Christianity, either directly in adverse comments about the shortcomings of Christianity or indirectly by showing Christians as hypocrites or fools."[35] Hillocks went on to note that the protestors in Kanawha County identified the humanist manifestos as the documents expressing the ideology pervading the texts.[36]

Some textbook bias may thus be inferred from what is ignored as well as from what is treated; this is what we call inculcation of humanism by elimination of theism. However, it might be argued that such evidence only points up the neutrality of the public school toward all religion, theism included. Since religion is what divides people, and since schools and textbooks deal with common beliefs and what binds a people together, religion must be omitted. This elimination is not due to an anti-theistic bias, but rather to the school's responsibility to pass on what is common and not what is controversial. Or it may be argued that the traditional religious communities in American society have themselves contributed to this state of affairs by failing to inspire the production of alternative textbooks and other learning materials reflecting the more traditional religious outlook, as well as by their sectarian rivalries and their militant opposition both to prevailing secular viewpoints and to the unfavorable light in which their position is often represented. The situation is therefore charged with ambiguities and the issues are not beyond dispute. The inculcation of humanism by the elimination of theism is less of a problem, however, than that which we now examine.

Inculcation by Affirmation

There is significant evidence that public schools increasingly promulgate, perhaps more unwittingly than by design, the religion of naturalistic humanism. That evidence can be examined by matching key beliefs in the humanist manifestos with those actively endorsed in a sampling of school textbooks.

Textbooks as teachers. Since textbooks are the chief evidence that naturalistic humanism is actively promoted in public schools, something should be said about the role and power of textbooks in reflecting a given educational perspective. Some extravagant claims have been made for their impact on the student. D. C. Heath, founder of the publishing house that bears his name, is reported to have said, "Let me publish the textbooks of a nation and I care not who writes its songs or makes its laws."[37] While acknowledging that such claims are extravagant, there is a common sense basis to the claim that textbooks and their point of view represent a powerful and pervasive factor in the school's overall goal. This is not to claim that the point of view of books is more, or less, powerful than the influence of the teacher or classmates.

There are several obvious reasons why textbooks are a crucial index of the perspective a school exhibits. First, they are *common* and *required*: *common* because all students confront them and *required* in that students exercise no choice in regard to them. They are thus separate from all other books in the classroom or library, which serve as enrichment materials for personal reading or research. Second, they are used for testing. They are thus not only read but also reviewed, discussed, and digested. Third, they often occur in a series, having a return engagement for as many as five or six years. While a child's individual teachers are usually replaced each year by others, and library books for the lower grades are replaced by those for the middle grades, the textbook series continues its effect on the learner. These three characteristics give them a cumulative impact on the learner that no other element of the school environment can muster.

In the last decade we have come to a greater awareness

that textbooks previously presumed to be neutral and objective were actually biased and slanted. Racism and sexism, for example, have now been shown to be pervasive in school materials long thought to be accurate, fair, and descriptive of our common beliefs. It took groups who felt misrepresented to expose what was hidden to the eyes of others. Thus, blacks and Indians revealed biases in social studies texts, and women played the major role in exposing basal readers as sexist. Today, therefore, we are more prepared than ever before to accept the possibility that texts may be biased in subtle but profound ways, and that they may aid and abet some ideologies and discriminate against others.

We shall examine selected texts in several curricular areas, focusing on those that have been granted a high degree of official endorsement. Scores of publishers compete with each other for the school textbook market. Some textbooks have more official standing than others, because they have been approved by a textbook adoption agency serving the state Board of Education.[38]* Others carry a more or less official endorsement because they were developed not by private textbook publishers but with tax grants from quasi-governmental agencies like the National Science Foundation.

Before proceeding to an analysis of a sampling of texts from several curricular areas, some mention should be made of the method of analysis. Much textbook criticism uses a bill of particulars approach. This consists of cataloguing a list of particular words, actions, or opinions and objecting to their inclusion. For example, when a sufficient number of words, particularly those that are sexual or profane, are catalogued, the book is assumed to approve of those words. Similarly, when a certain number of actions are depicted, particularly those that are sexual, violent, or criminal, the book is again assumed to advocate such actions. Finally, when opinions are expressed, whether they are opinions about politics, religion, or authority, the conclusion is that the book supports such opinions. Such criticism is inadequate for our purposes, since this method inevitably blurs the distinction between the pedagogical purposes of exposure to a word, action, or opinion and the inculcation of such concepts.

What is more difficult to detect is the perspective or point

---

*Twenty-one states have official machinery for identifying those textbooks that have been approved for state-wide use, and all public schools must select from the approved list. All other states leave the decision to county or local school districts. In a number of those twenty-one states parochial and private schools, if they are approved schools, must use state-adopted texts.

of view of a text. Point of view is equivalent to what was earlier defined as religion in the sense of life orientation. While more subtle and often implied rather than stated, a point of view may nevertheless pervade a given textbook series. It may appear in the Teachers' Manual, in the Preface, or in the major sections and chapter headings. It may be evidenced in what is not treated as well as what actually is stated. While our method incorporates elements of the bill of particulars approach, it goes beyond that to examine the fundamental premises, the point of view of the material.

Secondary biology. Biology is a required course in most secondary schools. The material we have selected for scrutiny is a group of four high school biology texts, each published by a different firm.[39] All were produced under grants from The National Science Foundation with funds appropriated by Congress; together they cost seven million dollars to develop. They are called The Biological Science Curriculum Study (BSCS) Texts and are reputedly used by more than fifty percent of American high school students studying biology.[40] Our own analysis of state adoptions reveals that of the twenty-one states requiring an agency recommendation, nine states have approved two of the books, eleven states have approved the third, and twelve have approved the fourth. The combination of their tax dollar funding, their development by a prestigious quasi-governmental agency, and their widespread official adoption and use gives this group of texts an official status and endorsement not accorded many school texts.

The point of view of these texts has been widely acknowledged to be one that actively teaches evolution, not as one theory among several, but as an established and settled fact. Hundreds of passages in all four texts demonstrate that the books embrace several key premises: (1) the origin of the universe through natural processes; (2) the naturalistic development of life from nonlife; (3) the evolution of present living forms through mutation and natural selection; and (4) the evolution of human beings from an ancestry common with apes.[41] A good deal of lower court litigation, in California and elsewhere, has attended the adoption of these texts,[42] and numerous complaints against their exclusive presentation of evolutionary theory have been filed with district and state boards of education.[43] Many people clearly agree that the texts have a consistent point of view, a point of view hostile to theistic understandings of the same data. This has been recognized not only by adherents of creationism but also by exponents of the theory of general evolution and by lower courts in California.[44]

In our summary of the creed expressed in the humanist manifestos, Doctrine 1 states that humanism holds to an evolutionary view of both human origins and development. Doctrine 2 states that humanism believes that the scientific method is the only means of validating truth in all areas of human concern. The evidence offered in the BSCS biology texts indicates that their outlook and that of naturalistic humanism are highly congruent. Indeed, The American Humanist Association has adopted "A Statement Affirming Evolution as a Principle of Science," which urges school boards, teachers, and textbook publishers to "resist and oppose measures currently before several state legislatures that would require creationist views of origins be given equal treatment and emphasis in public school biology classes and text materials."[45]

The U.S. Supreme Court has not been faced with the evidence of humanism as exhibited in these texts. It is hard to see how it could avoid acknowledging that the texts support a perspective legally defined as a religion, and that the books therefore fall under the ban of the establishment clause as presently interpreted. The case involving a textbook on Transcendental Meditation led to the conclusion by an appellate court that the book taught a secular religion.[46] That case seems to establish a clear precedent for a similar conclusion regarding the BSCS texts, if their status is tested in the courts.

Civics/government. This curriculum area is a required course in either junior or senior high in most schools; the textbook we selected has been identified as one of the "two current front runners."[47] Our analysis confirms that it appears on the adoption list of eight of the twenty-one states having such procedures.

Perhaps the most striking and explicit similarity between the creed of humanism and the viewpoint of this text is illustrated by humanist Doctrine 2, which says that humanism believes that the scientific method is applicable to all areas of human concern, and is the only valid means for determining truth. Both in the *Teacher's Guide* and the main text this view is explicitly underscored. The *Guide* says that one of the most important goals established for the text is "influencing students to value scientific approaches to the verification of factual claims and rational analysis of value claims" (p. 2). While admitting to some limitations of the scientific method, "social scientists feel that by emulating the scientific method to the greatest possible degree, they can uncover more of the regularities of human behavior than have previously been set forth" (p. 11).

In the student text the commitment is made even more explicit in the following:

> Scientific inquiry is the *best* method we have for making decisions about competing alternative hypotheses about reality. It is the best method, because it is the most useful and reliable. (p. 56)

This is a close paraphrase of Doctrine 2.

This explicit commitment leads consistently to several other key beliefs of humanism. Our summary Doctrine 4 is that humanism affirms an anthropocentric and naturalistic view of life. This is evident from the way the authors treat other nonscientific approaches to the study of political behavior, one of which is called "the method of Revelation." It is judged to be inadequate because:

> There is no easy way to confirm the claims of those who have experienced revelations. Ultimately, one must accept the word of the prophet on faith or reject his statements. (p. 55)

The authors state that they are not opposed to religion, its beliefs or values. Indeed they point out that many scientists are religious people who attend church (p. 53). However, as the previous passages show, revelational claims do not stand up to the test of the scientific method and are thus quietly discounted.

One looks in vain in the text for any serious treatment of the institution of the church and its role in society. Ignoring the church does not seem to be an oversight, but a conscious decision to discount the claim that the church offers a normative vision of life that has a bearing on social life and political principles. The claims of the church to a normative vision of life that has a bearing on society are discredited in the section entitled "Beliefs Based on Faith." Here the text says, "A belief based on faith cannot be tested scientifically, since it cannot be confirmed or rejected in terms of what exists" (p. 53).

The irrelevance of religious beliefs and the role of the organized church in political events is particularly striking in the treatment of the Montgomery, Alabama, bus boycott of 1955–56 (pp. 132–139). In a generally sympathetic treatment of the black cause the text tells the story of how segregation was fought and eventually defeated. The fact that Martin Luther King was a *pastor* and that the black *churches* played a key role is ignored. Political power and efficient organization are identified as the key factors. Thus the irrelevance of organized religion and theism are effectively taught by ignoring the church's impact on a political struggle in a very specific instance.

A different, but related, perspective of the text relates to Doctrine 3, which states that humanism affirms cultural relativism, the belief that values are grounded only in a given culture and have no transcultural normativity. This view appears in both explicit statements and in the book's overall treatment of various dissident groups in American politics. A general explanation of how values are grounded is provided:

> Through the process of socialization, an individual learns what is considered right and wrong political behavior in his society. Through socialization an infant born in the United States of America learns to behave politically in the American way. (p. 101)

Whether in a description of the Amish (pp. 91–99), the poor blacks in the Alabama bus boycott (pp. 132–138), the anti-war demonstrators (pp. 129–131, 155–158), or other groups, the beliefs, values, and priorities of any group are shown to stem essentially from the cultural conditioning of the group. Thus the student is taught that values are culturally bound.

The evidence suggests that this civics/government text does indeed exhibit a certain bias; the bias goes deeper than politics and covers fundamental ways of looking at society and its institutions. There is a great deal of congruence between the perspective of the text and at least three explicit tenets of humanism. The question is simply whether or not public schools using this text are exhibiting the religion of humanism, and whether humanism is thus the unacknowledged religion of such public schools.

Elementary social studies. One of the most controversial of the numerous elementary school textbook series is *Man: A Course of Study* (MACOS), designed for fifth grade. The series contains a wide array of teacher's manuals, student texts, student activity sheets, records, films, maps, and simulation games. It was produced in the middle sixties under a grant from the National Science Foundation, which in turn is funded by congressional appropriations. The series is reported to have cost over seven million tax dollars for its development and marketing.[48] Like the BSCS biology texts, the series thus can be said to represent a more "official" ideology than any published by private publishers.

Our analysis of state adoptions reveals that only one state, California, includes MACOS on its approved list, probably because of its controversial qualities. Objections to the materials are many and varied, and not all are relevant for this study. The charges most relevant to our study are that it aggressively teaches both cultural relativism (Doctrine 3) and environmental determinism (Doctrine 6).[49] Much of the controversy centers on the unit dealing with Netsilik Eskimos, the only unit dealing with humans. It is also the longest of the units. It is preceded by units dealing with the king salmon, the herring gull, and the baboon, in that order. One might wonder why units dealing with animals dominate in a social studies program named *Man: A Course of Study*; but what all the units have in common is a focus on the mating habits, infant rearing practices, and family structure in both animal and human social groupings, in order from simple to complex. One might also speculate whether or not the very sequencing of the units, starting with lower forms of social life and culminating in man, does not itself teach some aspects of evolution. This speculation is supported when one notes the parallels between the way the social groupings and "family" structure in the animal units are treated and the way they are treated in the unit on Eskimos. Thus there is considerable inferential evidence that humanist Doctrine 1 on evolution is the basic viewpoint of these materials.

There is also convincing evidence in both student and teacher materials that MACOS teaches ethical and cultural relativism. Doctrine 3 holds that values are grounded within a culture and have no transcultural normativity. Since the student materials are so varied, their ideological outlook is not readily apparent on the surface. However, a number of social practices in the Eskimo unit, such as cannibalism, wife-sharing, and senilicide (abandonment of the aged) are consistently portrayed as plausible and natural responses to the social situation. The student materials do not contain any negative evaluation, but merely describe these practices. However, the materials for teachers reveal a clearer ideological orientation. A separate publication, *Talks to Teachers*, contains explicit observations that signal congruence between the orientation of MACOS and the creedal formulation of humanism on ethical relativism. The project director states as the second major objective:

> Second, we hope that through this course children will come to understand that what we regard as acceptable behavior is a product of our culture.[50]

Elsewhere he has been even more explicit about whether values are transcultural. In describing one of the overall effects of the materials he says:

> For one thing, it questions the notion that there are "eternal truths" about humanity that must be passed down from one generation to the next.[51]

Clearly, the MACOS series intends to convey the message of humanist Doctrine 6, that humanism affirms cultural determinism.

When elements of the humanist doctrines of evolution, cultural relativism, and cultural determinism are present as shapers of curricular materials produced by a quasi-governmental agency, one may well ask whether MACOS does not indeed teach a civic religion that is banned under the current interpretation of the establishment clause.

History. Most states require a course in American history before a student graduates from high school, so nearly all students receive some formal instruction in at least one period of history. For our analysis we selected an American history text that has been approved by ten of the twenty-one states having adoption policies.[52] Estimated sales figures reveal that the text sold 200,000 copies in 1977 alone.[53] It is therefore a widely adopted and respected text — and one that unabashedly states its perspective.

Humanist Doctrine 1 states that humanism believes an evolutionary explanation of both human origins and development. While this book does not address the question of human origins, it does perpetuate notions of evolutionary development by stressing adaptation to an environment and natural selection.[54] For instance, in the sections on American colonization (pp. 54–96) the authors consistently point out that the settlers had to change their manners, language, techniques, and values, for the new environment demanded radically new emphases and techniques in the lives of the colonists. Either the colonists had to meet the challenges of the frontier or suffer dire consequences. Although undisguised and explicit passages revealing this bias are not abundant, the book consistently uses the evolutionary model of adaptation and change to a new environment to explain the failures and successes of various leaders and movements.

The text also has a strong commitment to the scientific method, not only as a valid means for determining truth in history but also as the only reliable method with which to understand all areas of human concern. First, the authors believe in using the scientific method in the writing of history. The student is told:

> Like the social scientist, the historian uses the scientific mode of inquiry in making his investigations. . . . In subjecting their sources of evidence to "the most severe and detailed tests possible," historians use scientific modes of inquiry. . . . (pp. 206–207)

Second, the authors favorably portray the advancement of the scientific method in American culture. For instance, the authors highlight the scientific method as it was applied to medicine, agriculture, and chemistry (pp. 556–559, 810–817). Another example of eulogizing the scientific method comes toward the end of the book:

> . . . by the 1970's the United States and other technologically advanced nations had the capability — or could acquire the capability — of doing just about anything men wanted to do. Stated concisely, through science and technology men had acquired Godlike powers. (p. 822)

Finally, the authors assent to the application of the scientific method to other areas of life. One of the striking features of this text is a series of essays, interspersed throughout the book, explaining the nature, methodology, and concepts of selected social science disciplines. Case studies in these areas are also provided that demonstrate how the findings of these investigations can aid us in understanding the issues and periods of American history. The authors emphasize that the scientific method is a common component of all these disciplines. For example, in the essay on "Sociology" the authors write:

> These are the scientific methods of inquiry developed and refined by sociologists. . . . The social sciences, then, although they differ greatly in the questions they ask, do not differ greatly in their methods of investigation. (p. 94)

In their defense, the authors might contend that they are merely attempting empirically to describe the present state of affairs in the social sciences and history. However, by highlighting and emphasizing the exclusive use of the scientific method in all areas of life, without paying due attention to other methods of determining truth, they are exposing a profound bias in their presentation. Their stance is therefore an epistemological commitment and not merely a commitment to scholarly accuracy.

Another tenet of naturalistic humanism is the belief that values are grounded only in a given culture and are not normative in another culture (Doctrine 3). Such cultural relativism comports with several points made in this text, especially in the sections dealing with the colonization of America. The authors discuss how much the values of the pioneers changed in their new environment; that this happened is understandable and plausible. However, the authors go a step further and suggest that all values are relative to a given culture.

Another principle of naturalistic humanism is the affirmation of an anthropocentric and naturalistic view of life (Doctrine 4). In various subtle and perhaps unwitting ways the text concurs with this creedal statement, as the following excerpts illustrate. Viewing history as "the record of mankind on earth" (p. 1), the authors describe "the freedoms we cherish, the material comforts we enjoy and the institutions that serve us" as the products of man (*Teacher's Manual*, p. 2). The history of America is regarded as "the most dramatic and significant story in all human history" (p. 6). The Constitution is regarded as "the supreme law" (p. 189). In reflecting on the bicentennial, Americans should celebrate that:

> . . . through understanding and through participation in the democratic political process, they have been able to solve their problems. (p. 843)

In the preface to the *Teacher's Manual*, the authors express this statement of purpose:

> But if we can help our students to face these problems courageously, intelligently and with humanity, we may hope that they will create a richer and more meaningful life for themselves and future generations. (p. 1)

Man is always at the center of the picture the authors paint. What this picture reveals is more than just an absence of God or the Christian religion. It asserts an optimistic faith in the ability of man to both create and shape the world he lives in and to solve his own problems. Like the adherents of naturalistic humanism, the authors seem to believe that man is autonomous.

Our study has found varying degrees of consonance between four tenets of naturalistic humanism and the biases of this text. Furthermore, these biases are not small matters of omission; rather, they are evidence of a pervasive and fundamental social philosophy, a philosophy that bears several striking resemblances to naturalistic humanism as a set of assumptions about the nature of man, society, and how to find truth.

Humanist religion in "secular" textbooks. Several observations and reminders regarding humanist religion and public school textbooks are in order. The texts selected are only a small sample of those used in American schools. The sample, however, was not a random sample, but a selection of those texts that met some of the following criteria: wide approval by state adoption agencies, wide use in schools (based on sales estimates), and full or partial funding of their development with public money. A more comprehensive sampling of texts in use in public schools may be necessary to validate more definitive conclusions, but the texts we examined are representative of those that have more "official" approval than is typical.

A second observation is that these materials have all been developed by reputable scholars in their respective fields, and we do not intend to impugn either the scholarship or the motives of the authors. We have no desire to engage in an exposé, or to suggest that criticism of these specific texts is intended. Our purpose is not to aid and abet any groups who wish to engage in textbook burning or censorship, but rather to add some empirical evidence to the charge that public schools teach humanism.

We must also note that no given text or collection of materials was found to exhibit all the tenets congruent with those of humanism. While collectively they represent a commitment to the full range of tenets in a humanist creed, each curriculum area reflects only those humanist beliefs appropriate to that subject field.

The upshot of this evidence is that the public schools are not neutral; they reflect a religious perspective as defined by the courts. Naturalistic humanism is that religion, and the courts, if faced with the evidence, must conclude that the public schools stand in violation of the Supreme Court's present interpretation of the establishment clause. And at that point, the public funding question puts the courts in a serious quandary.

FUNDING AND THE FIRST AMENDMENT

The Supreme Court has several times stated the principle that the Constitution prohibits policies in education that discriminate against one religion or that prefer one over another, and that this principle refers not only to theism, but also to nontheistic religions like humanism. The compulsory flag salute case yielded this explicit declaration:

> If there is any fixed star in our constitutional constellation, it is that no official, high or petty, can prescribe what shall be orthodox in politics, nationalism, religion, or other matters of opinion or force citizens to confess by word or act their faith herein.[55]

A specific prohibition against aiding a "religion of secularism" has been introduced in at least one ruling, holding that if such were taught in public schools it would constitute an illegal establishment. Justice Clark in the *Schempp* case said:

> . . . the state may not establish a religion of secularism in the sense of affirmatively opposing or showing hostility to religion, thus preferring those who believe in no religion over those who do believe.[56]

133

Justic Goldberg wrote in a concurring opinion an even more explicit warning:

> Untutored devotion to the concept of neutrality can lead to a . . . brooding and pervasive devotion to the secular and a passive, or even active hostility to the religious. Such results are not only not compelled by the Constitution, but it seems to me, are prohibited by it.[57]

The most recent ruling, that Transcendental Meditation is such a secular religion whose teaching falls under the ban of the establishment clause, is a clear instance of the application of the principle.[58] The grounds for a funding dilemma, and the need for a solution, are glaringly apparent.

The Quandary

If the Constitution forbids, as the courts have repeatedly said, the use of tax funds to prefer one religion over another, and if tax funds and official endorsement have gone into the production and adoption of teaching materials that clearly inculcate a religious ideology, then the courts have two choices. They should conclude either that tax money cannot go to public schools, or they must admit that the present formulation of the secular-religious distinction is faulty and that therefore tax money can constitutionally go to all accredited schools. In either case they must break long-standing precedent, both legally and legislatively. This is the dilemma that the courts and the American people must face, a dilemma created by the courts themselves by both ruling against support of religion in schools, and at the same time broadening the meaning of religion. We conclude that the secular-religious line is no longer tenable as a legally or educationally meaningful distinction for constitutionally deciding questions of educational funding.

The Solution

The general solution lies in recognizing that the present paradigm of collectivism is inadequate for dealing with the actual plurality of views in American education. The solution also requires acknowledging that while the state has a legitimate role to play in education in ensuring that all citizens obtain an education, it is not the single locus of educational authority, nor should its funding power be used to discriminate against those who hold that the church or the family is the locus of educational authority.

The logical way out of the quandary is to acknowledge in

education what we have always acknowledged in politics and in worship: multiple institutional expression. The choice of a school in the future must be made as free as the choice of church or political party is now, with the state acting only with malice toward none and with charity for all. Our society must come to acknowledge that religious commitment, seriously held, affects not only the choice of ecclesiastical affiliation but of educational affiliation as well.

In our vision of educational pluralism each system of schools would work out its educational ideology as freely and as clearly as it wished, with all having equal status and rights before the law. No American family, theist, nontheist humanist, or agnostic, would be denied the right to choose, without fear of economic penalty, a school most clearly reflecting its own value system.

A move toward multiple school systems entails abandoning several cherished notions long held by sincere Americans. It means abandoning more than the legal fiction that religious affairs and secular affairs are distinguished by a wall of separation. It means abandoning the notion that any single "stretch sock" school could ever honestly and impartially reflect our religious and ideological multiformity, and the notion that America's future strength lies in a single melting pot school, with the state acting as central school board and arbitrator between conflicting visions of education.

The solution also requires that we abandon the notion that white Anglo-Saxon Protestantism has a moral mandate to fight courts and enact legislation in order to retain its hundred-year hold on the public school, while subjecting other minority religions to subtle persecutions or second-class-citizen status in protest schools of their choice. Society must accept religious freedom in education for the Jewish vision, the Muslim vision, the humanist vision, the Protestant vision, the secularist vision, the Catholic vision—in short, for all the confessional visions Americans hold. Finally, we must accept the principle that since government cannot aid one religion in education or prefer one over the other, it must find ways to aid them all, both legislatively and financially. There is some hope that the American people will come to see that this is a possible solution to the dilemma of religion and education that the stance of the courts now reflects. When the American people catch the vision, the courts will not be far behind.

Solutions will not come early or easily. Our specific recommendations for enhancing pluralism are spelled out in terms of legislation, litigation, and the possibilities of a constitutional amendment in a final chapter.

THE COMPARATIVE CASE FOR FUNDING

Many who accept the argument of this chapter concerning the quandary of the courts may not agree with our solution on practical social policy grounds. They may firmly believe that pluralism is but another term for social chaos, and that no society can survive the near anarchy that pluralism suggests to them. Our final argument is an attempt to answer this legitimate concern for social stability. For this argument we turn not to legal American theory or to social theorists, past or present. We turn instead to the empirical evidence of other contemporary societies. Through such comparative analysis it should become apparent that social stability can be maintained by societies committed to pluralism. Of course, not all the features of these alternative systems are applicable to the United States; nevertheless, they do serve as useful models for a thoughtful examination of the direction for constructive change.

Canada

Under Canada's "acting" Constitution, the British North America Act, the responsibility for education lies chiefly with the several provinces. However, those school systems in operation at the time of confederation were guaranteed that their funding would continue. Two large school systems existed at that time — Protestant and Catholic. While the Protestant has since become secular and serves as the "catch-all" for almost all non-Catholic students, the Catholic schools have retained their identity. Today, the larger system in a given province is called "public" and the smaller one is called "separate."

Those provinces that joined Canada after the time of confederation were allowed to choose their own type of educational structure. Thus, some provinces have established a single school system whereas others have recognized and funded separate as well as public school systems. Moreover, some provinces have also recognized and funded a third kind of school system — the independent schools. While the B.N.A. Act safeguarded the establishment of a dual school system in the Canada of 1867, no clause prevented provincial legislatures from acknowledging a third alternative. Six out of ten provinces have now chosen to aid independent education. For the sake of brevity, we will survey three of ten: British Columbia, which recognizes both in law and in funding the rights of independent schools; Alberta, which funds independent schools as a matter of public policy, but has given no legislative guarantee to its appropriations; and Ontario, which steadfastly resists both recognizing the rights of independent schools and funding them.

Ontario. Since Ontario was one of the four provinces existing at the time of confederation, its separate (Catholic) schools are protected by the B.N.A. Act. The third alternative, independent schools, has been neither legally recognized nor funded. While the independent schools still must comply with numerous regulations, as other schools do, they receive no provincial support.[59] It funds numerous "public" experimental schools with widely varying philosophies. Moreover, a number of judicial decisions have opened the way for government funding of its independent schools. As one knowledgeable observer has pointed out:

> Clearly the Legislature in Ontario has not kept up with the judicial interpretation of the B.N.A. Act. It is a case in which the Courts have opened the doors for progressive change but the Legislature has failed to walk through them.[60]

Alberta. In recent years Alberta's independent schools have received increasing financial support from their provincial government. Contrary to what some feared, this support has neither weakened the autonomy and quality of the independent schools nor has it jeopardized the public school system.[61] Nevertheless, this substantial support from the hands of the ministry of education comes without any legislative recognition of the rights of alternative schools. Only two designations of school status are allowed under present legal conditions: public and separate (Catholic). Other schools exist only by the grace of the Cabinet; they must make annual applications to the provincial government in order to maintain their lease to operate.[62]

Since 1961 there has been a gradual development of greater provincial assistance in direct grants, in indirect grants, and in permitting local authorities to assist independent schools. Realizing that this was an implicit recognition of the legitimacy of independent schools, various factions of the independent school movement have worked for even greater equity. Their efforts have been successful in gaining more aid for independent schools. Besides some property tax exemptions, and the use of public school buses and discounts on textbooks, the provincial government gives to each independent school student fifty-five percent of what a public school student would receive. Furthermore, the provincial government has hinted that the grant may go as high as eighty percent.[63]

While the motivations for increasing these grants may have been pragmatic,[64] these significant developments have taken place without upsetting the educational system in Alberta. Perhaps this is why there has been only minimal opposition to the increased financial support of independent schools. In fact, according to some school officials, including the Minister of Education himself, the competition among various school systems may actually be helping the public schools improve their quality. Alberta's Minister of Education recently said:

> I don't see that a move in that direction will in any way jeopardize the public and separate school systems in this province. In fact, I see it as assisting those jurisdictions. Quite often a monopoly could use a little competition in terms of alternate forms of delivery. We've seen the benefits of that to date.[65]

British Columbia. In September 1977 the British Columbia government passed the Independent Schools Support Act. Prior to this Act, for one hundred years British Columbia had officially recognized only one unified school system. This landmark legislation gave recognition and substantial aid to independent (including Catholic) schools. By passing this Act the British Columbia government recognized that parents have a right to send their children to schools in harmony with their beliefs. Through the Independent Schools Support Act the freedom of parents, rich and poor alike, to form associations and operate schools is protected and supported.

Under the legislation, a two-tiered funding program is offered to independent schools. Harro Van Brummelen, a specialist on independent education, states that Group I funding applies to

> schools that have existed for five years, that have adequate facilities, and that sign a statement that they will not teach programs of racial or ethnic superiority, religious intolerance or persecution, or social change through violent action. This latter clause does not affect our Biblical Studies programs nor our school's admission and teacher hiring policies.[66]

Group II classification is only accorded schools already accepted by the Group I program. Additional requirements must be met, such as balanced curricula, adequate testing programs, and teacher certification. The purpose of these requirements is to make sure that independent schools satisfy at least the core of public school requirements. Independent schools continue to have complete independence in structuring their own curricula and programs. In the 1977–78 school year the per pupil grant for students in independent schools was set at thirty percent of the per pupil public school cost. It is estimated that this percentage may go up to seventy percent or more, depending on the approval of the cabinet and the independent school representatives.[67]

Three strikingly different educational systems are at work in these three Canadian provinces. Contrary to what one might expect, however, the provinces that give financial stipends do not impose substantially more regulations on independent schools than Ontario, which, much like its American counterparts, gives nothing to its independent schools. One can also see, on the word of the people in power themselves, that the public schools have not been threatened, undermined, or enfeebled by granting justice to the independent schools.

Israel

In Israel all schools are supervised by the Ministry of Education and Culture. The State Education Law, passed in 1953, established a unified school system within which various other school systems operate. Under this plan all schools receive almost one hundred percent of their payroll budget for teachers and other personnel. This is true for the Hebrew and Jewish schools as well as for Arab, Moslem, and Christian schools. In addition, all schools, whatever their affiliation, receive full financial support for their "secular" programs.[68] While this distinction between the religious and the secular is faulty in our view, the support Israel gives to all confessional schools is noteworthy, especially when one considers the highly diversified and often precarious nature of Israel's society. After suffering hardship and persecution in many countries, the Israelis have learned the value of educating their children in schools whose views are akin to their own beliefs. As the declaration issued upon the establishment of the State of Israel states:

> The State of Israel will foster the development of the country for the benefit of all inhabitants; it will be based on freedom, justice and peace as envisaged by the prophets of Israel; it will ensure complete equality of social and political rights to all inhabitants, irrespective of religion, race, or sex; it will guarantee freedom of religion, conscience, language, education and culture.[69]

England

Independent schools in England, although controlled primarily by confessional societies, are a recognized and subsidized part of the overarching governmental educational system.[70] Optional religious instruction is also provided in the public schools.

The system allows a great deal of diversification and complexity. The societies, local authorities, teachers, and parents retain most of the control of the independent schools. The Ministry of Education oversees the general structure of the system, but the other groups determine the specific details of education.

The present system of education in England is in accord with the Act of 1944 and its subsequent Amendments. Based on this Act, English schools may be divided into three general classes: (1) maintained schools, which belong to the system of education financed by the state and local authorities; (2) private schools, which do not receive any direct support from the state or the local authorities; (3) direct grant schools with partial support from the government.[71] Sectarian schools can be found in all categories. Categories (2) and (3) have limited relations with the government and so need no further mention. One component of category (1) is the "aided" independent schools, which are in some cases run by churches or other confessional associations.* For a school to become aided, a proposal requires both the approval of the Ministry of Education and consultation with local authorities. As long as there are sufficient pupils of the confessional group concerned and the building involved meets certain requirements, permission is usually granted to the applicant school and aid is begun. In some cases seventy-five percent of the construction costs are paid by the local authorities.[72]

In most instances the full cost of running independent schools is met by the local authority or ministry. This applies to expenses such as salaries, books, furniture, equipment, lighting, and cleaning.[73] Ownership of the school remains with the association responsible for it, and the religious instruction is of course that of the denomination concerned. Two-thirds of the managing body of the school are appointed by the confessional association, one-third by the local authority. This managing body has power over the appointment and dismissal of teachers, but the local authority retains veto power with respect to teacher qualifications. The day-to-day running of the school is controlled by the managing body, as is the admission of pupils.

One of the striking features of the English educational system is that it has retained in great measure the tradition of voluntary initiative in founding and managing schools. The structural diversity that exists within the English school system is both le-

*In recent years the educational system in England has undergone some profound changes; however, the funding of independent schools has remained the same.

gally sanctioned and financially supported. A considerable degree of parental choice in freely choosing the appropriate type of education is also maintained and fostered. Finally, the teachers and supporting associations exercise a great deal of control over the curriculum, thus ensuring substantial freedom for all schools.

Belgium

Although Catholics comprise ninety-five percent of the Belgian population, they have had to struggle for recognition and fiscal justice for their schools. Since 1958, however, parents have had the right to decide the nature of education that their children will receive. To make this ideal a reality, the state is committed to a dual system of schools — official (state) and free (nonstate) — in which the free schools are sponsored and controlled by various associations.[74] Most of the free schools are Roman Catholic. Although other schools, such as Protestant and Jewish, exist, they are unsupported. The central government pays for all the personnel costs of the free schools, including pensions and sick benefits, at state school levels.[75] The free schools also receive a graduated, per pupil subsidy. However, the government pays none of the building or maintenance costs of the free schools.

Under the Belgian system, the free schools are not completely autonomous. Local, provincial, church, and national education authorities all have an influence upon them. New regulations come only by common consent. The usual practice is to provide guidelines for such matters as curriculum and length of school years, while leaving each educational authority free to make its own specific arrangements.[76] Fifty-seven percent of the student population attends free schools at the primary and secondary level. For some specialized technical and commercial secondary education, the free schools enroll nearly seventy percent of all students.[77]

The Netherlands

The history of the modern Dutch educational system goes back to the last century. After the Reformation, education in Holland was predominantly Christian. Slowly, however, it became secularized, culminating in the institutionalization of the monopolistic, centralized state school system of the late nineteenth century. Already in 1840, Guillaume Groen Van Prinsterer delineated the root of the problem when he said in Parliament:

> Parents who, with or without sufficient grounds, are convinced that the religious orientation of the teaching in a

particular school is un-christian, must not, either directly or indirectly, be hindered from giving their children the kind of education that they feel is necessary before God. Such coercion, I say it plainly, is intolerable and must cease. It is presumption that springs from the doctrine of the French Revolution which views the children as the property of the State.[78]

This pivotal issue of family rights versus state control of education was to remain at the center of the dispute between the free school supporters and the state school supporters for years to come.

In 1888 a coalition of Roman Catholics and Protestants came into power. In 1889 legislation placed the free schools on a basis similar to that of state schools. Although full financial parity was not yet achieved, state schools were no longer officially assumed to be suitable for all people. Although some funds were now available for free schools, they were woefully insufficient and caused leaders such as Prime Minister Abraham Kuyper to argue that the right to establish a free school was in practice available only to the rich, for only they could afford it.[79] Thus the school struggle continued for another thirty years until complete equity both in funds and in recognition was established.

The Primary Education Act of 1920 implemented a constitutional amendment of 1917. Subsequently, the traditional distinction between public and private schools was virtually erased, since all schools were recognized as part of the common or public effort to provide education.[80] The constitution itself now states that parents have the "natural right and duty" to determine the kind of schooling that their children will have.[81] Furthermore, financial parity between the free schools and the state schools was ensured:

> Private general elementary education fulfilling conditions to be imposed by law shall be defrayed from public funds according to the same standards as public education.[82]

The present educational system in the Netherlands functions in this way: any group of parents may form a school association providing they have at least 50 students for a city whose population is up to 50,000, or 100 students for a city whose population is between 50,000 and 125,000 or more.[83] If there are not enough children to form a new school, the parents may send their children to a neighboring town to the school of their choice. The government will pay for the transportation costs. Once a proposal for a new school has been submitted, the government has a month to respond. If the proposal is approved, the government pays for the entire cost of the building and its furnishings. The government also pays for lighting, heating, cleaning, books, and maintenance. Each year the school board draws up a budget (excluding teacher salaries, which are paid by the national government) that must be approved by the local authorities. The amount of the fiscal need is determined by comparison with state-run schools. If the budget is approved the city pays for all costs.

Thus, the national and local governments in the Netherlands pay equally for all schools, whether they be state or nonstate. Recipient schools must meet certain conditions. Government inspectors of various faiths have free access to classrooms in order to check on the following:

1. Teacher-pupil ratios
2. Teacher certification, qualification, and health
3. Basic curriculum design (i.e., certain core subjects must be taught)
4. Building safety
5. A minimum number of classes per year for each student[84]

These conditions are necessary to ensure proper academic and health standards and the wise use of tax money. Complete freedom remains in:

1. The appointment of all personnel
2. The nature and orientation of instruction
3. Teaching methodology
4. The admission and retention of pupils[85]

Thus it is safe to say that nonstate schools in the Netherlands enjoy complete freedom in the essential matters of education. Whereas in 1850 seventy-seven percent of primary school students attended state schools, seventy-three percent now attend nonstate schools.[86] The Dutch people are aware and proud of the precedent-setting character of their educational system. A 1971 government publication states:

> The Dutch public regards it as a prized possession because it enables every section of the population to give expression in its own way to the spiritual values that it considers of fundamental importance and to make its own contribution to the development of the community.[87]

Educational pluralism exists and works in other democratic countries. We should also realize that the United States is an exception in the Western world in that it grants virtually no aid to its independent schools.[88] The questions, problems, and fears we outlined at the beginning of this section must be assessed in the light of our comparative study. First, countries such as Canada, Israel, Belgium, and the Netherlands place regulations on independent education not unlike the regulations placed on independent education in the United States. Yet these countries provide substantial aid to their independent schools. Thus the adage that increased aid to independent education necessarily brings with it increased government control is not supported by our comparative data.

Second, the pluralist vision is not a utopian ideal. Rather, pluralism is a plausible, realistic, and coherent philosophy of society that works in education, as evidenced in the countries we have cited.

Third, rather than being divisive, independent schools make unique contributions to society. They also offer strength, diversity, and healthy competition to other schools. In these and in other ways independent schools build up a culture.

Fourth, independent schools in a pluralist framework are not undemocratic. On the contrary, they are more democratic than the present American unified and monopolistic education system. True freedom implies freedom of choice. Under the present American system this freedom cannot be realized by all, for there is only one real choice: state-run education. True democracy offers a variety of alternatives; this criterion is fulfilled only in a structurally pluralist society.

Finally, governmental schools do not suffer under the pluralist view of society. In the countries we have examined the governmental schools have not been hindered, crippled, or deprived of their function in society. The purpose of educational pluralism is not to usurp the government schools, but to give all schools a fair chance in order that rich and poor alike may experience true justice and freedom in education.

CHAPTER 6

A BIBLICAL CASE
FOR STRUCTURAL
AND CONFESSIONAL
PLURALISM

IN successive stages and with a kind of cumulative pressure we have signalled repeatedly the need for an alternative to the prevailing individualist and collectivist notions of how to structure society. Pluralism, we submit, offers a better way of living together in society, the state, and the schools. It stands as a realistic hope for a more just social order. Both structurally and confessionally it accounts for the social realities of contemporary American society better than the two dominant social paradigms.

We have discussed the advantages of pluralism as a social paradigm with its public policies; now we examine pluralism at the level of fundamental commitment and confessional vision. At the close of Chapter One we argued that all social paradigms are at bottom anchored in one or another world-view. Ours is no exception. The revival of a pluralist paradigm is deeply rooted in a Biblical view of reality, one that takes the pattern for a just social order from an ordered and meaningful creation.[1]

BIBLICAL FOUNDATIONS

Privatizing the Bible

The very idea of proposing a Biblical view on the social order is often regarded as an exercise in futility and irrelevance. After all, we are dealing here with very complex social-political-economic-educational problems. What has all this to do with the Bible? Scripture is concerned with only very limited matters of a very extraordinary kind. It speaks in no direct and decisive way to issues of society, the state, and the schools. These rejoinders therefore force upon us the question, What kind of book is the Bible? What may we rightly expect of it in our address to the public-legal order? Does it offer any help for working out a Christian social philosophy? Is there actually a divinely ordained pattern for societal life? Granting that the Scriptures do comment in passing on public affairs in ancient Israel and among first-century Christians in the Greco-Roman empire, are such data even remotely relevant to the twentieth-century situation in our secular Western society?

This sampling of critical questions reflects the problems that confront us in developing a pluralist paradigm from within a Biblical perspective. Immediately we are confronted with a controversial excursion into hermeneutics, in this case Biblical hermeneutics, which considers the basic principles and methods for understanding and interpreting the Bible.

Our case for pluralism is not based on a proof-texting approach to Scripture. We resist fragmentary appeals to isolated passages scattered throughout the Bible. Such a piecemeal approach assumes that the Bible is a collection of timeless truths with built-in, ready-made applications for every situation. Accepting such a hermeneutic might imply, for example, restructuring contemporary American society on the model of ancient Israel. Rather, Scripture opens up principles and directives which hold for life in every age. We therefore rely on the comprehensive meaning of the Biblical message. Though couched in ancient forms, the Scriptures carry with them universal norms that can not be ignored with impunity.

Our case for pluralism is clearly not based on the popular American opinion and the standard public policy, both strongly conditioned by Enlightenment dogma, that the Bible as a religious book deals only with narrowly religious matters. Conventional wisdom assumes religion to be a personal and private affair, not integral to life as a whole. Public life is then assumed either to be nonreligious, operating on the secular principle of religious neutrality, or to be governed by a civil religion common to all. Such affirmations are often accepted as self-evident truths. Accordingly, the right to "the free exercise of religion" is taken to mean no more than that each citizen is at liberty to follow whatever religious beliefs he chooses, or none at all. In this sectarian sense, to be or not to be religious, just as to be or not to be interested in art, is an option open to each individual. Thus both religion and the Bible are privatized.[2]

Strangely, many evangelicals share this position with secularists. They are quite willing to restrict the Bible to the privacy of inner religious experience. They regard the Bible as irrelevant to public life. In no significant way is it normative for public policy.

146

It has nothing essential to do with society, the state, and the schools — except perhaps devotionally to promote greater piety and better morality. Consensus politics, they argue, demands such a stance. Thus confessional pluralism is acknowledged, tolerated, even extolled, on condition that it be excluded from public policy. Attempts to grant it legal structural standing and funding rights in the public domain always meet with stiff resistance. Official recognition of confessional pluralism, so the argument goes, poses an ominous threat to the unity of society, the state, and the schools; it would be a divisive intrusion of the religious into the secular realm. This dualism between the private-religious and the public-secular is so deeply woven into the very fabric of the American consciousness as to constitute an unquestioned article of faith. This mind-set also dominates the courts in the decisions they hand down concerning the respective rights and nonrights of so-called public and private, secular and religious schools. The freedom of nonstate schools to exist is upheld in law. But on the crucial question of funding discrimination prevails. Such discrimination is a direct assault upon religious and educational freedom, for freedom that must be purchased at a price so dear is no longer true freedom.

When consistently applied, American public policy therefore seeks to rule out both the Bible and religion from the public domain. Other criteria prevail in the public-secular realm, such as majoritarian decisions arrived at by consensus politics. The Bible is alien to the public life of society (except for "wholly other" churches), the state (except for occasional prayer breakfasts), and the schools (except for released time religious activities). The Bible, like other "holy books," deals with saving souls, not society. On matters of contemporary social reconstruction it is silent. Obviously, then, if we accept a privatized Bible, it makes no sense whatever to speak of a Biblical paradigm for society, the state, the schools — or any other public institution or association.

A Word for the World

A very different understanding of Scripture lies behind the pluralist description of the social order being advanced in this book. The Bible is indeed a religious book, but to reduce religion to some (large or small) part of life is not a self-evident dogma. All of life falls within that revelation-response framework that constitutes the very structure of religion. Religion is that unbroken series of ongoing human responses — both just and unjust — to the Word of God, which holds for our entire life in the world. These unavoidable religious responses give form and direction to the flow of history. Religion is therefore not a choice, but a given. Men are all "incurably religious" (John Calvin). A community's multi-faceted culture is the concrete embodiment of its deepest spiritual allegiances. Every social issue is a human issue, and every human issue a religious issue. At bottom all public policy is shaped by some "ultimate concern" (Paul Tillich). The dichotomy between the private as religious and the public as secular therefore draws through life a wholly arbitrary and unreal line of demarcation. The public affairs of society and the state, including its governmental schools, are not less religiously qualified than the so-called private affairs of personal, church, home, and non-governmental school life. Henry Zylstra explains:

> The fact is that education is a human affair. It represents a human awareness of reality and a human appropriation of it. And this is a further fact: whatever is human is religious. . . . To be human is to be scientific, yes, and practical, and rational, and moral, and social, and artistic, but to be human further is to be religious also. And this religious in man is not just another facet of himself, just another side to his nature, just another part of the whole. It is the condition of all the rest and the justification of all the rest. This is inevitably and inescapably so for all men. No man is religiously neutral in his knowledge of and his appropriation of reality.[3]

Since all of life is religion, and since the Bible as a book on religion speaks to life as a whole, the question is not *whether* the Bible speaks to issues of society, state, and schools, but *how*. It is not a question of whether Scripture addresses matters of public justice and educational equity, but what is the nature of its address. Clearly the Bible is not a handbook on social theory, nor a textbook on public policy. It offers no systematic treatment of such issues. Nor does it deal with them scientifically. Yet no aspect of life is exempt from its message of judgment and renewal; its address is universal. How then does it speak meaningfully and normatively within the full range of all our life relationships?

Biblically directed social thought begins with the confession that the Bible confronts us as an urgent Word from beyond our own universe of experience. It is God's Word for a broken world, which comes as a message of healing and reconciliation. It is couched in the language of renewal and redemption. It aims at the reordering of the life we live together in the world. As Richard Mouw puts it, the Bible is "the locus and record of God's address to human beings in their wholeness, including the entire network of relationships, institutions, and projects in which they participate."[4]

We must somehow define more sharply the nature of Biblical authority in its address to life's issues. What is its unique focus? One way of putting it is this: the Bible speaks to politics, but it does not speak politically. It speaks to social concerns, but without using sociological concepts. It speaks to education, but not in educational language. The language the Bible employs in its universal address is the language of *re*demption. Note that in this context the prefix *re-* is very crucial. It denotes a follow-up action, something done over again. Thus the Bible is not God's primary, but secondary revelation. It is, therefore, the *re*articulation, *re*publication, *re*iteration of the divine will for societal life. It has to do with *re*demption as the *re*storation of creation, which, originally good, fell into sin, and is now being *re*conciled (II Corinthians 5:18–20; Colossians 1:15–20). First creation, then *re*creation—that is the ordered pattern in the Bible's perspective on world history.

One point must be clarified. All interpreters, whether they interpret the Bible or anything else, bring certain pre-understandings of reality to bear upon their work. No man perceives reality in a perceptual vacuum. Social theories are always constructed along the lines of certain confessional visions of life, shaped by certain hermeneutic principles and methods. Some may object to this assertion in the name of objectivity. Objectivity, however, is a myth, an impossible ideal. No method of reasoning is capable of taking us outside ourselves. Nor can we by reason get on top of things to examine them in a detached way. We all wear perceptual glasses of some sort that shape our perspective of reality. This acknowledgment requires no apology. It is just a profoundly simple recognition of our creaturely existence in a state of total dependence upon created reality the way it confronts us. The only question is, What kind of glasses shall we wear? That choice belongs freely to every community, for world-views always have a communal dimension. They are never the fruit of individual insight alone. They are formed within the context of supporting communities of like-minded people, and are not individualistic or religiously neutral.

Now a right understanding of creation is basic to a right understanding of *re*-creation. Implicit in this stance is the conviction that, while Scripture is the Word of God, it is not God's only Word for the world, nor is it his first Word. God's original Word harks back to the very beginning, to creation. To counteract the effects of sin upon the world, however, God gave his follow-up Word in the Scriptures. Taking this transcribed Word seriously as the Word of God leads us to recognize that Scripture itself points to a reality beyond itself that it identifies as also the Word of God, namely, God's Word for creation. Scripture therefore does not exhaust the meaning of God's Word. It also witnesses to Jesus Christ as Word of God incarnate (John 1:14; Hebrews 1:2; Revelation 19:13). It testifies to the cosmic significance of Christ's creating, sustaining, and redeeming work. In John 1 it confronts us with a Christological rewrite of the Genesis 1 account.

Thus, the Word of God in all its fullness comes to bear upon our life in the world. The one Word in its various manifestations converges upon creation and highlights its abiding significance. Then and there, at that undateable date that marks the dawn of history, God's dynamic Word of creative power brought all things into existence and gave them order and meaning. Listening to the creation drama recorded in the Genesis narrative, we hear the resonance of that commanding series of "Let there be's," which gave to all created reality its richly diversified, yet integrally unified structure and task. To be a creature, therefore, of whatever kind, and to each after its own kind, is to be subject to the creative Word in its original and abiding authority. Creatureliness means subservience to a transcendent norm. This norm also holds for the creature man, whose very existence is insinuated into and defined by an astonishing web of relationships. God's Word therefore holds for human beings in all their many ways of being human. Life is not self-explanatory or self-justifying. The world is not an independent substance, a self-sufficient and self-determining entity. In all its complex unity it points beyond itself for answers to the questions of origin, structure, meaning, and purpose. Its ultimate reference point lies in God's Word, which holds transcendently for all creation.

Christians acknowledge the reality of both the Creator and the created. The relationship between them, however, is often either not addressed at all or else only alluded to rather nebulously. This relationship, the link between the Creator and created reality, which is simultaneously both boundary and bridge, is God's Word revealed in the creation order. This Word is not open to generic definition. It transcends rational explanation. Ultimately its reality is a matter of commitment and confession. Its recognition instils a sense of stability, guidance, and certainty, without which there is a continuing sense of crisis and social unrest.

Such a Biblical world-view calls for the acknowledgment that structure precedes and defines function. Most contemporary thought assumes an opposite starting-point: all structures, organic and social, as we know them today, are the products of an infinite series of evolutionary functions. Functions therefore create de facto structures. From the Biblical standpoint, however, things are made to function in keeping with their established structures. Therefore the possibilities for, as well as the limitations upon, historical-cultural development are given with creation. There is a constancy to the creation order that holds for the social order. The life of a community cannot unfold arbitrarily or capriciously. The structural options open to mankind in ordering society are not infinite; the boundaries are circumscribed, and a community gives shape and form to its social order within them.

Thus understood, Biblical religion offers the most practical way of life in the world. It alone conforms to actual experience. That is, as men seek consciously to order their life relationships in keeping with divinely established norms, they experience a certain affinity with the very nature of things. Antinormative ways of structuring society run into resistance. They create anomalies, injustices, inequities. They tend to become self-serving, and in the end self-defeating and self-destructive, because they work at cross purposes with the built-in meaning of life. Biblical religion aims rather to keep the structures *of* society in line with the structures *for* society, and within that framework to work out the functions of a Biblically structured society.

Scripture describes the creation Word as the decrees, commands, ordinances, and statutes of the Lord. God's Word brings into existence, upholds, and directs the creation order as it unfolds dynamically in history. Communities in every age respond concretely to these transcendent norms in their social contours and configurations. Every culturally formative activity is therefore a response — affirmative or negative — to this symphony of creation Words. The most comprehensive Word of God is that which covers the entire range of our life relationships: "Love your neighbors as yourself." That universal command, which is central to God's Word, takes on specific form in the directives given for the various spheres in society: a Word of fidelity for families, of justice for the state, of proclamation for churches, and of learning for schools. Social structures therefore find their ordered beginnings and their legitimate existence in the creative acts of God. The social order is not an autonomously functioning reality or an artificial creation of sovereign people. It is a functioning order dependent upon and answerable to the sovereign will of the Creator.

This priority of the creational Word is reflected in the words of Psalm 33:6, 9: "By the Word of the Lord were [all things] made. . . . For he spoke, and it came to be; he commanded, and it stood forth." Scripture does not share the disjunction that Western thought has introduced between words and deeds. Word and work reinforce each other in the Bible. Often the two are used in parallel constructions, synonymously, as equivalents (cf. Psalm 33:5). Words in Scripture are not mere lingual symbols, audible sounds, or pious wishes. They are efficacious; they make thoughts happen. The creative Word of power by which God in the beginning called the world to order is as truly revelational as his Word in Scripture. Therefore we do not honor the source of both by playing off his words and works, which comprise his one Word, against each other. The creation order reveals God's working words, his resounding works. This Old Testament insight is updated and restated in the language of the New Testament by the writer of Hebrews: "By faith we understand that the world was created by the Word of God . . ." (11:3). Within this Biblical perspective, life in God's world, from beginning to end, is unthinkable apart from that Word, which creates its very possibilities and which also preserves its structures even in the face of disintegrating powers. The apostle witnessed to the scoffers of his day in these words: "They deliberately ignore this fact, that by the Word of God heavens existed long ago, and an earth was formed out of water . . . [and] by that same Word the heavens and earth that now exist . . . are being kept until the day of judgment" (II Peter 3:5– 7). Creation and the final consummation of all things are held together by the Word of God.

Creation and re-creation. In thus reflecting on the Biblical world-view as the basis for a pluralist view of society it is crucially important to grasp as clearly as possible the intimate connection between Biblical and creational revelation. Scripture cannot stand alone. Seeking to derive from it alone a full answer to all the questions of social theory is to overload, and thus to short-circuit, the Biblical message. Reading the Bible alone leads to biblicism. On the other hand, looking to creation alone apart from Scripture leads to secularism. When therefore the Reformers spoke of *sola Scriptura*, they did not mean that Scripture is God's only revelation. God also reveals his will in creation and providence. In fact, the creation Word remains his fundamental and abiding revelation. According to Genesis 3, however, distortion entered our world. Scripture was therefore given as a corrective, *re*inforcing the original revelation upon our minds, *re*directing our attention to the meaning of it all, *re*focusing its intent and purpose. The basic message is ever the same, but it comes in different modes. Its author does not engage in double-talk. Though the *form* of revelation is variable, its *norm* is constant. The Word holds, even when men do not discern its giver. Its normativity is not dependent upon human response, but upon the will of God.

Thus the Bible functions within the framework of the historical sequence of creation, fall, redemption, on the way to the consummation of all things. Revelation is ongoing. It is not once-for-all-time or static. It is existential in the sense that it addresses us where we are and as we are. After the fall, however, the original and continuing creational revelation proved to be no longer adequate. Not that the revelation itself failed or lost something of its force and clarity. The shortcoming is not on the revelation side, but on the response side. John Calvin's "spectacles" of Scripture are therefore now indispensable for reading aright the meaning of the creation order in its bearing on the social order.

In the ontological and historical order of all things, God's first Word in creation remains basic, neither abrogated nor withdrawn. By it God maintains his abiding claim on all men and all societies, including the institutions of state, church, home, school, and all other associations in society. The wholeness, peace, and justice built into the unified diversities of the original creation order still rest upon our societies as a continuing summons to obedience and hope. Through the fall the human situation has indeed changed radically—and for the worse. But the guiding authority of God's Word has not fallen. The cultural mandate is still in force, because the giver is faithful. His Word, first published in creation, then republished in Scripture, is for the healing of our life relationships in society, the state, and the schools.

In one sense, the concept of redemption stresses the discontinuity in history, and thus also in revelation, which was made necessary by that radical break called sin. There is no unbroken, uniform, evolutionary movement in history. Scripture is a representation of God's will, representing his renewed initiative calling the social order back to its intended design. Republication, however, stresses the continuity in history, and therefore also in revelation, between creation and Scripture. The Bible is the second revised edition of God's Word, but it is still at heart the same Word. God's good will for life in his world is constant. Yet, Scripture is not merely a repetition of that unchanging Word. The creational *norms* are forever the same, but in Scripture they are expressed in different *forms*. God accommodates the mode of his revealed will to a radically altered world situation. To begin to understand the continuity in the norm of God's Word in relationship to the discontinuity in its form we must bring to the fore the distinction between *structural* and *confessional* analysis.

God's Word for creation establishes the structures of life. It sets the bounds, tasks, rights, and freedoms of men within their various social relationships—for example, in marriage and family, in worship, work, government, learning, and all the rest. Creational laws for societal life are not announced for the first time in the Bible. They antedate the laws written in the Old Testament; they are embedded in creation (Romans 2:14–15). The Bible can address them precisely because they have existed since the beginning; and it does address them because, though still in force, man's response to them has become distorted. The structures *of* society fail to live up to the structures *for* society. Scripture therefore has to do with these structural norms not in their *objective* reality (for by God's will they remain permanent), but on their *subjective* side. It deals with man's response to them, with the direction we choose to take in our life together. It addresses the *confessional* pluralism that has resulted from man's turning away from God's will. Scripture points to the reformation of society that is possible in and through the re-creating work of Christ Jesus. The aim of Scripture is to counteract the suppressive effects of human unrighteousness, including social unrighteousness (Romans 1:18–25). Such distortion has the whole creation groaning as it awaits its final restoration (Romans 8:18–25), causing painful conflicts in society. This is so precisely because God's original Word still holds. Evil always opposes that Word, fighting a losing battle against the indestructible will of God, combating the ineradicable transcendent norm, unaware that the very possibility of developing distorted structures *of* society is dependent upon the unfailing structures *for* society.

The intent of the Bible then is to redirect our misdirected responses to the creation order, to reorder human social relationships and institutions according to God's will for our life together in his world. We are therefore called to restructure the life of society, the state, and the schools in accordance with the only guideline that corresponds to the real nature of things. All manmade norms for society are artificial, fictitious, illusory. The Bible takes them seriously, because sinful people do, but our attempts to respond to them as guidelines for society result only in oblique and unsatisfying imitations of the only social pattern there really is. This is the case with both individualism and collectivism. Each in its own way constitutes a life-disrupting response to the only life-enriching norm there is. Pluralism, understood in both its structural and confessional dimensions, offers what Robert Nisbet calls the "last best hope" of bringing the structures *of* society back in line with the divine structures *for* society.

Of course, the nature of a social philosophy depends upon what set of values it accepts as normative. Fundamentally, the choice is limited to two basic kinds of ultimate appeal. Some locate

154

the norm immanently, in the world itself. Thus individualists locate it in the unique identity of every individual; collectivists find it in some social megastructure such as the totalitarian state. The alternative is to seek the norm in a transcendent reference point. Our case for pluralism is born of the conviction that the social order refers and points responsively to an ultimate normative order beyond itself as the source and criterion of its meaning.

God's Word maintains its claim upon society even in the face of a powerful tendency to render ultimate authority immanent. Many individualists sense this, even as they declare that the norm resides in the individual. Hence their declaration that the rights of the individual are divine rights. Many collectivists sense it too, even as they seek to locate the norm in the collectivist state. Hence their affirmation of the divine right of the state.

A Biblical view of pluralism resists such impulses toward the immanent and insists instead that the norms for society are and ever remain transcendent. The norm, say, for the state is the impartial administration of public justice. Accordingly, in the state's relationship to schools, public justice calls for educational equity. All social tasks are measured against the creation ordinances, which impinge upon us with an abiding authority. No specific social theory, including the pluralist paradigm, is itself the norm nor may the norm be reduced to and identified with any specific social structure. A pluralist social philosophy, like all others, is a subjective response to those objective guidelines. It is our contention, however, that pluralism answers to the transcendent norm more consistently than the other views. This conviction lies behind our case for structural and confessional pluralism as a social pattern that seeks to reflect the Biblical perspective on the way God's Word is authoritative for the social order.

A normative beginning: its unity. From the Biblical vantage point, then, we need Scripture as a pair of glasses to refocus our view of society, the state, and the schools. But glasses are meant to be used. No one in his right mind spends all his time examining and polishing his glasses. Once cleaned, they must be put on. Thus Scripture too serves a much needed and very practical purpose. It sheds its light upon the complex paths which intersect to form societal life (Psalm 119:105). In its light (Psalm 36:9) we can begin to understand more clearly how the creation order serves to direct the social order.

Scripture is therefore our noetic key. It is "profitable for instruction in righteousness" (II Timothy 3:16–17) — including social righteousness. Scripture serves as our guide through the social landscape of our times, as we pay special attention to those two landmarks that now loom so large, the state and the schools.

Let us begin at the beginning. The Genesis account of creation forms the prologue to the rest of the Bible's unique commentary on the meaning of life in the world. In the first chapters of Genesis the stage is being set. Creation is covenanted into being. Principles (in the sense of *principium*, meaning a starting-point that governs all that follows) are enacted that constitute abiding norms for the future structures of society. The Biblical narrative moves from a rather simple, undifferentiated beginning toward more highly differentiated social structures. In the Biblical account of the successive acts in this historical drama, we first recognize the original creation mandates. We then learn how, after sin, these mandates become re-creation mandates that open up in the course of time, giving formative direction to the institutions and associations of today's highly structured society.

God never asks of man what he does not first give. The cultural mandate (Genesis 1:26–31) therefore comes to us not only with authority as a duty, but first of all beneficently as a gift. Man was made to *be* what he was also called to *do*: as a social being he was natively equipped to live socially. To this end all his habits were inclined. Made in God's image, man was (and still is) called to reflect his maker's image by carrying forward into history the work decisively begun in creation. As worker he was to continue the tasks of the first worker. God's original works established the pattern for man's later works. Thus all the historical-social-cultural potential of creation came to increasingly fuller realization. Creation is indeed the beginning. But beginnings call for follow-through, which is man's task in community. Creation is God's work, quite apart from man. Structuring society and forming culture is man's work, but never apart from God. Man can only act in dependence upon the divinely established creation order.

Man's working out of this creation order in history has resulted in sharply contrasting paradigms of society and culture. This situation does not, of course, reflect the original meaning of creation. Still, it is very real; it must therefore be reckoned with seriously and be given recognized status in public life. The pluralist paradigm envisions greater public justice and educational equity by granting confessional pluralism structural rights in the social order.

In the beginning, however, not only was there confessional unity but also a structurally undifferentiated social setting. At first there were no sharp lines of demarcation between marrying, parenting, governing, worshiping, learning, and the rest. God's Word, calling the creation to order, first came to concentrated expression in the cultural mandate, man's assignment in the world. God's many Words were focused in a single Word. Life was basically of one piece. All man's many tasks were at bottom but one task. Structurally as well as confessionally, therefore, the Biblical emphasis falls first on undifferentiated unity. The undifferentiated social pattern was a unified model of social interaction. This is the truth expressed in the idea of sphere universality—the unity of the various spheres of social activity. The pivotal point of this unity is man's heart (Proverbs 4:23), the concentration point of life as a whole. When this unifying life vision was later lost, social fragmentation, political polarization, and educational inequities set in—the very problems we face today.

A normative beginning: its diversity. From the very beginning, an historical process of gradual differentiation came about. Different aspects and dimensions of life came into their own with increasing clarity. Man's response to the command that he love opened up into (a) loving God above all, as servant-partner; (b) loving fellowman as oneself, as guardian; and (c) loving all creation by "subduing" it and "having dominion" over it as a good steward. As a single ray of light passing through a prism gets refracted into a multifaceted array of colors, so man's single office as God's vicar on earth began to manifest its richly diversified social and cultural potentials. Vertically, all human authority in every life relationship manifests itself as God-given and therefore derived and delegated. Office carries with it the idea of a sovereignty and authority that is subservient to the absolutely sovereign authority of God. All human authority and sovereignty is therefore limited—limited by its dependence upon God and limited also by the rightful exercise of other authorities and sovereignties in life. Second, the Biblical idea of office also highlights our responsibility to the giver of sovereign authority for our exercise of it within the various zones of life. Accountability is built into the very texture of creation. As a third basic dimension of office, Scripture stresses the truth that every office—parent, government official, cleric, educator—exists in order to serve. These three qualities of office—subservience, accountability, and service—all enter into a Biblical view of society, especially as it bears on the role of the state and the schools.

Mankind, then, is endowed with a deeply unified, yet also richly diversified cluster of tasks. These mandates are woven into the very fabric of our life in the world. Scripture offers a running commentary on them, their beginnings and their development. Revelation is always intensely historical; therefore its portrayal of these tasks reflects the cultural setting of its first recipients, ancient Israel and the early Christians. Accordingly, the Scriptural description of man's life in society reflects the agrarian and pastoral life-style of those times. Yet these revelational forms embody norms that have an abiding authority for social theory and practice even in today's highly complex, technical, politicized society.

Scripture, being the kind of book it is, may not be pressed for an exhaustive listing of all these core tasks. Rather, shedding its light on their meaning within the total structure of created reality, it simply illustrates a sampling of them. Among the original nuclear tasks that we can perceive dimly and from a distance in the Genesis narratives are the following: marrying (cf. Matthew 19:3–9), family living (Adam, Eve, Cain, Abel, and Seth), working (tilling the soil), learning (naming creatures after their kind), governing (guarding the garden), and worshiping (walking with God in the cool of the day). Each task has its own identity and integrity; one is not reducible to another. Each has its own right of existence and reason for existence. This truth is captured in the idea of sphere sovereignty—namely, that each of these spheres of social activity has an inalienable authority and sovereignty of its own.

Regarding these original nuclear tasks we may claim neither too much nor too little. They claim too little who assume that world history sprang from a raw, formless, and unstructured beginning. From the Biblical perspective, creation is not amorphous. Life began as a cosmos (an ordered whole), not chaos. On the other hand, we must also avoid claiming too much. Take education as an example. God made man as an educable and educating, a teaching and learning creature. By native impulse man set out spontaneously to exercise that talent. For a long time, however, the task of education took place very informally, within the life of the family, carried on by an oral tradition that was suited to the demands of everyday living. Clearly, therefore, God did not create a middle-west consolidated school system, nor even a little red schoolhouse. These are products of historical development. But man was made a learner. This was and remains the normative beginning for all our educational enterprises. This is the abiding basis for the many attempts throughout the ages to give culturally formative expression to this built-in educating impulse.

Similarly, one can also claim both too much and too little for man's worshiping and governing tasks. God did not create the World Council of Churches or even a local congregation. But man, as one of his several callings, was made a worshiping creature. Building upon the authoritative guidelines of this beginning, history reflects a steady build-up of ecclesiastical structures. Also, of course, the American government does not go back to the beginning; God did not create and hallow the three branches of government or the two-party system. From the beginning, however, man was endowed with a governing task. He is, among other things, a political creature. Thus the normative beginning of state life is also rooted in the creation order. The central mandate for the state is the impartial administration of public justice. This is an abiding norm for every society in every age, which must come to expression in positive law as a people gives historical-cultural form to the role of the state in society and its schools.

The genetic origin of every social sphere therefore goes back to the nuclear tasks embedded in the creation order. The creation order defines the nature of these core tasks within each sphere. It is also the abiding basis for the way various historical traditions developed their views of societal structures, both in continuity and in discontinuity with the original mandates. A Christian view of society must therefore take history seriously, because history is the appointed way of leading creation to the realization of its intended potential. History is the record of faithful and unfaithful responses to the creation order within various human communities. The structures *for* society take on concrete form in the structures *of* society. As we allow the Biblical narrative to enlighten this unfolding process of historical differentiation, we see these nuclear tasks, originally clustered in a highly unified way around the family, gradually coming to their own in more sharply focused, highly specialized ways, each with its own structure and function.

Differentiation of Tasks

Let us briefly retrace the historical process through which man's several mandates came increasingly to more differentiated expression. In the early chapters of Genesis, Adam is simply the general worker, equipped for every job, a man of all trades. In time, however, a degree of specialization becomes evident. Cain is a farmer, Abel a herdsman, Nimrod a hunter, Tubal a metal worker, and Tubal-Cain a musician.

Differentiation did not, however, follow a constant, progressive, evolutionary pattern. A little later in Genesis we meet Abraham, whose colorful career reflects a stage of development as yet largely undifferentiated. He acts as husband, father, leading educator, chief liturgete, land developer, patriarchal head of his political community, top herdsman, well-digger, and commander of a military task force — all of these functions concentrated in a single person. Moses illustrates a similar case. Nearly all leadership functions in Israel during the exodus era were concentrated in him, to the point that he was advised to delegate some of his authority. Samuel, too, played a rather undifferentiated leadership role during a crucial transitional period in Israel's history as it moved politically from tribal independence toward a united kingdom. Traditionally, Hebrew society had recognized its allegiance to a threefold office, that of prophet, priest, and king. All three were embodied in Samuel, reflecting thus an undifferentiated distribution of authority. Gradually, however, the respective tasks of the prophet, the priest, and the king were delegated to distinct individuals. Saul, as king, was rejected for usurping the prerogatives of the priesthood; Uzzah was later guilty of a similar presumption.

During the reign of David, Samuel's successor, sharper lines of demarcation begin to emerge with increasingly greater clarity. David the king is rebuked by the prophet Nathan, while the priest Abiathar carries on his work in the temple. Thus, this threefold task, rooted in creation and long exercised in an undifferentiated way, gradually came to a more clearly differentiated expression as it was restored to a redeeming function in Israel. As the Old Testament narrates the unfolding salvation history, these official tasks gradually gain a firmer structural footing in Israelite society. This is evident, for example, in the schools of the prophets, the palace as the royal residence, and the temple as cultic center. Each of these established institutions with its unique task had its own God-given rights. This process of historical differentiation reflects the development of the principle of sphere sovereignty in Hebrew history. Varying degrees of strain and tension as well as cooperative partnership accompanied its evolution. Israel's neighboring nations underwent formally similar patterns of historical development, often involving very bitter rivalries among kings, priests, and prophets.

During the Inter-Testamentary era a case arose within the Jewish community that reflects a retrogressive movement in this historical process of differentiation, marking a setback in the development of the principle of sphere sovereignty. The year was 142 B.C., the place Jerusalem. The Macabbean revolt had succeeded in freeing Israel from Syrian oppression. As a reward, Simon the Jewel, one of the sons of the Macabbean family, which had spearheaded this war for liberation, was crowned governor of Judea. But the Maccabees were also priests. Now they acted both as priests and kings, resulting in a kind of church-state coalition. This represents a violation of the principle of sphere sovereignty, disrupting the historical process of vocational differentiation and the normative development of institutional life in Israel. Were this merely an abstract illustrative case, it might be interesting enough. However, it had a significant, concrete repercussion in New Testament history. This bit of Macabbean history is essential background for understanding the role of Annas and Caiaphas, high priests and presiding officers in the Sanhedrin, in the trial of Jesus: they were "church" functionaries acting politically on behalf of state government. Such distortion is unthinkable except as a radical departure from the established principle of a normative distribution of tasks in society.

The writings of the New Testament indicate renewed progress in the unfolding process of differentiating tasks. Within the early Christian community Christ commissioned certain men to the office of apostle. As we learn from the book of Acts, almost all activity among believers centered at first on those twelve apostles. Soon it became clear that this apostolic office was being overloaded with responsibility. This led to a redistribution of tasks. The single office of apostle was differentiated into the threefold office of deacon, elder, and minister. This opening-up process caused various elements of the church's ministry to come increasingly into clearer structural focus. In the New Testament letters we find a similar recognition of multiple spheres of societal activity, each sphere with its own distinctive norms. Yet altogether their functions were interrelated and coordinated within a unified pattern of communal life — reflecting again the complementary principle of sphere sovereignty and sphere universality. In his letter to the Ephesian Christians, Paul emphasizes this unity in partnership: "Be subject to one another out of reverence for Christ" (5:21). In writing to believers in Colossae he emphasizes the importance of their several distinctive callings when he says, "Whatever your task, work heartily, as serving the Lord and not men" (3:21). In both contexts Paul sets forth specific guidelines for various life relationships, such as those between husbands and wives, parents and children, slaves and masters (cf. I Timothy 6:1–2). Romans 13:1–7 stands as a classic passage on the relationship between rulers and citizens; norms for this relationship are also given in I Peter 2:13–17. Similarly, the principles that govern the relationship of officers and members of the church are spelled out by Paul in I Timothy 3.

Thus, by the close of the first century the spheres of home, church, work, and state activity had come to rather clearly differentiated expression. Schools as well-structured institutions for general education, had, however, not yet developed. It is natural then to find the New Testament pervasively offering its redemptive commentary on these various life relationships with a view to restoring them to their creationally intended ends.

HISTORICAL DEVELOPMENTS

As its book of faith, the Bible served to guide the church down through the ages in shaping its social paradigms. The pluralist perspective of the Scriptures, embracing the idea of differentiated social structures within community, helped to counteract excessive intrusions by both individualist and collectivist ideologies. Yet often the church failed to grasp clearly this pluralist world-view and to live up to it consistently. During the medieval era it borrowed heavily from the collectivist ideals of Greek social philosophy. During the modern period it succumbed all too readily to the pressures of Enlightenment individualism. Such synthesizing of its own Biblical standpoint with alien patterns of thought resulted in the emergence of a number of competing social paradigms within the Western Christian tradition.[5]

This is apparent, for example, from the history of the university. Early medieval universities were structurally free in the sense of having their own academic sovereignty, free of control by either church or state. By the high medieval era they had become largely church institutions, dominated by the ecclesiastical hierarchy. During the modern period universities became mostly state owned and operated, governed by the prevailing world-views and social paradigms of their sponsoring governments.[6] One instance of a dramatic restoration of the university to its own rightful sovereignty came in Amsterdam in 1880. That was the year Abraham Kuyper founded the Free Reformed University, free of both state and church control, free to find its own place structurally and confessionally within society and thus to fulfill its own calling.[7]

Views of the State

In the medieval era the role of the church was crucial to a Christian view of society. In the modern world, the role of the state is equally important. Yet fundamentally different points of view persist among social thinkers concerning the origin of the state, its norm, its place in society, and therefore also its relationship to schools. This is true among Christian social thinkers as well, where we encounter at least three significantly divergent views.[8]

Some root the state in the order of redemption. According to this view, since all reality must be viewed Christologically, the state too must be viewed as related to Christ Jesus. The state then exists as a provisional analogy and embodiment of the coming kingdom of God. It must reflect, though indirectly, the faith of the church. It looks forward toward its future justification, not back to a normative beginning in creation. Therefore its present status is laden with dialectical tension and ambiguity. Structurally, this view tends to move toward collectivism.

Others anchor the state in the order of preservation. It belongs neither to the original creation order nor to the future order of redemption. It has only an interim status. It forms a kind of historical parenthesis between the beginning and the end. In the meantime the state is necessary because of human sinfulness to protect social institutions from destructive forces and to curb ruthless powers. This view holds to a basically negative, even demonic outlook upon the state. Often it goes hand in hand with individualism.

A third view grounds the state in the order of creation. Like all other social realities, the state participates in the Biblically illumined historical drama of creation, fall, and ongoing restoration, moving toward the final re-creation of all things. In this view, the original mandate for the state as given in the creation order still holds — namely, to regulate social interaction and promote good order. Now, because of sin, it is also called to restrain evil. All this is in the interest of fulfilling its abiding task of administering public justice evenhandedly among all institutions in society. Of these three views, clearly the third stands as the most constructive approach. It alone offers positive structural guidelines for normative change. Therein lies the best hope for social and educational reform directed toward a more just society. This is the Biblical view with its accompanying social paradigm that is being developed in this book.

Within this pluralist paradigm we recognize the norm for the state as the Biblical principle of justice and righteousness. In its address to political issues, Scripture's comprehensive and cumulative emphasis consistently strikes this central theme. The state can indeed, and often has, become the horrendous beast of Revelation 13. There we meet the state at its worst, as the very epitome of social injustice, embodying the kind of radical anti-normativity that can overtake any contemporary institution. Such an apostate condition is not necessary, however. It is not intrinsic and essential to statehood. By way of contrast, Romans 13 describes the positive norm for the life of the state. There we meet the state at its best — the way it ought to be. The key is always justice, in this passage and throughout Scripture. With powerful

impact the minor prophets of the Old Testament speak out tire-
lessly in recalling the state to its central task — do justice, act righ-
teously, deal equitably with all, especially the weak.

If then the administration of public justice is the abiding
norm for defining the social responsibility of the state, and if a
pluralist paradigm represents the most adequate response to that
norm, both structurally and confessionally, how then shall we
define what social justice is? In Western history justice has had at
least four substantially different meanings. One view goes back
to ancient Greece. It defines justice as giving men their *due*, what
they have coming to them, what they may rightly expect and
claim. This definition does little more, however, than beg the
question, for what is man's due? A second view holds that justice
means giving to each man what he deserves, rewarding each
according to his personal *merit*. The measure of human merit,
however, is said to vary from one individual to another. Accordingly there are different classes of men in society. This understanding of justice is typical of modern individualism, especially
in the West, where people appeal to it in vindication of the capitalist free enterprise system. There is also a third view, which
prevails generally in the East, especially in socialist countries. It
defines justice according to human *need*. From each according to
his ability, to each according to his need, as the familiar slogan
goes. This view is characteristic of the collectivist tradition.

These three views all represent understandings of public
justice as the central task of the state that arise out of certain pre-
accepted social paradigms. They also reflect the problems that
arise from affirming various forms of individualism and collectivism. Is there an alternative? It is our contention that a pluralist
paradigm based upon a Biblical view of society helps to break
through the false dilemmas of these other views. It is rooted in
the Biblical idea of *office*, as previously sketched in this chapter.
By virtue of the Word of God which establishes and maintains the
regularities of the creation order, man as crown of creation is
called to be God's image, his officer in the world. He is, in Biblical
terms, chief steward (I Corinthians 4:1; Galatians 4:2; I Peter 4:10),
one placed in charge of the household, that is, of the several
rooms in this creational habitat. Accordingly men hold a diversity
of offices, such as those of parents, teachers, students, citizens,
church members and leaders, magistrates, workers, and state
officials. In this pluralist view, public justice as the central task of
the state means enacting and administering public policy in such
a way as to safeguard and encourage men in the fulfillment of
their manifold offices and callings in society, the governing task

of the state itself being only one of our many offices in society. Neither the state, therefore, nor sovereign individuals create the social institutions or confer upon them their offices and tasks. Rather, the state is obligated to safeguard them in the exercise of their divinely prescribed rights, freedoms, and duties. It must assure them of the room they need to fulfill their respective offices. The state functions as the balance wheel in society, balancing out as equitably as possible the conflicts of interest that arise among different institutions (structural pluralism) and among different faith communities (confessional pluralism).

Pluralism therefore affirms the importance of a clear distinction between state and society. This means that the state too must be respected in its office, not as an artificial creation of sovereign people by way of a social contract (individualism), but as the coexisting agent of public justice within the ordered structures of a free society. Liberty and justice for all institutions and all social groups encapsulates its normative role in society. It must mete out justice impartially, or become an agent of injustice. What it secures for one, it must insist upon for all—both structurally and confessionally. Given the complexities of a highly differentiated society, without a stable guiding norm the state is bound to act arbitrarily, even capriciously, or to succumb to the political pressures of the most powerful lobbying groups, rather than implement justice and safeguard the rights of all.

While the state must act impartially, it cannot act in a religiously neutral way. We are therefore compelled to consider seriously the religious vision that shapes a state's understanding of public justice. A basic step in the direction of a more just society follows from the open acknowledgment that public policy is always shaped by some social paradigm and some religious vision. This being the case, it is crucially important to examine carefully various alternative social paradigms in order to determine which one leads to public policies that assure the greatest possible justice and freedom for all the individuals, groups, and institutions that make up a pluralist society.

Our point is not first of all to petition the state to replace its individualist-collectivist paradigm with a pluralist paradigm. Nor are we asking that the Enlightenment mind be abandoned in favor of that earlier American outlook called the Puritan mind. Rather, what we are asking is this: that the state acknowledge its own deeply entrenched world-view; that it also acknowledge the resultant social paradigm that shapes its public policy; that it further acknowledge that its prevailing world-view and social paradigm is not neutral; that it then cease to impose its world-view and social paradigm upon society as a whole as its test of public orthodoxy and its standard for public funding; that it recognize the fundamental rights of confessional communities holding to other world-views and social paradigms to give structural form to their commitments publicly in the social order; and therefore, most importantly, that the state and its citizens, while allowing competing world-views and social paradigms the right to interact freely, reflect upon this decisive question: which world-view and which accompanying social paradigm offers the state the best promise of living up to its norm and central task, namely, to administer public justice evenhandedly with respect to all social structures and all confessional groups in society.

New Directions for Schools

The implications of this pluralist social paradigm for the relationship of the state to the schools can now be briefly drawn. Social justice translated into public policy for schools means placing the resources of the state on the side of educational equity. What equity means for schools needs to be worked out carefully, giving all parties involved a voice in the planning. Our final chapter offers some concrete proposals for implementing this pluralist view. At this point we shall simply draw some initial conclusions from the pluralist paradigm by sketching a few guiding principles embedded in it.

Consider first the principle of structural pluralism. The state is the state, and a school is a school. Each has its own unique structure and task, its own rights and sovereignty; this clear distinction between the state and the schools must be observed. Society must be led to respect the proper structural distance between them — each having its own office, social identity, and integrity. The growing state monopoly in education must be broken. Schools must be depoliticized. Ways must be found to reduce the "excessive entanglement" of government in education. Rather than acting as the national educator, the state must play a different role, a positive but more limited one, seeing to it that schools enjoy the rights and freedoms they need as academic institutions to do their work; seeing to it also that the needed resources and revenues are available, and that basic educational standards are honored. These and similar considerations grow out of the state's central task of shaping a just public policy in education that honors the normative social realities embedded in the idea of structural pluralism.

More specifically, the state stands in a roughly threefold relationship to the schools. Each of these relationships entails a different set of tasks. First, the state must safeguard the right of all schools to freely determine their own religious commitments and philosophies of education — whether Roman Catholic, Lutheran, Amish, Hebrew, Baptist, Calvinist, Secular, Atheist, or any other. Second, in pursuit of its task to execute public justice, the state must assure itself of the health, safety, good order, equitable treatment, and well-being of both the teaching staff and the student population in its various schools. Third, decisions on issues that are specifically academic belong rightfully to and should therefore be made, not by state officials, but by representatives of the academic community. This involves particularly such matters as the formal content of the curriculum, teacher certification, basic student achievement, length of school terms, etc.

Thus every possible effort should be made to promote self-regulation by educational leaders on matters that concern the essential internal operations of schools. The state should, accordingly, see to it that there be qualified accrediting agencies to regulate specifically academic affairs. Further, it should assure itself that all schools have an equitable voice in shaping the policies by which they are to be governed. Moreover, the state should see to it that every reasonable effort be made to allow all equity-sharing schools to comply with such regulations, and that, within such accrediting procedures, the right of appeal for all participating schools be safeguarded in accordance with due process of law.

In such an arrangement the state plays a see-to-it-that-it-gets-done role, while schools play a see-to-the-doing-of-it role. The basic principle is this: to each its own. The state should deal with the specifically political dimensions of school life. Schools should regulate those academic functions that pertain uniquely to their own structural right of existence and reason for existence within society.

Finally, the principle of confessional pluralism must be reevaluated in very concrete ways. Paying lip service to American toleration of its many faiths is poor compensation for the practice of privatizing religious differences, or for the identification of religion with church and then exiling it from the public domain, or for the insistent failure to grant confessional pluralism structural rights in society as a matter of just public policy. In education this requires the state to open up official relationships with all schools. The religious-confessional plurality of school systems within society must be granted structural standing before law. This must be done equitably, evenhandedly, impartially. Implied in this is clearly an end to the state's discriminatory policy toward so-called nonpublic schools. All schools would become public schools, thus laying to rest the untenable public-private, secular-religious distinction. The state could still operate schools along the lines of the present public school system. But the privileged status and favored financial treatment of a single school system would make way for a multiplicity of school systems, each enjoying the right and freedom to determine its own philosophy and to regulate its own internal academic affairs without financial penalty.

Such a pluralist paradigm recognizes as a matter of just social policy the legal right of each faith community in society to work out its own world-view in a structured program of education. No school community would be coerced, either overtly or subtly, to adopt another's view concerning the locus of educational authority. Views on this differ widely. Some locate it in the state, others in the home, or in the church, or in the school itself. This plurality of viewpoints could remain and should be respected. The principal matter of concern to the state in administering a just public policy in education is simply whether a school is really a school. That is, does it meet the basic structural standards of adequate educational achievement as defined by the demands of public justice in contemporary society? Once this legitimate concern of the state is met, confessional pluralism in education will be able to flourish.

CHAPTER 7

STRATEGIES FOR CONSTRUCTIVE CHANGE TOWARD PLURALISM

IN this final chapter we look hopefully to the future. We take the vision of structural and confessional pluralism that has been articulated in this book, and translate the theory into an outline of political action to achieve educational pluralism. We believe that if public justice, as outlined in our theory of pluralism, is to become more than a catchword for expressing discontent it must not remain a utopian dream but be made a political possibility. It must be so in touch with social realities that even those not committed to our confessional basis can see its socially constructive quality, and can see that our proposals are not self-serving but will lead to a revitalization of the structures of the family and the school for all.

We believe that constructive political action is conceivable on three fronts simultaneously: legislation, litigation, and a constitutional amendment. One kind of action need not wait on the others for implementation; all three can proceed simultaneously and can mutually support each other.

The legislative front must focus on those kinds of legislation that are most possible within present political realities and judicial precedents. At the same time, plans must be laid for advancing on the judicial front. Our analysis of past Supreme Court decisions has exposed its past bias against freedom of associations, particularly school associations, by striking down legislative funding proposals favorable to family choice. Litigation must be undertaken that will cause the judicial system to reexamine its long-standing bias against the rights of such associations and to redress their grievances. Such litigation would have as its objective the changing of the climate of court opinion about what is constitutionally permissible. The achievement of a landmark Supreme Court decision on the rights of families and schools would have the effect of broadening the scope of what is legislatively permissible, removing from such legislation the present cloud of constitutional prohibition. Meanwhile, efforts to amend the Constitution itself must be undertaken. Apart from a constitutional amendment to secure forever the full rights of families and school associations, both legislation and litigation will be subject to the vagaries of both the legislative process and of Supreme Court justices. Structural and confessional pluralism need to be guaranteed in the Constitution itself.

We have sketched the broad outlines of action on these three fronts, a blueprint for educational funding reform for the recognition of structural and confessional pluralism in American society.

LEGISLATIVE INITIATIVES: GUIDE FOR THE PERPLEXED

In the last twenty-five years much legislation relating to nongovernmental schools has been passed at both the state and the federal level. It is clear from the record that the majority of legislators, the two major political parties, and most of our recent presidents have sought some way to reform the funding of American education, and in the process to preserve nongovernmental schools as a vital part of that total system. The record is equally clear that while the legislative and executive branches of governments have proposed, the judicial branch has disposed. While limited and peripheral forms of aid to nongovernment schools have survived and continue in effect, the vast majority of such legislation has been struck down by various kinds of judicial action, some at state Supreme Court and some at the U.S. Supreme Court level. Some reform proposals have also been struck down by public referendum.

We must examine both the small successes and the large failures to achieve educational equity in order to discover those forms of legislation that will survive judicial scrutiny. Since most of the legislation has been struck down as being in conflict with the establishment clause of the First Amendment, legislation that minimizes the likelihood of its being snared in the tangle of church-state relations must be brought to the fore, and the old forms laid aside. That which is permissible under present court interpretation of the First Amendment must now be pursued.

Income Tax Legislation

One form of legislation that has been repeatedly proposed at both state and federal levels is either an income tax credit or a deduction for tuition paid at nongovernment schools. Tax credits must be distinguished from tax deductions. While tax credits are subtracted directly from the tax due, and thus are worth 100% of their face value, deductions are subtracted only from gross income in arriving at taxable income, and hence are worth only a certain percentage of their face value. Some of the proposals have embraced only college tuition, while others have included elementary and secondary school tuition.

The attempt to use the present income tax system as a means of reform of educational funding has a relatively recent history and has taken several forms. A brief history of these efforts is needed to understand its present status in terms of its constitutional acceptance and its future political feasibility.

Tax credit legislation. In the sixties a citizens' group called CREDIT mounted an effort to obtain relief for tuition-paying parents by adding to the federal income tax form an additional line under credits (rather than deductions). The organization had a national director located in Washington, D.C., and lobbied congressmen for legislation. It failed to get any proposals out of committee to see what Congress would do with such a plan. Another citizens' group called CEF (Citizens for Educational Freedom) also publicly endorsed such legislation and lobbied on its behalf for a number of years.

In New York state one formal attempt was initiated by the legislature itself. Legislation passed in 1972 provided for tuition reimbursements in the form of a state income tax credit for those parents paying tuition for private schooling. At almost the same time, in Pennsylvania legislation was enacted that allowed parents who had paid tuition for elementary and secondary school children to claim a tax credit under a tuition reimbursement plan.

In two separate actions in 1973 the Supreme Court struck down both state plans. It ruled that both legislative acts failed the test of constitutionality concerning establishment of religion.

Several attempts have been made at the federal level. Several tax credit bills were introduced in both the Senate and the House. The most publicized version, known popularly as the Packwood-Moynihan bill, was introduced in the Senate in September, 1977, in a bipartisan effort. It was cosponsored by fifty Senators, twenty-six of whom were Republicans and twenty-four Democrats. It was a bill "to amend the Internal Revenue Code of 1954 to permit a taxpayer to claim a credit for amounts paid as tuition to provide education for himself, his spouse, or for his dependents, and to provide that such credit is refundable."[1] It was designed to embrace both college and pre-college level expenditures for education, and as the last phrase indicates, to include a refund for those whose taxes were less than the credit allowed.

A companion bill was introduced at the same time in the House of Representatives. Subsequently a Senate-House Conference Committee was unable to iron out difficulties, particularly the inclusion of elementary and secondary tuition, and the threat of a presidential veto hung over the bill if it were passed. The bill thus died before the adjournment of Congress in 1978.

Tax deduction legislation. Some recent state legislation has focused on tax deductions for tuition. A New Jersey state income tax provision in 1976 allowed a $1,000 per child tax deduction for parents who pay tuition to send children to school. Even though the legislation resulted in an estimated saving of only $20 for a family with a $20,000 yearly income, it was struck down by a Federal District Court on February 1, 1978. That court held that it had the direct effect of aiding religion, since most of the schools to which the legislation applied were religiously oriented, mostly Roman Catholic.

Subsequently the United States Court of Appeals for the Third Circuit affirmed that decision, relying in part on previous U.S. Supreme Court decisions in 1973. The state then appealed to the U.S. Supreme Court, arguing that the law granted only "in an even-handed manner a meager amount of tax relief to parents whose children attend all schools which normally charge tuition."[2] The case was not heard by the U.S. Supreme Court because four votes are needed to hear such cases, and only Burger, White, and Rehnquist voted to hear the state's appeal. The decision had the effect of making the lower court's ruling binding.

Another state has similar legislation, but with one key difference. A Minnesota law, on the books since 1955, allows a state income tax deduction for tuition and other fees paid to either public or private elementary and secondary schools. A ruling by a federal district court in *Minnesota Civil Liberties Union* v. *Roemer* (1978) held that allowing deductions for educational expenses such as tuition, transportation, and secular textbooks did not violate the First Amendment, because it provided benefits to parents of both public and private school children alike. At the time of this writing the decision has not been appealed to the U.S. Supreme Court.

Critique of tax legislation. Fifteen years of tax legislation have produced only negligible results and have cast a cloud of unconstitutionality over all such efforts. One may speculate about why the Minnesota case has not been appealed and what the decision would be if it were. It may be that the amounts involved are small, being only deductions and not credits, and it may be that the inclusion of public school expenses prevents it from falling under the ban of *Nyquist* and *Lemon*. The facts are that all such efforts are constitutionally suspect, at least as they are seen by a majority of the present justices.

A version of tax credit or tax deduction legislation similar to that in Minnesota might very well survive Supreme Court scrutiny. The legislation would have to include benefits to all parents of school age children and not just those attending schools which charge tuition. Provisions of the bill would have to allow all such taxpayers to specify as tuition that part of the local property tax which is the school tax. The credit allowed could be some specified maximum related to the average cost per student in the state. Thus all parents would receive some tax funds for their discretionary use in the education of their children. Some could use it to provide transportation to a different public school of their choice within a district. Some could gain admission to their preferred school outside their district by paying the tuition charged by public schools for students who reside outside the district. Those who prefer some form of nonpublic education could also use their tax funds for tuition to such schools.

Such legislation, if properly drafted to include public as well as private school parents, would be a significant step toward enhancing freedom of choice. If such legislation could be designed to move toward full parity of the cost of education, it would enhance even more the free choice of public or nonpublic school for parents. It would require a provision that where the actual cost of education exceeded the actual tax owed, a refund would be provided.

If benefits went to parents regardless of their choice of school, such legislation would probably survive Supreme Court scrutiny under the establishment clause. Several signals have come from the Supreme Court suggesting that where all have been aided, public school clients and private school clients, the aid will be proper by establishment clause standards.*

A larger and deeper problem with all legislation geared to Internal Revenue Service rules is that it leaves untouched the more basic question of structural pluralism. While it would enhance confessional pluralism, such an approach would not even

*Such signals from the Supreme Court in recent funding cases will be discussed further in this chapter in our discussion of vouchers and their constitutional acceptability.

raise the question, much less resolve it, of whether or not the state is the sole locus of educational authority. We have sought to raise the larger question of the rights of associations and the recognition of sphere sovereignty as applied to schools. Until legislation is premised on such rights of family and of schools, it will give only token assent to family choice in education. It will leave the power of the present monopoly of the state in education unquestioned. It will leave nonpublic schools defenseless against the increasing expansion of state power to dictate the details of nonpublic school operation. Such legislation may produce tax reform but not educational reform.

We conclude that income tax legislation, whether state or federal, is less than fully satisfactory for achieving public justice and educational equity. Persistent pursuit of these small measures may direct energies and attention away from the larger tasks of funding reform to which this book is committed.[*]

The Voucher System

Various proposals for the voucher idea and experiments with it are a phenomenon of the sixties and seventies. Common to them all is the idea of placing in the hands of parents and other consumers of educational services an amount of tax money for the purchase of the educational services of their choice. An analysis of these plans will reveal the extent to which the voucher idea, whether the payment is called an education stamp, a certificate, or a voucher, contains the seed of more basic reform.

We believe that the voucher concept is an idea whose time has come, politically speaking. It represents a coming together of a wide variety of both tax reform and educational reform ideas. For about twenty years now it has been the subject of vigorous scholarly discussion, as well as political debate; indeed, a federally funded experiment in Alum Rock, California, has been carried out. Basically, the voucher concept involves a change in both the collection and disbursement of taxes for school purposes. We shall focus only on the second of these processes, assuming that the collection of such taxes must move away from local property taxes and toward a state-wide progressive income tax, sales tax, or such other equitable taxation as the respective states may de-

---

[*]No mention has been made of loans and grants to students for educational purposes. Presently limited to the college level, and available only to those who can prove financial need, they also leave untouched the deeper question of the state's role in education, and therefore the larger questions of structural pluralism.

vise to replace the present tax. We recognize many problems connected with the question of how the school tax is best collected, but our present concern is only with its disbursement.

The disbursement of the voucher places in the hands of parents of each school-age child a voucher or certificate with a given face value. That amount covers all or a substantial part of the cost of education at any accredited school of the parents' choice, whether it be under public, private, or church auspices.

Political feasibility. While all reform legislation should be designed to meet the test of constitutionality, it must also be politically feasible. It must be acceptable to a wide range of persons who approach it with different social and economic priorities and differing motivations. Such we believe is the case with the voucher concept. While the adherents of various ideologies and motivations may prefer different formulas and stipulations regulating the use of the voucher, they agree that the concept is a more equitable form of disbursing taxes for education than the present system.

There is every indication that the American people at large are ready for a reform of educational funding. The property tax has become the focus of much citizen discontent and has already resulted in some state level legislation. This discontent is germane to the voucher concept only because in many areas over fifty percent of the local property tax is actually a school tax. Any reform in the collection and disbursement of the school tax will thus have a large impact on the property tax. The voucher concept, when presented as a tax reform, is therefore likely to gain the attention of the average American home owner.

The political feasibility of the voucher concept does not rest solely on this connection with tax reform. Much of its support comes from a coalition of those who see it mainly as a lever for social and educational reform. At present four major identifiable views converge in support of the voucher concept. They are what we call free market theory, social equality theory, civil liberty theory, and religious freedom theory.

A father of the free market approach to educational reform through vouchers is the University of Chicago economist Milton Friedman. Friedman's basic scheme runs through the proposals of most others who wish to increase consumer choice in the educational marketplace through a voucher, education stamp, or other means of placing purchasing power in the hands of parents. The logic of free enterprise in economics applied to education makes this plan plausible to a segment of the population. The case has been put succinctly by Friedman:

Here as in other fields, competitive private enterprise is likely to be far more efficient in meeting consumer demands than either nationalized (publicly run) enterprises or enterprises run to serve other purposes.[3]

In this view both profit-making corporations and nonprofit organizations, such as churches or associations of parents, can compete in the marketplace for the consumer of educational services, with the free enterprise principle acting as the chief lever for educational improvement. As in business, so in education, the state will not operate schools but will encourage them by appropriate legislation that gives grants to consumers to purchase the educational services of their choice. In this business model of education the present monopoly of governmental schools is broken. The present public schools compete with other forms of schooling on an equal basis. Thus, the voucher becomes the mechanism for reform of education through competition.* The Center for Independent Education has also published a position paper endorsing the voucher concept from this viewpoint.[4]

A leading spokesman for the social equality theory is Christopher Jencks, a social psychologist at Harvard University and former member of its Center for the Study of Public Policy. The heart of Jencks's support of the voucher form of funding lies in his belief that present public education funding perpetuates both racial and economic segregation, and therefore discriminates against the poor and minority groups. School districts with wealthy clientele spend far more per student than those that are real estate poor. Minority group members who are also poor are victims of a double discrimination, because of both racial and economic factors. Jencks proposed the voucher system to the U.S. Office of Economic Opportunity, which funded an experimental voucher program in Alum Rock, California, in the early seventies. He has written extensively in support of the concept.[5]

Those who wish to equalize educational opportunity through equalizing expenditures for education thus see in the voucher an opportunity to achieve social reform through educational funding reform. While this view proposes details and amounts for the voucher that differ from Friedman's proposal, it joins the free market theory in seeing in vouchers the best mechanism for funding education.

*Parenthetically, it should be noted that there is a large element of similarity between this free market concept of the state and that which we have described in the social theory called individualism. To the extent that both these ideologies join in supporting the voucher system the idea becomes more politically feasible.

The civil liberty view stresses the liberty of individual citizens and freedom from government control of education. Lawyers like Stephen Arons of the University of Massachusetts and Coons and Sugarman of the University of California have written extensively on the need for increasing citizen power in education as a case of civil liberty. All have supported vouchers as a mechanism for returning to citizens the right to select the kind of education appropriate to their needs. Coons and Sugarman have proposed experimenting with various forms of the voucher.[6]

A fourth view supporting the voucher concept may be called the religious freedom theory, and comes mainly from those already committed to religiously oriented schools. They ground their views in a religious conception of the rights of parents to direct the education of their young. Accordingly, they view the school as an extension of either home or church values, and support parochial or parental schools to guarantee them. They support the voucher concept because it guarantees religious freedom to the poor as well as the rich.[7] Spokesmen for this view have come from Roman Catholic, Missouri Synod Lutheran, Reformed, and Seventh Day Adventist schools. These groups collectively make up the vast majority of those in the nonpublic school sector. As recently as 1978 in the state of Michigan these groups joined in a coalition with others and generated a public referendum on a version of the voucher concept. While their proposal was not adopted, it did provide evidence that political support is present.

Other groups, not specifically representing any of these theoretical points of view and using various arguments, have also seen in the voucher a way to reform funding for America's schools. The present Director of the Congress of Racial Equality (CORE), for example, has publicly announced his support, arguing that inner city schools will be revitalized if parents are given more direct influence on their schools.[8]

The coalition of support that has been generating for two decades leads us to the conclusion that the voucher idea is one whose time has come. While in some sense it is still a concept in search of a wide constituency, once the concept is more clearly understood it will bring together varying groups into a political coalition. It is likely to gain the support not just of scholars who understand the issue as a problem of social philosophy,[9] but also of businessmen who accept the free market idea of improvement through competition. It is likely to be supported by many minority groups when they see that it gives them choice in the selection of schools, enabling them to vote with their feet. It will be viewed favorably by those whose religious convictions have led them to support their own schools, and who feel not only the burden of double taxation in present practices but also the second class citizen status their beliefs have placed upon them. And finally, it will gain the support of all who feel alienated from the centers of power in education, who feel helpless before the many layers of educational bureaucracy that serve to blunt the effect of any citizen impact. They will come to see that a voucher in the hand is worth two bureaucrats in the bush when it comes to securing the kind of education for their children that they believe is best.

The members of this coalition of otherwise conflicting ideologies and groups recognize in the voucher idea the realization of some central tenet in their respective systems of belief. They will differ on the precise details of implementation, either in terms of the amount of the voucher or in terms of the stipulations attached to schools that qualify as voucher schools. Many legislative details remain to be determined; among them is the crucial pragmatic question of what form of the proposal may be ruled constitutionally acceptable.

Constitutional acceptability. The voucher system we envision involves a basic change in the structuring and funding of a state's educational system. The change is so basic that it renders inapplicable for the purposes of challenging the new system existing establishment clause case law on aid to nonpublic elementary and secondary education. True, no Supreme Court decision could ignore the history of all such case law, but a boldly conceived voucher system will render that history only tangentially relevant.

The proposed system shifts the focal center of the American educational system from state dominance to family choice within the framework of multiple schools. Its intention is to promote educational variety so that the family's ideals, the child's needs, and the nature and offerings of the school can be more readily matched than is now possible. It would not be to reimburse a relatively small number of parents for the cost of education in nonpublic schools — the alleged aim of much "parochiaid" legislation of past years. The device for realizing our goal is a plan to give all parents and students a free choice among schools: one public school rather than another with a different emphasis, a public school rather than a nonpublic school, a nonpublic school of one sort rather than any school of another sort. All schools will be compelled to seek supporters and to find ways of showing their effectiveness to parents as well as to be attractive to pupils. Schools will become agents of their clientele, not agents of the state. These purposes should be spelled out forcefully in the section of the state statutes on legislative intent. The state's role in education will be:

1. to empower parents for effective choice;

2. to empower present and yet to be organized schools, public and nonpublic, to create a diverse educational system reflecting diverse educational goals and styles;

3. to foster such standards for all schools as would protect its citizens from inadequate education and from fraud;

4. to operate such public schools as the free-choice system required.

A court challenge to such a voucher system will raise issues other than the familiar church-state question. On the one hand, they will be issues that relate to the power of the governments to shape and to fund a fundamentally new kind of educational system. On the other hand, they will be issues of freedom of choice for all families and students to choose an education that best fits their educational goals and life commitments. The church-state issue will be clearly secondary to these matters of state power and family and student rights.

There can be no doubt that the government has the power to create a voucher system. We list the accepted powers at stake merely to show that some long-established governmental powers are not in jeopardy.

1. All states have the power to devise and administer a general educational system. Since the middle of the nineteenth century the normal powers of the states have been specifically detailed in most state constitutions.

2. All states have ample taxing and spending powers to fund their educational system.[10]

3. The federal government's spending powers permit it to supplement state educational funding.[11]

4. Respecting both state and federal governments, the power to assist families and persons for a public purpose is likewise beyond constitutional question. A host of assistance programs for health, welfare, and education have done so for decades.[12]

5. Both prior to the *Pierce* decision of 1925 and especially since the Supreme Court approved the practice in that case, the states have had power to regulate nonpublic education.[13]

6. Such regulation demonstrates, as several recent Supreme Court opinions have reaffirmed, that nonpublic education serves a public purpose, and can thus be granted public assistance.[14]

Respecting the rights both of nonpublic schools and of parents to choose those schools there also can be no doubt. Several such rights have long been settled.

1. Nonpublic schools have a right to function within the compass of "reasonable regulation."[15]
2. Parents have the right to use these schools.[16]
3. Parents also have a related right grounded in freedom of belief and life-style to control in some immediate ways the education of their children. The recognition of these rights has been demonstrated by the victory of the Amish to educate their youth informally after the age of fifteen and the victory of the Jehovah's Witnesses in the flag salute case.[17] In addition, in 1978 in *State of Iowa* v. *Sessions*, a family won the right in a state District Court to educate its own child in the home, because, though not having the services of a "certified teacher," the education was found to be the "equivalent" of mandated state education.[18] This case, and others like it springing up across the land, show that parents are willing today to challenge the state's system of monopolistic public education. These challenges are attracting attention as disenchantment with public schools grows.[19]

Perhaps many will ask: What of all the decisions on state aid to nonpublic elementary and secondary education in recent years that turned on the establishment clause? Would these not prohibit the inclusion of church-related schools in any voucher plan? Our answer is "No," for several reasons. First, as we have just shown, the voucher system we propose is a novel device for using state funds for education. It shifts the focus to the state's authority to establish a voucher plan and to parental freedom, rendering the establishment issue unimportant by comparison.

Second, even if challenges were made to the inclusion of religiously controlled schools in the voucher system on establishment grounds, the Supreme Court has wisely left the way clear to distinguish such a system from earlier cases. Actually, repeated Supreme Court comment fits very nicely with a voucher proposal. Programs that have aided all the public using different sorts of schools have long been upheld. Justice Powell points this out sharply in *Committee* v. *Nyquist* by showing that where all have been aided, public school clients and private school clients, the aid has been proper by establishment clause standards:

In *Everson*, the Court, in a five-to-four decision, approved a program of reimbursements to parents of public as well as parochial school children for bus fares paid in connection with transportation to and from school. . . . In *Allen*, decided some twenty years later, the Court upheld a New York law authorizing the provision of *secular* textbooks for all children in grades seven through twelve attending public and non public schools. Finally, in *Tilton*, the Court upheld federal grants of funds for the construction of facilities to be used for clearly *secular* purposes by public and nonpublic institutions of higher learning.[20]

Thus, the Court can point to precedents that support tax expenditures for the education of all as it reacts to the proposed voucher system.

Third, Justice Powell, who wrote the *Nyquist* majority opinion, made careful exception for such a general support plan as we have proposed. This qualification appears in a footnote to his opinion:

> Because of the manner in which we have resolved the tuition grant issue, we need not decide whether the significantly religious character of the statute's beneficiaries might differentiate the present cases from a case involving some form of public assistance (e.g., scholarships) made available generally without regard to the sectarian-nonsectarian, or public-nonpublic nature of the institution benefitted.[21]

Thus, the majority opinion in the most crucial case of the Burger Court on state aid to nonpublic education reserves judgment on general state grants such as vouchers. The Court has avoided putting itself in a box that excludes a voucher system.

The fourth reason for saying the establishment clause would not control the outcome of a voucher case is this: as Chapter Four showed, the Supreme Court has not been united on establishment clause cases during the Burger era. Although the totals are a bit debatable, the Court has written opinions in some fourteen cases related to aid to nonpublic education at all levels since 1971. In those cases the Court frequently voted on the subaspects of some state or federal government aid law. All told, one can count up twenty-five separate votes on these fourteen establishment clause cases. Only three of the decisions were unanimous. Twenty-two found the Court divided, with the most common split being six to three. Three of those six to three decisions concerned major state assistance of nonpublic education by means of general tuition reimbursements, tuition reimbursements for poor families, and tax benefits for moderate income families.[22]

This means that for the present Court the distinctive free

choice features of a voucher plan need be persuasive to only two of the "moderate separationist" judges to shift enough votes to leave a pro-voucher majority on the Court. Of course, this assumes that the three accommodationist justices would accept such a voucher program. We are confident that they would, because, as noted in Chapter Four, they have repeatedly approved those state measures that give assistance to either parents or students. The analogy they made was to the G.I. Bill's education benefits.[23] A well-devised voucher program would fit that analogy.

Since the two passages by Justice Powell, who is one of the three "moderate separationists," cited above give him room to shift position gracefully, we think there is reason to suppose a voucher plan could produce a change in his stance. Unfortunately, neither Justice Blackmun nor Stewart, the other two "moderates," wrote opinions for the cases on tuition reimbursements or tax benefits. As a result, we cannot scrutinize their exact words on the cases most analogous to the one the voucher plan would raise. We can only note that both justices accepted Justice Powell's opinion on both cases.

Fifth, implicit in the last point is another that merits separate notice. The elements of a full opinion supporting a voucher plan have already been written and rewritten by justices of the Supreme Court. Without meaning to sound flippant about the serious business of Supreme Court drafting, any person generally familiar with the issues could, with scissors and cellophane tape, piece together on short notice a fairly respectable opinion upholding a voucher plan from the past opinion of the justices. It would contain at least these elements that justices have developed in their opinions:

1. Families have the primary responsibility for care and nurture of children.[24] As Chapter Three showed, family rights are better protected today than in the past.
2. Families can choose nonpublic schools for their children's education.[25]
3. Nonpublic schools *as associations* are protected by freedom of religion and freedom of and for associations to reflect their educational preferences.[26]
4. Educational pluralism is a valued part of American society.[27]
5. The necessary public purposes promoted by all education and required for state financing of nonpublic education can be ensured by proper state regulation of schools.[28]
6. The government may not deny a benefit to a person oth-

erwise eligible for some public aid because of that person's religious belief.[29]

This last point merits special stress. It was the nub of *Sherbert* v. *Verner*, 1963. In that case the Supreme Court ruled that a Seventh Day Adventist who had applied for unemployment compensation from South Carolina could not be refused that compensation because she had rejected a job that required Saturday work, when the rejection was a product of her religious scruples.

Justice Brennan found the decisive issue to be one of the free exercise of religion. South Carolina's law interfered with that exercise by pressuring her to take up Saturday work. It was almost as if the government fined those who chose Saturday as their day of rest.

This case does not stand alone. Another of the Court's strict separationists recognized the point at issue in a different case as early as 1947. In deciding that a local school district could pay for bus rides to parochial schools, Justice Black wrote these lines for the majority in *Everson* v. *Board of Education*:

> [The free exercise clause] . . . commands that New Jersey cannot hamper its citizens in the free exercise of religion. Consequently, it cannot exclude individual Catholics, Lutherans, Mohammedans, Baptists, Jews, Methodists, Nonbelievers, Presbyterians, or any other faith, *because of their faith or lack of it*, from receiving the benefits of public welfare legislation. . . . We must be careful, in protecting the citizens of New Jersey against state-established churches, to be sure that we do not inadvertently prohibit New Jersey from extending its general state law benefits to all its citizens without regard to their religious belief.[30]

With two such strict separationists as Justice Brennan and Black writing these similar words of freedom and equality, it is obvious that the Court is but a small step away from shifting the focus of aid to church-related schools cases away from the establishment clause to the free exercise and equal protection clauses. In the Burger Court era minority justices have actually called for that shift. The Chief Justice as well as Justices White and Rehnquist have repeatedly done so, both separately and together.[31]

In sum, a principled opinion can now be written upholding a voucher plan such as that which we will sketch below. Government powers are ample for it, parental authority and school autonomy recognized in law exists for it, and religious freedom supported in relevant majority opinions urges it.

Contours of the concept. We come now to a description of

the specific features of the voucher system that we believe will encourage structural and confessional pluralism, stand the test of constitutionality, and be supported by a wide range of citizens with ideologies other than our own. It is important to underscore once again that the plan we propose is not simply to aid and abet some small segment of the American people; it is not made on behalf of some special interest group. It is not a case of special pleading. It is rather a proposal for reform that will revitalize the family and other social institutions like the church as educational associations. It is made on behalf of all schools as academic institutions, and not on behalf of certain schools. It is made on behalf of all churches or other ideological groups as social institutions engaging in education, and not just certain denominations or groups. Since pluralism represents a way of looking at old problems, and opens up new possibilities for reform of educational funding, the contours we present should receive the support of many ideologies and not of only those who subscribe to the Biblical vision outlined in Chapter Six.

While we cannot describe in detail the various specific features of legislation relevant to the voucher idea, we can suggest its main contours. We shall address ourselves to the two most controversial features that attach to any specific voucher concept. One concerns the face value of the certificate or voucher. The other concerns the stipulations and regulations attached to its use in schools.

The face value of a voucher may either be the same for all or may be adjusted to compensate for cultural and economic differences among the recipients. The flat rate voucher, with the same face value for all students, would either be related to the average cost per pupil in a state or be set at some other more arbitrary amount. The other option is a compensatory voucher with the face value adjusted to equalize actual educational access.

Our view of structural pluralism leads us to favor a compensatory voucher, with the amount adjusted to equalize opportunity between the rich and the poor. Whatever strengthens family choice thereby strengthens the family as a social structure. However, educational choice for some families can be made real only if the disadvantages of poverty do not inhibit free choice. In our conception of structural pluralism the state is to ensure that opportunity to achieve an equal education is available to all, and thus legislation that minimizes inequality is compatible with the state's role of ensuring justice. Per pupil expenditures vary widely from one school district to another, and from one state to another. Real estate tax poor districts spend less per pupil than tax rich districts. When low income families are trapped in tax poor districts, such families receive a doubly disabling blow in their struggle to achieve an equal education. Such inequality of access to quality education requires the use of the compensatory voucher as a matter of principle.

Our purpose is not to state a precise formula for such compensatory vouchers, which is not possible without a detailed analysis of the actual economic impact of a specific form of voucher legislation. We can only observe by way of principle that such a formula can be derived in two ways. The formula could take into account the income of the family, providing a higher amount for low income families. The formula could also be based on the cost per pupil in a given school district, with a higher amount going to tax poor districts. State-wide equalization formulas will have to be devised to enable students in tax poor districts to have as much expended on their education as those in districts with more school tax available. If both compensatory features are included in voucher legislation such students would be doubly attractive to any school, and give such schools extra funds to educate those who come from culturally and financially disadvantaged families. Other factors affecting the face value of the voucher might relate to the physically or emotionally handicapped and those with other special learning problems that affect the cost of educational services to them.

We are aware that many problems remain before a given piece of legislation can be written, but the principle is clear. While even flat rate vouchers strengthen family choice, thus honoring the integrity of that structure we call the family, the compensatory form gives added purchasing power to those families that need it the most. Our conception of the requirements of educational equity leads to the conclusion that the face value of the vouchers ought to be different for different families.

The second concern has to do with the degree of regulation of those schools that accept vouchers. While some supporters favor no regulation, letting supply and demand operate to ensure quality education, we believe that the state has certain though limited duties, relating to its positive role of enhancing family choice rather than directly operating the schools. If the state is to honor structural pluralism, then the school as an academic structure cannot be treated as an arm of the state, with all that this implies as to the control of its internal operations. Schools with varying educational philosophies governing curriculum emphases, goals, and pedagogy must be encouraged. Whatever strengthens the academic integrity of the school as a school strengthens structural pluralism, and the voucher system should not result in uniformity but diversity in the types of schools. In addition, if confessional pluralism is to be honored, then those schools with an explicitly religious vision can be neither eliminated as voucher schools nor can their integrity be destroyed by imposing regulations that standardize all admission requirements, teacher hiring practices, and curriculum emphases. The "reasonable regulation" that the state can impose, to use a legal phrase, must be limited to that which minimizes the likelihood of fraud and guarantees that schools meet health and safety standards.

Two types of regulations are appropriate. First, the civil government may:

1. Require all school buildings to meet minimum health and safety standards. Regulations that apply to other buildings should also apply to schools. To require specific physical facilities, such as swimming pools and manual arts equipment, directly related to given curriculum emphases does not fall under state jurisdiction.

2. Enact appropriate compulsory attendance laws for elementary and secondary education.

3. Require that schools be in session for a stipulated number of days. Since this regulation does not impinge on the goals of education or dictate curriculum emphases, it frees the schools to be schools, while preventing possible fraud by unscrupulous fly-by-night educational entrepreneurs.*

4. Require that teachers be certified or hold licenses to teach. We believe that the state can best exercise its role by seeing to it that academic accrediting agencies determine the standards, while the state issues the license. The licensing of professionals is a long-established use of state power to protect citizens against incompetent practitioners. Since such certification speaks only to the amount of training and to competence in certain professional areas, such regulation does not inhibit structural and confessional pluralism. Such certification does not dictate the educational philosophy of the professional, but leaves to the professional an academic and religious freedom. A voucher school could thus be required to have certified teachers without the state infringing on either academic or religious freedom.

*It is interesting to note that colleges and universities have never been regulated by the state as to the number of days they must hold classes. However, since elementary and secondary schools fall under compulsory attendance laws, while postsecondary schools do not, this difference can stand.

5. Require that voucher schools have a practice of open enrollment, that is, the acceptance of all applicants. Acceptance of all clientele who express agreement with the educational ideology of the school does not significantly interfere with the academic integrity of the school. It is possible that parental motivations for selection of a school might be based on geographical proximity, or attractive buildings, or antipathy toward another school. As long as such parents both understand and accept the uniqueness of that particular school, there is no interference with structural or confessional pluralism.

Another regulation often suggested is evidence of racial balance in the student body. Such a requirement inhibits confessional pluralism. Confessional or ideological identity, not racial identity, should qualify a student for acceptance in a school. Some schools with an explicit religious confessional identity, such as Jewish day schools, are unable to meet racial balance quotas because of the relatively few minority race members in such a community. A school sponsored by a Black Muslim group represents the other side of the racial coin. The denial of voucher status to either of them because of a failure to meet racial quotas is a denial of confessional pluralism in education.

The rejection of all but the five stipulations given above applies only to the state and its power to exercise "reasonable regulation." Other forms of regulation to ensure academic integrity of schools are appropriate to structural pluralism, which recognizes the academic sphere as a sphere in its own right. Structural pluralism requires that regional academic accrediting agencies, not the state, determine which schools act responsibly toward their students. Such agencies now exist for colleges and secondary schools, and work reasonably well in informing parents and students about which schools meet the minimum standards of an educational program. Their role could be expanded to include all schools that wish to be voucher schools. Such regional accrediting agencies have always recognized a diversity of educational philosophies; they judge schools on how well they implement their own educational goals, and not on whether they conform to some single uniform educational program. Schools under church auspices are judged the same as those under other agencies. The agencies make no distinction between sacred and secular content in the curriculum, or between religious and civic goals. Thus, placing accreditation of the school program under academic accrediting agencies also enhances confessional pluralism.

Many other matters, both administrative and political, remain to be resolved in order to legislate a fully operational voucher system. Among the other legitimate considerations that legislative bodies, with the assistance of various academic communities, should study is the matter of the actual economic impact of various forms of the compensatory vouchers. The "add-on" or compensatory feature requires careful study by economists. Such further study should also consider the possibility that voucher schools be required by legislation to provide a report to authorities that the money is spent for its designated purposes, again to prevent fraud or mismanagement. Another factor is the creation of what has been called an Education Voucher Agency (EVA). This agency will resemble a traditional public board of education except that it will operate no schools of its own. That responsibility remains with existing school boards. The EVA will function simply as a clearing house, determining which schools qualify as voucher schools by meeting both state regulations and academic accreditation standards. It will also function as a source of information about the nature of each of the alternative schools available in that geographical area. The EVA cannot tell schools whom to hire, what to teach or how to teach it, but must confine itself to collecting and disseminating information about what each school offers as its special educational identity. This agency will ensure that families are aware of all the choices open to them. It will also help discourage misleading advertising on the part of schools themselves.

Significant progress toward implementing a pluralist system of education can result from new and creative legislation. Those efforts, however, must be supplemented by selected judicial action if they are to stand the test of constitutionality.

LITIGATION INITIATIVES: CHALLENGE TO THE COURTS

In the American legal system the courts have the power, through judicial review, to declare legislation and administrative actions unconstitutional at both the state and federal level. In such a system litigation is a potent political weapon. It is especially potent when a Supreme Court, federal or state, is composed of judicial "activists," who are disposed to use their power to reshape existing public policy, as distinguished from judicial "self-restraintists," who are more disposed to let legislators and executives lead.[32]

The Warren Court of the 1960's was an activist court. The

Burger Court in the 1970's has been less activist overall, but in some areas of law its activism has been marked. We earlier noted that it pioneered by holding that freedom of expression was a right of associations, thereby overturning long-accepted precedents.[33] Its decisions on abortion were in impact and style of opinion as activist as any in American history.[34] Further and more directly relevant to our concerns, its three accommodationist justices on church-state relations have in several angry dissents signaled that they will override long-settled precedents on aid to church-related schools in the best activist tradition. A change of the "right" two justices could bring a new era in school funding.

Therefore, any group that wants educational equity for all schools should be prepared to litigate. That preparedness should be concerned with a wide range of issues, for any and all litigation that affects such crucial legal definitions as "religion," "school," "reasonable regulation," and "establishment of religion" may arise from many different sources under many circumstances.

This preparedness has been inadequately achieved in the past on the part of those who support nonpublic schools. The lack may have cost them dearly, because its effects may last decades. Frank J. Sorauf, a well-known political scientist, has written a meticulously detailed volume on two decades of church-state litigation. He repeatedly notes that the strict separationist groups were more active, better organized, and more effectively integrated for the judicial battles they either initiated or joined than their opponents were. While the accommodationists were not without some legal resources and successes, their efforts lacked an overall sense of direction. He concluded:

> In sum, therefore, two conclusions stand out. First, the diffuseness of the Roman Catholic support and the absence of any other accommodationist organization or nucleus seriously hampered the defense in these cases. There was little or no coordinated plan of defense, no agreed-on set of litigation priorities, no efficient allocation of resources for the defense. Secondly, where no Roman Catholic interests were apparent, the collective support for accommodationism broke down. Its interests were then far less well organized than those of separationism. In general there was nothing approaching the interest group division of effort—the "system"—one could find in the separationist camp. As a result of all this, the battle over church-state issues in American courts was a very unequal one.[35]

The Sorauf study describes how these cases arose and how groups on both sides became involved in four distinct ways: (1) as initiators who brought suits; (2) as intervenors in suits, that is, as fully participating third parties who showed that some suit raised questions that directly affected their interests; (3) as *amicus curiae*, that is, as "friends of the court" who submitted their own legal brief; and (4) as supportive agencies that provided expert resources, financial and legal, for one of the parties. The separationists acted more frequently and more systematically in all four ways, thus affecting the outcomes more heavily. One may observe that each of the four routes has its advantages and disadvantages and is subject to some judicial control.[36] Deciding on the form of participation is not a simple matter, but all four methods are possible, and the separationists pursued each vigorously.

If those interested in a more pluralist structure of education are to succeed in altering the precedents of the Supreme Court on the First Amendment, they must be prepared at all times to play some role in the courts. Not only must they undertake litigation, they must also take part of its burden out of the inept hands of some who begin it. Many persons, groups, or nonpublic schools who become involved in these disputes do so without sound counsel. The attorneys they hire are often amateurs on the establishment clause. The groups that support educational pluralism must supply expert advice and offer specialized counsel to them. Even in what is clearly a losing case, this must be done, for a case can be lost in irredeemable or in redeemable ways. A lawyer who helps a justice write a skillful dissent or forceful concurring opinion has sometimes done more in the long run than a lawyer who helps shape a poorly written majority opinion.

Ideally, the larger agencies that promote and assist private education should coordinate their legal efforts more than they have done in the past. Defenders of the status quo have bridged wide ideological gaps in some joint legal efforts, as Sorauf's work shows.[37] The coordination should settle on a long-range litigation strategy that will attempt to bring step-by-step legal victories for the causes of alternative education. A model for this approach can be found in the remarkable work of the NAACP. Some of that association's victories from the 1930's through the 1950's were carefully orchestrated toward a goal: to have restrictive covenants in real estate contracts, which prohibited sales to blacks, declared unconstitutional. The one-step-at-a-time strategy was successful.[38] Perhaps its greatest, though indirect and unplanned success, was that one of its leaders, Thurgood Marshall, later became a justice of the Supreme Court. His reputation had been created by the effectiveness of the execution of the NAACP's long-term plans. The need for an overall strategy will become more obvious when we explore the issues that are now being litigated and that seem likely to be litigated in the foreseeable future.

Issues and Future Litigation

William B. Ball, one of the few nationally known lawyers specializing in cases in the defense of educational freedom, has developed a taxonomy of litigation now before the courts and likely to occupy courts in the future. His headings are: (1) compulsory attendance; (2) state control of private education; (3) denial of distributive justice in the use of tax funds (including enforced contribution to programs insupportable in conscience); and (4) rights of conscience in public education (including the problem of value impositions).[39] The first three of these items raise questions directly related to schools that are organized on a consciously religious perspective; we will examine each for the purpose of describing both the legal issues at stake and the constitutional arguments that can be made respecting them that will be most likely to serve the end of educational freedom.

Compulsory attendance. Issues of compulsory attendance might be raised in two ways: first, they will surface when families or groups of families educate their children at home on grounds of conscience; second, they will be raised when private schools are declared by state officials to be inadequate to earn state approval as alternatives to public schools. Thus, attendance at such unapproved schools could not meet compulsory education regulations; this is in fact a matter of state control of private education.

Unquestionably, the state has the constitutional power to require that the youth be educated. This point is so well settled in American law that any attack upon it would be quixotic. An attorney who argues for parents or for unaccredited schools should argue other issues.

Whatever other issues are raised, however, the issue of freedom of religion is crucial to the argument against forced attendance in only state-certified schools. Freedom of religion has already been broadly defined to include freedom of schools to teach their world-views, and freedom of families to select schools. When other issues are put in the judicial balances, freedom of religion can be especially decisive. It is a First Amendment freedom. While debate on the issue of priority of constitutional passages has never ended, much scholarly writing and many Supreme Court opinions have called the First Amendment freedoms "preferred freedoms," because they are essential to the open discussion required in a free society.[40]

The most important precedent for the argument that freedom of religion overrides a compulsory attendance law is *Wisconsin* v. *Yoder* (1972). The decision was unanimously grounded in the religious freedom of the Old Order Amish to educate their high school age children in their own communities.[41] Critics have conceded its importance by bewailing that in it, ". . . for the first time in our history the Supreme Court has made inroads on the power of the state to compel formal schooling beyond primary grades."[42] So it did. It is true that the Yoder decision can be read narrowly to refer only to such unique groups as the Old Order Amish. But where other confessional communities can demonstrate that their own educational programs are grounded in their basic beliefs, are necessary to their way of life, and are effective in achieving educational competency by their own standards, no reason exists to suppose that the next group would have to be similar to the "plain folk" to benefit from the Yoder precedent.

Further, that decision gives still more support to educational freedom. At its very center the rights of parents come to the fore. In Justice Burger's words, at issue are ". . . the traditional interests of parents with respect to the upbringing of their children."[43] This passage reminds us that the Supreme Court has refined and expanded the rights of the family and other associations in recent years, as we have explained in Chapter Three. From well-established and repeatedly quoted opinions in the freedom of association cases come such words as these:

> It is cardinal with us that the custody, care and nurture of the child reside first in the parents, whose primary function and freedom include preparation for obligations the state can neither supply nor hinder.[44]

Thus, to freedom of religion can be added freedom of the family as an association to control the destinies of its children. These are powerful legal weapons that have settled cases on the side of freedom where the state indisputably had a constitutional power to act. The Supreme Court has handled this head-on collision of group freedom and state power by reserving to the state the authority of only "reasonable regulation."

State control of private education. The Supreme Court in *Pierce* v. *Society of Sisters* announced that:

> No question is raised concerning the power of the state reasonably to regulate all schools, to inspect, supervise and examine them, their teachers and pupils; to require that all children of proper age attend some school, that teachers shall be of good moral character and patriotic disposition, that certain studies plainly essential to good citizenship must

be taught, and that nothing be taught which is manifestly inimical to the public welfare.[45]

As the passage indicates, the right to operate private schools was not a right to autonomy. What did "reasonably to regulate" mean? The schools took a long time learning. State education officials tended to adopt a hands-off attitude toward regulation of private education both in developing standards and in enforcing those that were developed. In 1947 the Supreme Court, while treating another matter, said ". . . the State has power to impose secular educational requirements on private schools."[46] One authority says that some three-fourths of the states require that the education offered be the "equivalent" of public school education. However, specifics are not often spelled out in the statutory law.[47]

In recent years there has been an increase of government controls, most of which are developed as state or federal administrative regulations. Some of these regulations clearly threaten the very existence of some private schools. For example, in 1978 the Internal Revenue Service set stringent and unattainable guidelines respecting the racial integration of nonpublic schools, backed by the threat of withholding tax exempt status from those not in compliance.[48] The arbitrary nature of the original guidelines produced a storm of protest. The IRS reacted by revising its demands, but even the revised regulations were so criticized that a House committee sponsored hearings on them.[49]

As such regulations increase, so does the tension between nonpublic schools and government. If negotiations cannot resolve the tensions (and polite negotiations are almost always the best starting-point), lawsuits may very well result. Attorneys for private schools in such suits should usually look first for a way to challenge the state regulations as improperly drafted; "void for vagueness" is the common phrase.[50] Or they should attempt to show that the regulation is beyond the legal authority of the agency that wrote it. In 1979 the Supreme Court struck down a National Labor Relations Board ruling respecting labor relations that was of concern to teachers in Chicago-area parochial schools, because, it held, the NLRB ruling exceeded that agency's statutory powers.[51] Such defenses, however expedient in the short run, do not get to the more fundamental issues of the rights of families, schools, and churches to be free of government regulations that hinder their educational discretion. These major constitutional issues must be introduced in every litigation by lawyers for private schools, even if they hope to win on the lesser grounds just described or hope to win only at the appellate level.[52]

Cases challenging the states' "reasonable regulation" of private schools can presently be won on freedom grounds. The federal Supreme Court has not yet handled a dispute squarely on this matter, but one state high court has: the Ohio Court of Appeal. That dispute is a model for those who litigate to ensure the freedom of private education. Its counsel argued all possibly useful issues, challenging the Ohio regulations for vagueness, and at the same time challenging them as a denial of religious freedom and of parental rights. The result was a spectacular success for educational freedom. Under Ohio truancy law, twelve parents of school children were indicted for failing to send their children to an Ohio-accredited school. They sent them instead to the Tabernacle Christian School, an integral part of a church. The school was not accredited, in part because the church's pastor believed the state's regulations for accreditation contradicted his group's beliefs.

In the majority opinion in *State* v. *Whisner* (1976), the Ohio court agreed. In Justice Celebrezze's strongly worded opinion the state's regulations were said to violate the natural rights of parents and the free exercise of religion. The court could not find any proof that a compelling state interest existed for several regulations that offended the consciences of those who used the church school. From their perspective the regulations unnecessarily forced the school to limit time for Bible study, to participate in activities and goals of the larger community that they did not share, and to foster social attitudes they believed were the products of humanism.[53]

Since then, lower court decisions in other jurisdictions have both followed and rejected the logic of *Whisner*.[54] This is to be expected, for *Whisner* was a bold opinion, and few lower courts act so boldly until their own appellate courts have done so.

The *Whisner* case shows that freedom of religion and parental rights can be used to strike down state regulations. It also shows what can be done by skillful litigations under decisive leadership. Counsel for Whisner, William B. Ball, must have advised against attempting to obtain a compromise settlement with the state Board of Education. Such a settlement may well have been possible — perhaps prudent in some states — but here it would have been half a loaf when a whole could be won, leaving Ohio and the nation without a freedom-building precedent.[55]

Denial of distributive justice. As Chapter Four demonstrated, the Supreme Court has so interpreted the establishment clause that nonpublic schools and their users have received nothing but a trickle of state financial aid. Taxes from all can presently be spent only on the education of some. This inevitably strikes those deprived of government funds as both unfair and, when they think about the phrase "equal protection under the law," constitutionally improper.

In this law-oriented society, more suits might have been expected in the face of such perceived wrongs, suits aimed at getting a "fair share" for all schools. Of course there were some, but in the tides of American history they have been discouraged by a combination of social and legal pressures. The strong forces that created a near monopoly of public education by the mid-nineteenth century have been suggested in Chapter Three. State schools were, in fact, agencies that promoted a popular, lowest common denominator Protestantism. Other schools were put on the defensive, because they were commonly seen as schools designed to promote a tolerated, not welcomed, culture, which was perceived as predominantly Catholic and often foreign. Still other private schools were widely regarded as preserves for the elite, somehow suspect in a land whose schools were to be the center of the democratic melting pot.

The constitutions of many new states reflected this climate of opinion. Almost identical passages specifically forbidding funding of church-related education appeared in the constitutions of many of the new western states, in part because their drafters were eager for the required approval of the Congress. In 1876 a similar passage was offered as the "Blaine Amendment" to the federal Constitution. Although it passed the House, it failed to receive Senate approval. That it advanced as far as it did shows the temper of the nineteenth century on this matter. That temper continued well into the twentieth century, climaxing in the voter-approved Oregon initiative that required public school attendance of all children. The *Pierce* decision of 1925 struck down that initiative as unconstitutional. It showed that courts could defend private education, but it was at best a victory for the mere continued existence of such schools. As such, it could scarcely encourage supporters of government aid to nonpublic schools to use litigation to gain their due.[56]

Later, when the federal Supreme Court for the first time defined the meaning of the establishment clause with respect to parochial schools, it did so in a way that was very discouraging to those who hoped for aid to all schools. By a bare majority it said free bus rides to parochial schools were a permissible "child benefit," but a benefit that was on the verge of the unconstitutional.[57] Thus, the first clearly relevant precedent made litigation aimed at obtaining just funding seem pointless.

As a result, legislation seemed more attractive to those who sought aid than law suits. In some states favorable legislatures passed laws benefiting private schools or their students. Since almost all victories of this sort were quickly challenged in the courts by strict separationist forces, attorneys for these schools found themselves defending state programs, often alongside state attorneys whose defense was half-hearted.[58] When such defenses produced the limited overall results documented in Table I on page 104, it was inevitable that litigation should seem an unattractive device for those who believed that educational equity was denied by state action.

However, litigation for educational equity is far from hopeless for several reasons. First, as noted, supporters of educational pluralism have never organized their legal forces as effectively as have their opponents, nor have they had a long-term strategy such as the NAACP once planned and executed.[59] If these defects are corrected, a long-term offensive in the courts may begin with hope of some eventual success.

Second, today the political climate is much more favorable to some sort of assistance for nonpublic education than it was when the separationists won their early and precedent-setting victories. Recent presidents, Republican and Democrat, have publicly committed themselves to aiding private education.[60] Powerful Senators have spoken, written, and introduced legislation to that end.[61] In 1978 both Houses of Congress passed a tuition tax credit bill, though final agreement failed in conference.[62] As the Burger Court church-state cases reveal, many state legislatures have passed a variety of aid measures and some have done so several times in an effort to adjust to adverse court decisions. Also, public schools, while strongly organized for political action, do not enjoy the same respect they once had in legislative halls. Indeed, they are under sustained criticism both from legislators and from the public at large. Gallup polls show public schools are less well received by the people today than a decade ago, while nonpublic school supporters can point to data from Gallup that show their causes are gaining understanding.[63] Further, the broad coalition described earlier in this chapter shows that new groups are in the field ready to contest for a new structure of educational funding.

Does a changed political climate signal change in judicial decisions? In the short run it need not, but in the long run it can. Since the 1930's one can count at least three major shifts in the general orientation of the Supreme Court and several dramatic overrulings of long-set precedents. These shifts and reversals have all been related in some degree to shifts in the political moods of the society. Justices read not only the election returns, but also Gallup polls and columnists.

Third, litigation for educational equity is far from hopeless because of Supreme Court precedents on the establishment clause. The Court's position at present is confusion confounded. Since 1947 justices have split bitterly over the clause's meaning, and since 1971 three three-judge blocs of Supreme Court justices have offered three general interpretations of how the clause should be applied in cases of state aid to private education.[64] Surveying their work, the newest justice, John Stevens, declared in an opinion, "Corrosive precedents have left us without firm principles on which to decide these cases."[65] The principle he offered to correct the Court's errors has been rejected for many years by the justices who make up the moderate separationist and accommodationist blocs. Confusion, therefore, continues. The time will someday be ripe for a perspective that breaks out of the rigid secular-religious distinction in education.

Suits related to compulsory education and to state regulation of nonpublic schools are now numerous in lower courts.[66] The Supreme Court will likely be faced with one or more of these in the foreseeable future. These cases might well be different enough from past establishment cases to cause the Court to find a new scheme for handling establishment clause limits. Such a prospect could spell a change of precedent. Attorneys for alternative schools, by helping shape that litigation, can harbor some hope for new precedents more conducive to their aims.

Finally and obviously, groups promoting pluralist education must continue to encourage and guide litigation relevant to educational equity because justices are mortal. A case begun today may not reach the Supreme Court for three years. By that time the Court's composition may change. With a three-to-three-to-three split common on church-state cases, one change of membership can be important. Two changes can be decisive.

Necessary Legal Strategies

Assuming that legislation favoring equitable state funding for all education will continue to be adopted, such legislation will be challenged by strict separationists before the courts. Legal experts for groups that support educational pluralism will join attorneys for the state in defending that legislation in one of the ways sketched earlier. When they do they will have to choose either a minimum or a maximum argument, or both. If legislatures fail to pass any favorable legislation, attorneys for such groups

197

eventually should initiate litigation, making the maximum argument when the time is ripe.

If a law is passed giving a tax credit or deduction to parents or some grant to a school, it will be challenged as an establishment of religion. In defending the law, attorneys can use the present minimal need arguments made by Justices Burger, White, and Rehnquist. These arguments would have upheld eighteen of twenty-three various aid programs voted on between 1971 and 1977, if there had been two more such judges.[67]

Minimum argument. Much of the education given in church-related schools has an essentially secular purpose. Support for this education has only a secular purpose, and its effects are also only secular. It thus meets two requirements of the famous three-part test. Justice White believes that payments for this portion of nonpublic education can be made *directly* to nonpublic schools. He believes this is payment only for publicly required, secular education given in those schools.[68]

Chief Justice Burger and Justice Rehnquist accept the argument up to the word "directly." They, however, are afraid of too much church-state administrative entanglement when money passes directly to such schools, because some of it might be spent for the religious education given there. Therefore, Burger and Rehnquist require the indirect route for aid. Tax deductions, tax credits, or tax reimbursements for tuition are appropriately indirect. Given the realities of such aid and state tax laws, the benefits the students and parents would receive are only part of the schools' total costs. That part does not do more than cover the costs of what for them is the secular dimension of private education. This indirect, secular support creates no church-state entanglement at all. If it is argued that such support creates a struggle in the legislative arenas between pro-aid and anti-aid forces that threatens to become dangerous entanglement, Burger and Rehnquist respond that not giving the support creates the same threat. They also trust the private schools to use state-loaned educational equipment for only secular purposes—a trust that obviates the need for entangling state supervision of such loans.[69]

Undoubtedly, careful legislators, relying on the opinions of these three justices, can find ways to give very substantial aid to private schools and those who use them. If supporters of non-public education think it prudent, and if changes in the thought or personnel of the Supreme Court allow it, they might very well decide to stress these already available arguments of the three accommodationist judges when future cases on aid arise.

It is important to note that these arguments accept the definitions and categories appropriate to what we have called Enlightenment thought. That thought equates public with secular and private with religious in constitutional matters. It assumes that these dimensions of life are separable.

In the course of events, some future Supreme Court may very well accept these minimum arguments to approve state aid that would be of great value to private schools. Notice, however, the aid will be given only as a matter of public policy, and not required as a matter of constitutional right.

Maximum argument. To win aid cases as a matter of right, a maximum argument needs to be made. Victory via this route will be difficult, because while Justices Burger, White, and Rehnquist have referred in passing to two parts of the maximum argument, that is, freedom of religion and equal protection of the laws, together their opinions stress a defense based on policy rather than a defense based on right.[70]

Two of the maximum arguments have already been offered to the Supreme Court. It has rejected them repeatedly with at least six negative votes.[71] But attorneys for nonpublic schools should continue to argue them in some cases and some courts for three reasons: first, they may help win close cases on the basis of the minimum argument, because some judge may be impressed by their force; second, they will help educate government leaders and the informed public about the deep-felt position of many private school supporters; third, they are arguments that use constitutional rights as an offensive weapon, and not merely as a defensive weapon. Implicit in this point is this: the maximum argument shifts attention from the establishment clause, centering it on the rights of the free exercise of religion, the equal protection of the laws, and freedom of association.[72]

As it has been presented to the Court in the past, the maximum argument rests on both freedom of religion and simple equity as guaranteed by the equal protection clause. It strikes us as simple and compelling. For people who have deep religious convictions about the nature of education, the use of public schools is unacceptable, because they believe such schools to be at odds with their basic world-views. Denying them the equivalent of the dollar aid that flows to public schools amounts to a denial of the free exercise of religion. The denial stems from their inability to obtain for their children the education their consciences require. Also, it stems from their view that the educational tax they pay is money spent entirely for a monolithic, public educational system they oppose ideologically. Their freedom is doubly assailed. Through the captivity of their children they are captives of schools hostile to their beliefs, and all their tax money goes to fund the instruments of that captivity. Thus, the First Amendment fails them.

Further, they are denied equal protection of the laws, because the law aids those whose beliefs are protected and promoted in the public schools and denies aid to those whose beliefs are not. Thus, the Fourteenth Amendment also fails them.

Of course, the anti-aid majority of the Supreme Court has attempted an answer to these two charges. In the answer concerning the free exercise claim Justice Powell has said:

> But this Court repeatedly has recognized that tension inevitably exists between the Free Exercise and the Establishment Clauses. . . . As a result of this tension, our cases require the State to maintain an attitude of "neutrality," neither "advancing" or "inhibiting" religion.[73]

The argument is faulty. Denial of aid *inhibits* the free exercise! Denial of aid for general education is not neutral; it is unjust because it does not treat all alike.

Of course, in practice tension exists between the two religion clauses of the First Amendment. Yet, in matters where state-regulated education is at stake —unlike church-controlled worship or seminary training—the tension obviously should be resolved in favor of freedom in a free society. After all, the two religion clauses of the First Amendment should be treated as a unity. The end is the "free exercise" of religion; the means is "no law respecting an establishment of religion."

As to the equal protection argument for state aid to non-public education a majority opinion has said:

> The Equal Protection Clause has never been regarded as a bludgeon with which to compel a state to violate other provisions of the Constitution. Having held that tuition reimbursements for the benefit of sectarian schools violate the Establishment Clause, nothing in the Equal Protection Clause will suffice to revive the program.[74]

These words are not convincing, for we believe that one clause is the equal of the other. If two clauses work against each other in some situation, then it is the duty of the Court to weigh the entire matter in the balance, with one clause in each arm of the balance at the start. Here Justice Powell can be charged with using the establishment clause as a bludgeon against the equal protection clause. Why not add the free exercise clause to the considerations in such a situation? That addition would make it possible to support school aids, for two clauses outweigh one. This is one of the points made by the dissenting justices in the *Nyquist* and *Sloan* cases.[75]

One further argument, not yet presented to the courts to our knowledge, should be used as a support for aid to nonpublic schools. It begins by noting four considerations: (1) school attendance is compulsory; (2) the state certifies those schools that can be used to satisfy its compulsory attendance law; (3) nonpublic schools are associations or institutions possessing fundamental rights; and (4) these associations are further protected in that they promote diverse points of view that the First Amendment is designed to foster. Points three and four are firmly grounded most recently in the decisions favoring freedom of and for associations. Together, these considerations mean that state action has occasioned the forming of voluntary associations of people into schools that have earned state approval. As such, they are legally equal to state-operated schools.

However, since state funding does not go to these schools, the freedom of association that is theirs under the First Amendment is a sham. To have their constitutionally protected freedom, state-approved schools merit state funding as a right of association.*

We recognize that some people claim that if tax funds went to religiously oriented schools, they would lose their freedom "not to be taxed" for religion. The point would be determinative in some circumstances, but not in these. If a variety of schools of different orientations were funded, the only reasonable assumption for the individual taxpayer would be that all were taxed to support the variety. All could think of themselves as equally offended, or as would be more socially constructive, all could say, "My small part of the total expenditure of educational revenue helps support that part of the varied educational program with which I agree."

If people cannot bring themselves to this level of social cooperation in a pluralist society, then they must recognize that hosts of taxpayers from prohibitionists, to anti-vivisectionists, to war resisters, to anti-nuclear protestors, to Christian Scientists, to nature preservationists, and to laissez-faire capitalists object to

---

*The right must be implemented, of course, through reasonable regulation. For example, the standards described above for a voucher system might be applied to these schools. A minimum number of pupils might be required to protect against unending proliferation of state-funded groups seeking what would amount to patronage positions. But these matters could be managed, for other nations have managed such a system successfully.

a wide array of government programs on grounds of conscience. The Supreme Court has handled such matters by almost casually affirming state taxing and spending powers. Many people give up much and pay for much they hate in order to live in modern society. Consciences ache every day. But they need not ache over a matter that can be corrected as simply and fairly as this one.

Necessary Legal Tactics

Those who attempt to manage litigation for educational equity should use the varied arguments presented here in ways that relate to the possible, not to the ideal. Suits that promote qualified recognition of freedom of religion and parental rights in education can be won now with respect to compulsory attendance laws, as the *Yoder* decision showed. Such suits should be supported and promoted to buttress further the rights already won on that issue. Victories in this area will help solidify the law of religious freedom and family rights in education.

Suits defending nonpublic schools against unreasonable state regulation can now be won on the basis of freedom rights, as the *Whisner* case demonstrated. These also should be supported and promoted, for they will not only reinforce freedom of religion in education but also gain more explicit recognition for the roles and rights of private schools.

In cases that involve the funding of nonpublic education, the minimum argument sketched above must be made when existing state aids are being defended. At the present time, the maximum argument probably should not be made before the federal Supreme Court, for it will surely be lost. Each loss means further reinforcement of the present precedents against the maximum view. If, however, from other church-state decisions it appears that the Supreme Court justices may be changing their views, or after new appointments have been made that seem to change the present voting blocs in favor of state aid, then the maximum argument might well be tried. It ought always to be tried in lower courts whenever it is relatively certain that it would be accepted by that unusual lower court judge who will decide against Supreme Court precedent.

In no case should lawyers for nongovernment schools argue that these schools are religious in the context of the secular-religious disjunction. By doing so they fall into the trap of being defined as religious schools, and are then forced outside of the public legal order. There will be a temptation to make that argument in order to protect a private school from unwanted state regulation. It is a poor argument, because all schools are religious, because it accepts a too narrow view of religion on the one hand and of public purpose on the other, because it does not clarify the rights of schools as institutions, and because it will be used later by anti-aid forces against state support of nonpublic education. In this connection it should be added that structuring schools as parts of churches to protect them from government regulation is short-sighted for the same reasons. Attorneys for private schools must keep in the forefront the theme that nonpublic education, including such unique education as that of the Old Order Amish, serves the public purpose fully. Unless that point is successfully made, confessional pluralism will suffer. In brief, attorneys must have all manner of education cases in mind when they argue any single case.

CONSTITUTIONAL AMENDMENT INITIATIVES: GUARANTEE FOR THE FUTURE

While legislative and litigative efforts proceed as means of achieving justice in the funding of American education, a constitutional amendment is also a necessary recourse. It is a recourse fraught with much difficulty. Yet, from the perspective of our vision of a pluralist society, it is potentially the best course of action, for it offers American citizens an opportunity to settle in a relatively permanent and authoritative way the roles of family, church, school, and state in education.

A Minimum Amendment

Any amendment to the federal Constitution permitting the alteration of both federal and state funding of all schools must be worded to control both levels of government. It might read as follows:

> Nothing in this Constitution or in any state constitution shall prohibit federal or state expenditures for education of all children in accredited schools regardless of the religious or ideological orientation of those schools.

The reason for including both federal and state power is this: under present interpretations of both federal and state courts, the limits of the First Amendment's establishment clause set only the narrowest degree of church-state separation. Each state under its own constitution is free to set wider degrees for its own separation. To illustrate: the federal Supreme Court has upheld state payments to parents for busing their children to parochial schools under the federal establishment clause. But after it did so a few state courts on the basis of their own constitutions prohibited such payments.[76] This difference is not unique to church-state law. In the last decade, a few state Supreme Courts have set "higher" standards of due process of law in some state criminal proceedings than the latest Burger Court decisions required.

A Maximum Amendment

Political prudence might indeed dictate that an amendment like that suggested above will be the greatest reform possible on this issue in the foreseeable future. We hope otherwise, for two reasons: First, it would only allow the states to adopt new policies that would aid all schools; it would not require it of them. That is, it would not make equity in education a *right*. State by state and federal legislative battles would then have to be fought to make substantial aid a reality.

Second, such a minimum amendment lacks the vision of structural pluralism in education. If the United States wishes to honor educational freedom for all people in their communities, it must do better than what the politically prudent amendment offers. It must make free education a fully protected constitutional right — a right that respects the educational preferences of all families and the integrity of all schools. Admittedly, such reform will not soon be politically possible. Our hope is in a long-term change of attitude. But we describe our hope here to expose it to wider consideration.

We begin our description with an introductory comment: The present Bill of Rights is clearly inadequate by both the standards of American practice and in comparison with other democratic nations.

The best statement on this matter is by Carl J. Friedrich, a much-published political scientist at Harvard. He argues convincingly that the American Bill of Rights is obsolete.[77] Its original provisions were, he notes, aimed at protecting individuals *against government*. They reflected both an eighteenth-century fear of the state and the individualism of the founding era. As ideas for democratic participation in government developed, state and federal constitutions were altered to ensure the right to vote and to run for office for adult males, for blacks, and eventually for women. These amendments and court decisions based on them promoted more democratic participation. Together this established what may be called rights *within government*. In the creation of constitutional rights both *against* and *within* government, the United States was a leader in the world.

Almost paradoxically, Friedrich continues, this nation was

slow to develop constitutional protection for state assistance or benefit for persons. Indeed, compared to the constitutions of several Western democracies, the American constitution is silent on benefit rights. True, much state assistance has been provided to persons by statutory law. The social security system is the most obvious example. That system and its protection by reason of public opinion and governmental commitment are as important as most constitutional rights; yet, it and other benefit programs have not been given the status of constitutional guarantees.

Friedrich urges the United States to modernize its constitution to include benefit rights, and specifically educational rights:

> The older constitutional systems are particularly in need of revision and radical innovation. Advance is needed, and it is more likely to be achieved at the polls or constitutional conventions than in courts; it is part of the *political* process to achieve them. The American bill of rights, so called, is no longer adequate. Not only has there been a certain attenuation of older rights which need to be reaffirmed and strengthened, but some of the new rights urgently require constitutional sanction. Thus the right to an adequate education, guaranteed in a number of the newer constitutions as well as the United Nations' *Declaration*, ought to be positively affirmed in the United States Constitution. It would provide the courts with the necessary ground for coping with certain grave abuses, such as the withholding of education from broad classes of citizens. . . .[78]

We agree. As soon as possible an amendment containing several provisions should be added to the federal Constitution. It should clarify the rights of persons as students and parents as well as the rights of associations such as schools, families, and churches with respect to rights *against* government, *within* government, and *to government* benefits.

Models for such purposes are readily available. Indeed, as Friedrich concedes, the one exception where benefit rights were commonly written into American constitutions is on the matter of education. Some states have long provided for free, public education in their constitutions. The proposed amendment should specifically require free education. Therefore, the phrasing of the state constitutions, including as it does the adjective *public*, cannot be followed. Article 26 of the *Universal Declaration on Human Rights* has a passage that serves the purpose better:

> Everyone has the right to an education. Education shall be free, at least in the elementary and fundamental stages.[79]

SOCIETY, STATE, AND SCHOOLS

The *Universal Declaration* wisely goes further in that it points the focus of education away from state domination and toward family control by adding a second provision:

> Parents have the prior right to choose the kind of education that shall be given to their children.[80]

These two provisions go a long way toward requiring funding of all kinds of education that families might choose for their children.

Still, more is needed. To make the point that all accredited schools would be funded equitably, to give constitutional protection against unreasonable state regulation of schools, and to promote full academic freedom for all schools, one provision should be concerned with the schools themselves. It might read as follows:

> All accredited schools shall be free to achieve their unique educational objectives and shall be assured such funding as is equitable with that given to other schools.

This provision would serve several objectives. First, it would moderate recent efforts by some state governments to develop and narrowly enforce detailed regulations controlling church-related schools that, in *Whisner* v. *Ohio*, have been judged to be destructive of the fruitful autonomy that free, church-related schools require.[81] Second, it would buttress by a constitutional reference point the freedom of association in education that the Supreme Court had to develop with so much effort, as seen in Chapter Three. Third, it would equalize educational expenditures among all schools within a state, including public schools, thereby promoting greater educational justice. This special reference to public schools is needed because in *San Antonio Independent School District* v. *Rodriguez* (1973), the Supreme Court, in a badly split decision, refused to require equalization of educational funds among public school districts in a single state. At the very center of the ruling was a five-judge majority's assertion that under the American Constitution education is not a fundamental right.[82] The opinion outraged spokespersons for the poor. Therefore, the proposed amendment gives common cause to supporters of private schools and to advocates of improved education in poorer public school districts.

The several considerations just discussed produce an amendment that might read as follows:

> Section 1. All persons have a right to a free education at the elementary and secondary levels of schooling.

Section 2. Parents have the prior right to choose the kind of education that shall be given to their children.

Section 3. Nothing in this or any state constitution to the contrary notwithstanding shall prohibit that all accredited schools be free to achieve their unique educational objectives and be assured such funding as is equitable with that given for other schools.

In combination, these three parts of a single amendment on educational rights identify the rights of students, of families, of all schools, and of the state. The provisions are adequate for a state that uses a voucher plan and for a state that uses direct funding of all schools. They provide a constitutional basis for the first time for free choice in education—choice for students, families, and for supporters of all alternative schools. They mandate equitable funding for all schools, including all public schools. In short, they make educational pluralism, educational freedom, and educational equity available to all Americans for the first time—not just to the few who live in the "better" public school districts or the few who can afford private schools or can benefit from other people's charity.

Clearly, none of these provisions is wholly novel or radical. Many states already give constitutional protection to a limited form of free education. The Supreme Court has long recognized the rights of parents and alternative schools. Very recently it has broadened the rights of all associations. For decades, several constitutions in other Western democracies have provided models for two of the three provisions. These proposals are only a small constitutional adjustment of the familiar, but they could very well enable a most useful change in an entire educational system.

Prospects for Amendment

The growing readiness of America for such an amendment is signaled by public opinion polls. In 1974 a Gallup poll of public attitudes toward education revealed that a majority of citizens is prepared to accept a constitutional amendment to achieve basic change on two questions relevant to funding. In a summary of statistics the editors had this to say:

> If these amendments were made the subject of nation-wide referenda at the present time, these majorities would likely be found: an amendment to permit government financial aid to parochial schools: in favor 52%, opposed 35%, no opinion 13%; an amendment to equalize amounts spent within a state on school children: in favor 66%, opposed 22%, no opinion 12%.[83]

Here is compelling evidence that the American people, and not just special interest groups, believe both that basic reform is necessary and that a constitutional amendment is an acceptable route to follow.

In any case, those interest groups that support educational pluralism must consider an amendment. Since the prayer cases of 1962 and 1963, many have been advocating amendments that would affect at least the broad meaning of the First Amendment's religion clauses. This agitation is not dead. If it appears possible that some "prayer amendment" might clear a committee of the Congress, the time might well be propitious for introducing the amendment suggested here, even though in substance their purposes would be contradictory. Calls for a constitutional convention, usually resulting from tax matters, are sporadically heard. Anti-abortionists also demand an amendment in their efforts to overturn the Supreme Court's abortion decision. Supporters of an equal rights amendment for women are already in the field. Just possibly, a convergence of unrelated forces might make the amending process much more open than it has been; such an opportunity should not be lost.

As alternative education interest groups press this matter, they will be educating themselves, their clientele, and the society at large on the issues surrounding educational funding reform. Judges, executives, and legislators read the newspapers. All sorts of political pressures, even in losing causes, are noted. Even unsuccessful agitation for an amendment could in some circumstances have indirect effects that might be welcome to supporters of all schools. If a voucher or similar amendment came close to proposal or ratification, new support for it might very well surface, and new support for other aids to private schools might appear. Therefore, while it is sound to say amendment is difficult, it is not sound to say serious preparation for it is impossible or a waste of effort.

Concentrated efforts on three fronts, legislation, litigation, and a constitutional amendment, may produce a new era in American education, and through it a revitalization of the social institutions of the family, the church, and the school.

EPILOGUE

We now rest our case. Throughout the preceding chapters we have set forth in a sustained way our argument in favor of structural and confessional pluralism. In various stages, from different points of view, and with a kind of cumulative effect we applied the principles of a pluralist world-view to the interrelated issues of society, the state, and the schools.

In the final chapter we have spelled out our strategies for constructive change. Such concrete proposals are always closely related to the state of affairs in a given society at a given point in history; ours, of course, are made with a view to the situation in American education in the late twentieth century. As is usually true for such specific recommendations, ours are tentative and subject to further elaboration. Changing circumstances will certainly call for changed strategies.

In closing, then, we invite response from our readers. The issues before us are significant enough to merit careful reflection and ongoing discussion by people from many walks of life. By means of vigorous interaction carried on in a spirit of mutual trust by concerned parties in an open forum we can work together to achieve a more just society, a more responsible state, and a more equitable system of education.

NOTES

CHAPTER 1

1. *To Empower People: The Role of Mediating Structures in Public Policy* (Washington, D.C.: American Enterprise Institute, 1977).
2. Berkeley: University of California Press, 1978.
3. In *Politics and Experience*, ed. Preston King and B. C. Parekh (Cambridge: Cambridge University Press, 1968), pp. 125–152.
4. *The Structure of Scientific Revolutions*, 2nd ed. (Chicago: University of Chicago Press, 1970).
5. Wolin, p. 148.
6. *Aid for the Over-Developed West* (Toronto: Wedge, 1975), pp. 14–15.
7. "The Nature of Voluntary Associations," in *Voluntary Associations: A Study of Groups in Free Societies; Essays in Honor of James Luther Adams*, ed. D. B. Robertson (Richmond, Va.: John Knox, 1966), p. 21.

CHAPTER 2

1. Leonard Boonin, "Man and Society: An Examination of Three Models," in *Voluntary Associations*, ed. J. R. Pennock and J. W. Chapman (New York: Atherton Press, 1969), pp. 69ff.
2. Ibid., p. 70.
3. Ibid., p. 74.
4. Ibid., p. 77.
5. Robert Horn, *Groups and The Constitution* (Stanford: Stanford University Press, 1956), ch. 1.
6. The list includes such titles as *The Sociological Tradition*, *The Quest for Community*, *The Social Bond*, *Social Change and History*, and *The Social Philosophers*.
7. *The Social Philosophers* (New York: Crowell, 1973), p. 7.
8. "Individu, gemeenschaap, eigendom," in *Verkenningen: Christelijke Perspectief*, No. 1 (Amsterdam: Buijten and Schipperheijn, 1962), p. 211.
9. Ibid., p. 162.
10. *Talks to Teachers on Psychology and to Students on Some of Life's Ideals* (New York: Holt, 1923), p. 301.
11. Curti, *The Social Ideas of American Educators* (Paterson, N.J.: Littlefield and Adams, 1959), pp. 451, 457.
12. *The Meaning of Truth* (New York: Longmans and Green, 1914), p. 125.
13. Ibid., p. 124.
14. Ibid., p. 161.
15. *Talks to Teachers*, p. 277.

16. *The Meaning of Truth*, p. 117.

17. Curti, *Social Ideas of American Educators*, p. 456.

18. *Some Problems of Philosophy* (New York: Longmans and Green, 1916), p. 61.

19. Ibid., pp. 141, 142, 229.

20. *Talks to Teachers*, pp. 169–196.

21. Ibid., pp. 89–90.

22. Curti, *Social Ideas of American Educators*, p. 448.

23. *Teachers College Record* (February 1978), p. 587.

24. *American Review of Reviews*, 34 (1906), 164–166.

25. C. P. Carey, *National Education Association Proceedings* (1910), p. 190.

26. "The Philosophic Aspects of History," *Papers of the American Historical Association*, 5 (1891), 247.

27. "Educational Needs of Urban Civilization," *Education*, No. 5 (1885), p. 449.

28. Curti, *Social Ideas of American Educators*, p. 336.

29. *Christianity and the Class Struggle* (Grand Rapids, Mich.: Piet Hein Publishers, 1950), pp. 47, 48.

30. Herbert Richardson, *Religion and Political Society* (New York: Harper, 1974), p. 3.

31. This point is well made in Karl Hertz, "The Nature of Voluntary Associations," in *Voluntary Associations: A Study of Groups in Free Societies; Essays in Honor of James Luther Adams*, ed. D. B. Robertson (Richmond, Va.: John Knox, 1966), p. 33.

32. Dooyeweerd, "Individu, gemeenschaap, eigendom," pp. 210–211.

33. New York: St. Martin's Press, 1974.

34. Nicholls, pp. 1, 4. Cf. also Nicholls's other book, *The Pluralist State* (New York: St. Martin's Press, 1975), esp. pp. 73–74.

35. MacIver is the author of numerous books on social philosophy, including *The Modern State*, *Society: Its Structure and Change*, *The Web of Government*, *Politics and Society*, and *Leviathan and the People*.

36. *On Community, Society, and Power* (Chicago: University of Chicago Press, 1970).

37. For a full bibliography see "Writings of James Luther Adams," in *Voluntary Associations*, ed. Robertson.

38. Encyclical Letter *Divini Illius Majistri of His Holiness Pope Pius XI* (New York: The American Press, 1936), pp. 6, 19.

39. *The Documents of Vatican II*, ed. Walter Abbot (New York, 1966), pp. 645, 644, 642, 644.

40. *Philosophy of the State as Educator* (Milwaukee: Bruce, 1959), pp. 55, 57.

41. 5th rev. ed. (Grand Rapids, Mich.: Baker, 1975).

42. Ibid., p. 129.

43. Ibid., p. 161.

44. Ibid., p. 135.

45. Ibid., p. 137, quoted from Ernst Troeltsch, *The Social Teachings of the Christian Church*, II (New York: Macmillan, 1931), 621.

46. *Ethics* (New York: Macmillan, 1959), p. 207.

47. The phrase reflects W. F. Graham, *The Constructive Revolutionary: John Calvin and his Socio-Economic Impact* (Richmond, Va.: John Knox, 1971).

48. John Calvin, *Institutes of the Christian Religion*, Battles-McNeill edn. (Philadelphia: Westminster, 1960), I, 2, 1; pp. 40–41.

49. Cf. Andre Bieler, *The Social Humanism of John Calvin* (Richmond, Va.: John Knox, 1964), p. 24.

50. *Institutes*, IV, 11, 1.

51. *The History and Character of Calvinism* (New York: Oxford, 1962), p. 234.

52. Cf. William Niesel, *The Theology of Calvin* (Philadelphia: Westminster, 1956), p. 230.

53. Cf. Gordon Spykman, "Sphere Sovereignty in Calvin and the Calvinist Tradition," in *Exploring the Heritage of John Calvin*, ed. D. Holwerda (Grand Rapids, Mich.: Baker, 1976), pp. 189–206.

54. *Commentary on Amos*, 7:10–13.

55. *Commentary on Ephesians*, 5:21–6:9.

56. *Commentary on I Peter*, 1:12–17.

57. "Calvyn en Zyn Academie in 1559," *Vier Redevoeringen over Calvijn* (Kampen, Netherlands: Kok, 1959), pp. 18–21.

58. *The Social Philosophers*, p. 399.

59. *Politica Methodica Digesta*, ed. Carl J. Friedrich (Cambridge, Mass.: Harvard University Press, 1932).

60. Cf. Otto von Gierke, *The Development of Political Theory* (New York: Fertig, 1966) and Frederick S. Carney, *The Politics of Johannes Althusius* (Boston: Beacon, 1964).

61. Herman Dooyeweerd, *A New Critique of Theoretical Thought* (Philadelphia: Presbyterian and Reformed Publishing Co., 1957), III, 662–663.

62. Cf. James Skillen, *The Development of Calvinistic Political Theory* (Ann Arbor, Mich.: University Microfilms, 1974), pp. 191–217.

63. Abraham Kuyper, *Lectures on Calvinism* (Grand Rapids, Mich.: Eerdmans, 1931), p. 78.

64. Ibid., p. 11.

65. Ibid., p. 85.

66. Ibid., p. 79.

67. Ibid., p. 87.

68. Ibid., p. 88.

69. Ibid., p. 89.

70. Ibid., pp. 96–97.

71. Anthony H. Nichols, "Abraham Kuyper: A Summons to Christian Vision," *Journal of Christian Education*, 16 (1973), 82.

72. *Lectures on Calvinism*, p. 94.

73. Ibid., p. 98.

74. Cf. Groen's *Unbelief and Revolution*, Lectures VIII and IX (Amsterdam: Groen Foundation, 1975).

75. *Lectures on Calvinism*, p. 90.

76. Cf. J. Verlinden, "Public and Private Education in the Netherlands," *The Educational Forum*, Nov. 1957, pp. 51–57.

CHAPTER 3

1. Edmund S. Morgan, ed., *Puritan Political Ideas* (New York: Bobbs-Merrill & Co., Inc., 1965), pp. 18–19.

2. John Cotton, "Copy of a Letter From Mr. Cotton To Lord Say and Seal in The Year 1636," in Morgan, p. 168.

3. Ibid., p. 169. (Italics added.)

4. "A coppie of the Liberties of the Massachusetts Colonie in New England," in Morgan, pp. 178–179. With respect to the rights of the church and the commonwealth the preamble of the *Body of Liberties* stated that "We doe therefore this day religiously and unanimously decree and confirme these following Rites, liberties and priveledges concerneing our Churches, and Civill State to be respectively impartialle and inviolably enjoyed and observed throughout our Jurisdiction for ever."

5. Ibid., pp. 199–200.

6. Ibid., p. 190. (Italics added.)

7. R. Baxter, in Peter Bulkeley, *The Gospel Covenant*, 2nd ed. (London: 1651).

8. N. Thorpe, ed., *The Federal and State Constitutions*, Vol. I (Washington, D.C.: Government Printing Office, 1906), p. 523.

9. William Perkins, "A Treatise of the Vocations or Callings of men, with sorts and kinds of them, and the right use thereof," in Morgan, p. 36.

10. Ibid., p. 38.

11. Cotton, p. 169.

12. Ibid., p. 172.

13. Perry Miller, *Errand Into the Wilderness* (New York: Harper & Row, 1956), p. 161.

14. *Pamphlets of the American Revolution*, ed. Bernard Bailyn, (Cambridge, Mass.: Harvard University Press, 1965), I, *1750–1766*, p. 118.

15. James Otis, *The Rights of the British Colonies Asserted and Proved*, in Bailyn, p. 472.

16. Ibid., p. 454. (Italics in the original.)

17. Bailyn, p. 413.

18. See, for example, Alexander Hamilton, *The Federalist Papers*, No. 22.

19. Thomas Paine, *Rights of Man*, in *The Complete Writings of Thomas Paine*, ed. Philip S. Foner (New York: The Citadel Press, 1945), I, 379, 388.

20. Ibid.

21. R. R. Palmer, *The Age of Democratic Revolutions* (Princeton: Princeton University Press, 1964), I, 228.

22. Ibid., p. 228.

23. Alexis de Tocqueville, quoted in Sidney E. Mead, *The Nation with the Soul of a Church* (New York: Harper & Row, 1975), pp. 89–90.

24. Ibid., p. 61.

25. Ibid., p. 55.

26. McCulloch v. Maryland, 17 U.S. 316 (1819).

27. Bank of United States v. Deveaux, 9 U.S. 61 (1809).

28. Strawbridge v. Curtiss, 7 U.S. 267 (1806).

29. Louisville, C. & C. R. Co. v. Letson, 43 U.S. 497 (1844).

30. Marshall v. Baltimore and Ohio R. Co., 57 U.S. 314 (1854).

31. Arthur Selwyn Miller, *The Supreme Court and American Capitalism* (New York: The Free Press, 1968), pp. 13–17.

32. Darmouth College v. Woodward, 17 U.S. 518 (1819).

33. Ibid.

34. *The Constitution of the United States: Analysis and Interpretation* (Washington, D.C.: U.S. Government Printing Office, 1973), pp. 396–407.

35. See, for example, Munn v. Illinois, 94 U.S. 113 (1877). By 1886

Chief Justice White opened the oral arguments of a case with the comment that there need be no discussion about the status of the corporation as a legal person under the Fourteenth Amendment, for all justices accepted that status; Santa Clara County v. So. Pac. R. Co., 118 U.S. 394 (1886).

36. Northern Securities Co. v. United States, 193 U.S. 197 (1904).

37. Pierce v. Society of Sisters, 268 U.S. 510 (1925).

38. 307 U.S. 496 (1939).

39. Watson v. Jones, 80 U.S. 679 (1872); Serbian Orthodox Diocese v. Milivojevich, 426 U.S. 696 (1976). In Wolf v. Jones, 443 U.S. 595 (1979) five justices of the Supreme Court held that when possible intrachurch disputes might be settled by religiously neutral principles of corporate law rather than by treating the church as "wholly other." This decision qualifies but for most purposes does not alter the major points made here.

40. Watson v. Jones, 80 U.S. 679 (1872).

41. See something of the Supreme Court's efforts to draw the religious-secular line in the discussion concerning government aid to education, pp. 93–102.

42. See, for example, Glenn Abernathy, *The Right of Assembly and Association* (Columbia: University of South Carolina Press, 1961); Arthur S. Miller, "The Constitution and the Voluntary Association: Some Notes Toward a Theory," in *Voluntary Associations*, ed. J. Ronald Pennock and John W. Chapman (New York: Atherton Press, 1969), pp. 233–262; Thomas I. Emerson, "Freedom of Association and Freedom of Expression," *Yale Law Journal*, 74 (1974), 1–35.

43. 357 U.S. 449 (1958).

44. Ibid.

45. Ibid.

46. 371 U.S. 415 (1963).

47. 381 U.S. 479 (1965).

48. Bigelow v. Virginia, 421 U.S. 809 (1975).

49. Virginia State Board of Pharmacy v. Virginia Citizens Consumer's Council, Inc., 425 U.S. 748 (1976).

50. 435 U.S. 765 (1978). See Pierce v. Society of Sisters, p.67 above.

51. 419 U.S. 477 (1975) (italics added).

52. 412 U.S. 94 (1973).

53. 407 U.S. 163 (1972).

54. 431 U.S. 816 (1977).

55. Ibid., citing Cleveland Board of Education v. Lafleur, 414 U.S. 632 (1974).

56. Ibid., citing Loving v. Virginia, 388 U.S. 1 (1967).

57. Ibid., citing Cleveland Board of Education v. Lafleur, 414 U.S. 632 (1974).

58. Ibid., at 844, citing Griswold v. Connecticut, 381 U.S. 479 (1965).

59. Ibid., at 842, citing Prince v. Massachusetts, 321 U.S. 158 (1944).

60. Ibid., citing Meyer v. Nebraska, 262 U.S. 390 (1923).

61. Ibid., citing Prince v. Massachusetts, 321 U.S. 158 (1944).

62. Ibid., citing Wisconsin v. Yoder, 406 U.S. 205 (1972).

63. Ibid., citing Moore v. East Cleveland, 431 U.S. 494 (1977).

64. Ibid., citing Village of Belle Terre v. Boraas, 416 U.S. 1 (1974).

65. Ibid., citing Stanley v. Illinois, 405 U.S. 645 (1972).

66. Smith v. Organization of Foster Families, 431 U.S. 816 (1977).

For another case illustrating the procedural rights of parents see May v. Anderson, 345 U.S. 528 (1953).

67. One widely cited article on free association is Thomas I. Emerson, "Freedom of Association and Freedom of Expression," *Yale Law Journal*, 74 (1964), 1–35. It includes a substantial bibliography of books and articles up to that time. For an article that stresses the rights of associations that are alleged to be subversive see Nathaniel L. Nathanson, "The Right of Association," in *The Rights of Americans*, ed. Norman Dorsen (New York: Pantheon Books, 1971), pp. 231–253.

68. Thomas I. Emerson, *The System of Freedom of Expression* (New York: Random House, 1970), p. 431.

69. 418 U.S. 683 (1974).

70. Amos J. Peaslee, *Constitutions of Nations*, 3rd ed. (The Hague: Martinus Nijhoff, 1970), III, 490.

71. Peaslee, III, 681.

72. Peaslee, IV, 1303.

73. See Egan Schwelb, *Human Rights and the International Community* (Chicago: Quadrangle Books, 1964), pp. 84–85.

74. See Karl Hertz, "The Nature of Voluntary Associations," in *Voluntary Associations: A Study of Groups in Free Societies*, ed. D. B. Robertson (Richmond, Va.: John Knox, 1966).

CHAPTER 4

1. Bernard Bailyn, *Education in the Forming of American Society* (Chapel Hill: University of North Carolina Press, 1960), p. 11.

2. Massachusetts Constitution of 1780, Ch. V, Sec. II. Reprinted in Francis Newton Thorpe, ed., *Federal and State Constitutions* (Washington: 1909), V, 467.

3. Thomas Jefferson, *The Writings of Thomas Jefferson*, ed. Paul Leicester Ford (New York: The Knickerbocker Press, 1892), I, 69.

4. Quoted in David B. Tyack, ed., *Turning Points in American Educational History* (Waltham, Mass.: Blaisdell Publishing Co., 1967), p. 91.

5. Ibid.

6. Ibid.

7. Benjamin Rush, "A plan for the Establishment of Public Schools and the Diffusion of Knowledge in Pennsylvania; to which are added, Thoughts upon the mode of Education, Proper in a Republic," reprinted in Frederick Rudolph, ed., *Essays on Education in the Early Republic* (Cambridge, Mass.: Harvard University Press, 1965), p. 10.

8. Ibid.

9. Ibid.

10. Horace Mann to Frederick Packard, July 2, 1938. Reprinted in Raymond B. Culver, *Horace Mann and Religion in Massachusetts Public Schools* (New Haven: Yale University Press, 1929), p. 267.

11. W. M. Oland Bourne, *History of the Public School Society of the City of New York* (New York: W. M. Wood and Co., 1870), p. 68.

12. Quoted in Michael Katz, *Class, Bureaucracy, and the Schools: The Illusion of Educational Change in America*, expanded ed. (New York: Praeger Publishers, 1975), p. 7. (Italics added.)

13. John Webb Pratt, *Religion, Politics and Diversity: The Church-State Theme in New York History* (Ithaca, N.Y.: Cornell University Press, 1967), p. 167. The full report of the law committee is reprinted in Bourne, pp. 713–21.

14. Daniel Patrick Moynihan, "Government and the Ruin of Private Education," *Harpers*, April 1978, p. 32.

15. Bourne, p. 134.

16. Ibid., p. 136. (Italics added.)

17. Hughes's evidence came from the Public School Society's 1827 Report. See Hughes, "The Petition of the Catholics of the City of New York," September 21, 1840, in *Documents of the Board of Aldermen of the City of New York*, VII, No. 40 (1840–1841), reprinted in Rush Welter, ed., *American Writings on Popular Education: The Nineteenth Century* (Indianapolis: The Bobbs-Merrill Co., 1971), p. 104.

18. Ibid. (Italics added.)

19. Ibid., p. 105.

20. Quoted in Moynihan, p. 33.

21. Ibid.

22. Ibid.

23. Ibid.

24. Wolman v. Walter, 433 U.S. 229 (1977).

25. Everson v. Board of Education, 330 U.S. 1 (1947).

26. Ibid.

27. Ibid.

28. Ibid.

29. Ibid.

30. Ibid.

31. McCollum v. Board of Education, 333 U.S. 203 (1948).

32. Ibid.

33. Ibid.

34. Ibid.

35. Zorach v. Clauson, 343 U.S. 306 (1952).

36. 175 U.S. 291 (1899).

37. 403 U.S. 672 (1971).

38. Ibid.

39. Hunt v. McNair, 413 U.S. 734 (1973).

40. Roemer v. Board, 426 U.S. 736 (1976).

41. Earley v. Dicenso, 403 U.S. 602 (1971).

42. Meek v. Pittenger, 421 U.S. 349 (1975).

43. See, for example, the opinion of Justice Brennan in *Tilton* v. *Richardson* that appears in his statement in Lemon v. Kurtzman I, 403 U.S. 602 (1971).

44. 413 U.S. 472 and 413 U.S. 825 (1973).

45. Ibid.

46. 413 U.S. 472 (1973).

47. 433 U.S. 229 (1977).

48. 433 U.S. 229 (1977; 421 U.S. 349 (1975).

49. Walz v. Tax Commission, 397 U.S. 664 (1970).

50. 403 U.S. 602 (1971); the two cases were considered together.

51. 421 U.S. 349 (1975).

52. 421 U.S. 229 (1977).

53. 413 U.S. 756 (1973).

54. 521 U.S. 349 (1975).

55. Ibid.

56. William Ball, "What is Religion?" *The Christian Lawyer*, Spring 1979, p. 12.

57. Richard E. Morgan, "Establishment Clause and Sectarian

Schools: A Final Installment," in Phillip B. Durland, ed., *The Supreme Court Review, 1973* (Chicago: The University of Chicago Press, 1974), pp. 57–98.

58. Committee v. Nyquist, 413 U.S. 756 (1973).

59. Ibid.

60. Sloan v. Lemon, 413 U.S. 825 (1973).

61. Justice Stevens has voted on only eight issues of church-state relations at this writing, so his position must be regarded as still a bit uncertain.

62. Meek v. Pittenger, 421 U.S. 349 (1975); and Wolman v. Walter, 433 U.S. 229 (1977).

63. Roemer v. Board, 426 U.S. 736 (1976); Tilton v. Richardson, 403 U.S. 672 (1971); Hunt v. McNair, 413 U.S. 734 (1973).

64. The Supreme Court handled 14 aid-to-private-education cases between 1971 and 1980. Several of these cases had distinct subissues on which the court voted. Thus, there were 25 separate issues requiring a vote in those years. The cases were: Tilton v. Richardson, 403 U.S. 672 (1971); Lemon v. Kurtzman, 403 U.S. 602 (1971); Earley v. Dicenso, 403 U.S. 602 (1971); Committee v. Nyquist, 413 U.S. 756 (1973); Levitt v. Committee, 403 U.S. 602 (1973); Sloan v. Lemon, 403 U.S. 825 (1973); Lemon v. Kurtzman II, 411 U.S. 192 (1973); Hunt v. McNair, 426 U.S. 734 (1973); Wheeler v. Barrera, 417 U.S. 402 (1974); Meek v. Pittenger, 421 U.S. 349 (1975); Roemer v. Board, 426 U.S. 736 (1976); New York v. Cathedral Academy, 434 U.S. 125 (1977); Wolman v. Walter, 433 U.S. 229 (1977); Regan v. Committee, 63 L Ed 2d 94 (1980).

CHAPTER 5

1. Quoted by Edward Gaffney, Jr., in *Freedom and Education: Pierce v. Society of Sisters Reconsidered*, Donald P. Kommers and Michael Wahoske, eds. (Center for Civil Rights, University of Notre Dame Law School, 1978), p. 86.

2. Philip Phenix, *The Scholars Look at the Schools* (Washington, D.C.: National Education Association, 1962), p. 17.

3. James Panoch and David Barr, *Religion Goes to School* (New York: Harper and Row, 1968).

4. Phenix, p. 18.

5. Educational Policies Commission, *Moral and Spiritual Values in Public Schools* (Washington, D.C.: National Education Association, 1951).

6. Educational Policies Commission, p. 46.

7. Will Herberg, *Protestant, Catholic, Jew* (New York: Doubleday & Co., Inc., 1960), p. 91.

8. Ibid., p. 92.

9. Martin Marty, *A Nation of Behavers* (Chicago: University of Chicago Press, 1976), ch. 8, "Civil Religion."

10. Quoted in Richard Neuhaus, "No More Bootleg Religion," in *Controversies in Education*, Dwight Allen, ed. (Philadelphia: W. B. Saunders Co., 1974), p. 78.

11. Ibid., p. 77.

12. See, for example, Onalee McGraw, *Family Choice in Education: The New Imperative* (Washington, D.C.: The Heritage Foundation, 1978), esp. her chapter on "Family Rights and the Courts." See also Virgil Blum, S.J., *Freedom of Choice in Education* (New York: Macmillan, 1958), pp. 98–101, as well as Daniel McGarry, "Secularism in American Public

Education and the Unconstitutionality of its Exclusive Governmental Support," *Educational Freedom*, Fall/Winter 1978– 79, and Spring/Summer 1979. See also Rousas Rushdoony in *Freedom and Education: Pierce v. Society of Sisters Reconsidered* (Center for Civil Rights, Notre Dame Law School, 1978).

13. Torcaso v. Watkins, 81 S. Ct. 1680 (1961).

14. 153 Cal. App. 2d. 673, 315 p. 2d. 394.

15. Francis Potter, *The Story of Religion* (Garden City, N.Y.: Garden City Publishing Company, 1929), p. xvii. He was also a signer of *Humanist Manifesto I* in 1933.

16. Quoted in Walfred Peterson, *Thy Liberty in Law* (Nashville, Tenn.: Broadman Press, 1978), p. 84.

17. Malnak v. Yogi, 440 F. Supp. 1284 (1977).

18. Quoted in *The Advocate*, Spring 1979, Center for Law and Religious Freedom (Oak Park, Ill.), p. 7.

19. A sampling of the literature has been given above, n. 12.

20. Leo Pfeffer, "Issues That Divide: The Triumph of Secular Humanism," *Journal of Church and State*, Spring 1977, p. 207.

21. Ibid., p. 209.

22. Ibid., p. 211.

23. Charles Potter, *Humanism: A New Religion* (New York: Simon and Schuster, 1930), p. 75.

24. *Manifesto I* was reprinted in *Religious Humanism*, Spring 1970, pp. 61ff., and *Manifesto II* in *The Humanist*, September-October, 1973, pp. 4ff.

25. *Humanist Manifestos I and II* (Buffalo, N.Y.: Prometheus, 1976).

26. *The Humanist*, September-October 1973, p. 5.

27. *Humanism as a Philosophy* (New York: F. Ungar, 1947), pp. xii and x.

28. John Dewey, *A Common Faith* (New Haven: Yale University Press, 1934), p. 87.

29. *Religion in the Public Schools* (Washington, D.C.: American Association of School Administrators, 1964).

30. Educational Policies Commission, p. 46.

31. Donald Oppewal, "Christian Textbooks? Yes!" *Christian Educators Journal*, April 1972, pp. 7–8.

32. Harold Pflug, "Religion in Missouri Textbooks," *Phi Delta Kappan*, April 1955, p. 260.

33. See George Hillocks, "Books and Bombs: Ideological Conflict and the Schools," *School Review*, August 1978; Clayton McNearney, "The Kanawha County Textbook Controversy," *Religious Education*, September-October 1975; for a different interpretation see the Inquiry Report published by the NEA: *A Textbook Study in Cultural Conflict* (Washington, D.C.: National Education Association, Teacher Rights Division, 1975). See also Edwin Welch, "Textbook Crisis in West Virginia," *Educational Forum*, November 1976.

34. Hillocks, p. 646.

35. Ibid.

36. Ibid., p. 642.

37. Quoted in J. Hefley, *Textbooks on Trial* (Wheaton, Ill.: Victor Books, 1976), p. 139.

38. Victor Durrance, "Public Textbook Selection in Forty-Eight States," *Phi Delta Kappan*, January 1952.

39. The four texts are: *Molecules to Man*, 3rd ed. (Houghton Mifflin

Co., 1976); *An Inquiry Into Life*, 3rd ed. (Harcourt Brace Jovanovich, 1973); *An Ecological Approach*, 3rd ed. (Rand McNally Co., 1973); *Modern Biology* (Holt, Rinehart & Winston, 1977).

40. Paul Hurd, "An Exploratory Study of the Impact of BSCS Secondary School Curriculum Materials," *American Biology Teacher*, 38 (1976), 80.

41. Wendell Bird, "Freedom of Religion and Science Instruction in Public Schools," *The Yale Law Journal*, 78 (1978), 521–522.

42. Ibid.

43. See, for example, J. Hefley, *Textbooks on Trial*, who documents the efforts of the Mel Gablers in the state of Texas and elsewhere.

44. Bird, p. 522.

45. *The Humanist*, January-February 1977, p. 4.

46. *Malnak* v. *Yogi*.

47. Ernest Lefever, ed., *Values in an American Government Textbook* (Washington, D.C.: Public Policy Center, Georgetown University, 1978), p. 3. The text is *American Political Behavior* (Boston: Ginn and Co., 1972).

48. Susan Marshner, *Man: A Course of Study —Prototype for Federalized Textbooks?* (Washington, D.C.: Heritage Foundation, Inc., 1975), p. 3.

49. George Weber, "The Case Against *Man: A Course of Study*," *Phi Delta Kappan*, October 1975, p. 82.

50. Peter B. Dow, *Talks to Teachers* (Cambridge, Mass.: Education Development Center, 1970), p. 6.

51. Peter B. Dow, "MACOS: The Study of Human Behavior as one Road to Survival," *Phi Delta Kappan*, October 1975, p. 80.

52. Lewis P. Todd and Merle Curti, *Rise of the American Nation* (New York: Harcourt Brace Jovanovich, 1972).

53. Martin Herz, *How the Cold War is Taught* (Washington, D.C.: Ethics and Public Policy Center, Georgetown University, 1978), p. 9.

54. Bird, "Freedom of Religion and Science Instruction in Public Schools."

55. West Virginia v. State Board of Education, 319 U.S. 624 (1943).

56. Abington School District v. Schempp, 374 U.S. 203 at 225 (1963).

57. Ibid., at 306.

58. *Malnak* v. *Yogi*.

59. T. Postema, "Unrealized Potential for Government Aid in Ontario," *Christian Educators Journal*, April-May 1979, p. 11.

60. Ibid., p. 32. See also Tom Malcom and Harry Fernhout, *Education and the Public Purpose* (Toronto: Curriculum Development Center, 1979), pp. 1–51.

61. G. Knoppers, "Independent Education in Alberta," *Christian Educators Journal*, October-November 1979, p. 16.

62. Ibid., p. 17.

63. J. Koziak, in *Alberta Hansard*, April 26, 1978, p. 848.

64. Knoppers, p. 17.

65. J. Koziak, responding to a question in the legislature, April 26, 1978.

66. H. Van Brummelen, "Government Funding of Christian Schools in British Columbia: Unique in North America," *Christian Educators Journal*, April-May 1979, p. 28.

67. Ibid., p. 29.

68. A. Mittleman, "Educational Freedom in Israel," in McGarry and Ward, eds., *Educational Freedom* (Milwaukee: Bruce, 1966), p. 101.

69. Ibid., p. 100.

70. R. F. Cunningham, "Educational Freedom in England," in McGarry and Ward, eds., *Educational Freedom* (Milwaukee: Bruce, 1966), p. 85.

71. Ibid., p. 88.

72. Ibid., p. 90.

73. Ibid., pp. 85–92.

74. R. McCarthy et al., "Disestablishment A Second Time: Public Justice for American Schools" (unpublished manuscript, 1979), p. 239.

75. Ibid.

76. G. Bereday and J. Lauwrerys, *Church and State in Education: The World Yearbook of Education* (New York: Harcourt Brace and World, 1966), p. 335.

77. B. Planche, "Belgium," in L. Deighton, ed., *The Encyclopedia of Education* (New York, Macmillan, 1971), p. 451.

78. E. Palmer, "Freedom and Equity in Dutch Education," in McGarry and Ward, eds., *Educational Freedom* (Milwaukee: Bruce, 1966), pp. 67–68.

79. Ibid., p. 70.

80. J.A.A. Verlinden, "Public and Private Education in the Netherlands," *Educational Forum*, November 1957, p. 53.

81. McCarthy, p. 242.

82. Amos Peaslee, *Constitutions of Nations*, 3rd ed. (The Hague: Martinus Nijhoff, 1970), III, 681.

83. Palmer, pp. 75–76.

84. Cf. McCarthy, p. 243; Palmer, p. 77.

85. Cf. McCarthy, p. 243; Palmer, pp. 77–78.

86. T. Reller, "Public Funds for Religious Education: Canada, England and the Netherlands," in D. Giannella, ed., *Religion and the Public Order: 1963* (Chicago: University of Chicago Press, 1964), p. 187.

87. *The Kingdom of the Netherlands* (The Hague: Educational Ministry of Foreign Affairs, Government Printing Office, 1971), p. 32.

88. For more information on aid to independent education in Western countries, see the following sources: Dubay, *Philosophy of the State as Educator* (Milwaukee: Bruce, 1959); Center for Field Research and School Services, Boston College, *Issues of Aid to Nonpublic Schools*, Papers submitted to the President's Commission on School Finance, June 1971; D. Giannella, ed., *Religion and the Public Order: 1963* (Chicago: University of Chicago Press, 1964); Nash, ed., *History and Education* (New York: Random House, 1970).

CHAPTER 6

1. In addition to the works cited in the notes to this chapter, the following works represent background materials consulted in the development of this chapter: G. C. Berkouwer, *General Revelation* (Grand Rapids, Mich.: Eerdmans, 1955); A. Bieler, *The Social Humanism of John Calvin* (Richmond, Va.: John Knox, 1964); D. Bonhoeffer, *Creation and Fall: A Theological Interpretation of Genesis 1–3* (New York: Macmillan, 1959); E. Brunner, *Christian Doctrine of Creation and Redemption* (Phil-

adelphia: Westminster, 1952); E. Brunner, *Justice and the Social Order* (London: Lutterworth, 1945); O. Cullmann, *The State in the New Testament* (London: SCM Press, 1967); J. H. Dengerink, *Critical Historical Analysis of the Sociological Development of the Principle of Sphere Sovereignty in the 19th and 20th Centuries* (Kampen, Netherlands: Kok, 1948); J. H. Diemer, *Miracles Happen: Toward a Biblical View of Nature* (Toronto: ICS, Academic Papers, nd); H. Dooyeweerd, *The Christian Idea of the State* (Nutley, N.J.: Craig, 1975); J. Ellul, *The Theological Foundation of Law* (London: SCM Press, 1960); J. Gibbs, *Creation and Redemption* (London: Brill, 1971); L. Gilkey, *Maker of Heaven and Earth* (New York: Doubleday, 1959); A. Kuyper, *Lectures on Calvinism* (Stone Lectures) (Grand Rapids, Mich.: Eerdmans, 1970); H. Meeter, *The Basic Ideas of Calvinism*, 5th rev. ed. (Grand Rapids, Mich.: Kregel, 1956); J. Olthuis, *The Word of God and Creation* (Toronto: ICS, Academic Papers, 1975), and *Visions of Life and Ways of Life: the Nature of Religion* (Toronto: ICS, Academic Papers, 1978); H. E. Runner, *Scriptural Religion and Political Task* (Hamilton, Ont.: Guardian, Christian Perspectives, 1962); J. Skillen, *The Development of Calvinistic Political Theory* (Ann Arbor, Mich.: University Microfilms, 1974); E. H. Taylor, *The Christian Philosophy of Law, Politics, and the State* (Nutley, N.J.: Craig, 1966); H. Thielicke, *How the World Began: Man in the First Chapters of the Bible* (Philadelphia: Muhlenberg, 1961); G. Groen Van Prinsterer, *Unbelief and Revolution*, Lectures VIII & IX (Amsterdam: Groen Fund, 1975); H. Van Til, *The Calvinistic Concept of Culture* (Grand Rapids, Mich.: Baker, 1959); G. Wingren, *Creation and Gospel* (Toronto: Mellen Press, 1979); G. Wingren, *Luther on Vocation* (Philadelphia: Muhlenberg, 1957); A. Wolters, *The Foundational Command: "Subdue the Earth"* (Toronto: ICS, Academic Papers, nd); A. Wolters, *Veenhof on Nature and Grace in Bavinck* (Toronto: ICS, Academic Papers, 1977); N. Wolterstorff, *Religion and the Schools* (Grand Rapids, Mich.: Eerdmans, 1966).

2. Cf. H. Blamires, *The Christian Mind* (London: S.P.C.K., 1966), pp. 25–27.

3. *Testament of Vision* (Grand Rapids, Mich.: Eerdmans, 1958), p. 145.

4. *Politics and the Biblical Drama* (Grand Rapids, Mich.: Eerdmans, 1976), p. 11.

5. Cf. H. R. Niebuhr, *Christ and Culture* (New York: Harper and Row, 1951), pp. 39–44.

6. Cf. H. Van Riessen, *The University and Its Basis: Christian Perspectives*, No. 3 (St. Catharines, Ont.: ARSS, 1963), pp. 24–28.

7. Cf. A. Kuyper, *Souvereiniteit in Eigen Kring* (Amsterdam: Kruyt, 1880).

8. Cf. W. Herberg, "Introduction—The Social Philosophy of Karl Barth," in Karl Barth, *Community, State and Church* (Gloucester, Mass.: Smith, 1968), pp. 22–38.

CHAPTER 7

1. Senate Bill 2142, September 22, 1977.

2. *New York Times*, May 30, 1979.

3. Milton Friedman, "The Role of Government in Education," in Robert Solo, ed., *Economics and the Public Interest* (New Brunswick, N.J.: Rutgers University Press, 1955), p. 129.

4. See, for example, David Friedman, *Toward a Competitive School System* (Wichita, Kansas: The Center for Independent Education).

5. Christopher Jencks, "Giving Parents Money To Pay For Schooling: Education Vouchers," *New Republic*, July 4, 1970, pp. 19– 21.

6. See Stephen Arons, "The Joker in Private School Aid," *Saturday Review*, January 16, 1971, pp. 45ff. See also John Coons and Stephen Sugarman, *Education By Choice: The Case For Family Control* (Berkeley: University of California Press, 1978), and Stephen Sugarman, "Education Reform at the Margin: Two Ideas," *Phi Delta Kappan*, November 1977, pp. 154– 157, in which he advocates school stamps modeled after federal food stamps for the poor.

7. For a summary of the arguments see Virgil Blum, S.J., "Quality Education for Inner-City Minorities Through Education Vouchers" (Milwaukee: Catholic League For Religious and Civil Rights).

8. Roy Innis, "How to Save Inner-city Schools," *Lincoln Review*, Spring 1979, p. 38.

9. See *Parents, Teachers & Children: Prospects for Choice in American Education* (San Francisco: The Institute for Contemporary Studies, 1977). A wide range of scholars speaks to the importance of providing parents with entitlements rather than services.

10. See, for example, the chapters on state education powers and spending powers in Newton Edwards, *The Courts and the Public Schools* (Chicago: University of Chicago Press, 1955), pp. 23– 46.

11. See, for example, the material on federal spending powers in *The Constitution of the United States of America: Analysis and Interpretation* (Washington, D.C.: U.S. Government Printing Office, 1973), pp. 136– 141.

12. Ibid.

13. Pierce v. Society of Sisters, 268 U.S. 310 (1925).

14. In addition to *Pierce*, see Committee v. Nyquist, 413 U.S. 756 (1973).

15. Pierce v. Society of Sisters, 268 U.S. 310 (1925).

16. In addition to *Pierce*, see Runyon v. McCrary, 427 U.S. 160 (1976).

17. Wisconsin v. Yoder, 406 U.S. 205 (1972); West Virginia Board of Education v. Barnette, 319 U.S. 624 (1943).

18. "Parents Win in Iowa," *Tidbits*, No. 4, 1978, p. 3. (This is the newsletter of the National Association for the Legal Support of Alternative Schools, Sante Fe, New Mexico.) The state of Iowa dropped its appeal to the state Supreme Court. See "Sessions Case Resolved," *Inform*, No. 9, 1979, p. 3. (This is the newsletter of the Center for Independent Education, Wichita, Kansas.)

19. For a statement of the issues involved and a case study see Stephen Arons, "Is Educating Your Child a Crime?" *Saturday Review*, November 25, 1978, pp. 16– 20.

20. Committee v. Nyquist, 413 U.S. 756 (1973).

21. Ibid.

22. Committee v. Nyquist, 413 U.S. 756 (1973); Sloan v. Lemon, 413 U.S. 825 (1973).

23. See Justice Burger's dissenting opinion, Committee v. Nyquist, 413 U.S. 756 (1973).

24. Prince v. Massachusetts, 321 U.S. 158 (1944); Farrington v. Tokushiga, 273 U.S. 284 (1927).

25. Pierce v. Society of Sisters, 268 U.S. 310 (1925).

26. Ibid., and Runyon v. McCrary, 427 U.S. 160 (1976).

27. Committee v. Nyquist, 413 U.S. 756 (1973).

28. Pierce v. Society of Sisters, 268 U.S. 310 (1925).

29. Sherbert v. Verner, 374 U.S. 398 (1963).

30. 330 U.S. 1 (1947).

31. See, for example, the dissents in Committee v. Nyquist, 413 U.S. 756 (1973) that also applied to Sloan v. Lemon, 413 U.S. 825 (1973).

32. For a discussion of judicial activism and restraint see Alexander M. Bickle, *The Least Dangerous Branch* (Indianapolis: Bobbs-Merrill, 1962).

33. See Chapter Three above.

34. See Roe v. Wade, 410 U.S. 131 (1973).

35. Frank J. Sorauf, *The Wall of Separation* (Princeton, N.J.: Princeton University Press, 1976), pp. 203–204.

36. Ibid., pp. 91–129.

37. Ibid., pp. 59–90.

38. A book describing this long-term legal offensive is Clement E. Vase, *Caucasians Only* (Berkeley: University of California Press, 1959).

39. William B. Ball, "Litigation in Education: in Defense of Freedom," Studies in Education, No. 5 (Wichita, Kansas; Center for Independent Education, 1977), pp. 4–5.

40. For a discussion of this see Henry J. Abraham, *Freedom and the Court*, 2nd ed. (New York: Oxford University Press, 1972), pp. 200–201.

41. 406 U.S. 205.

42. Philip Kurland, "The Supreme Court, Compulsory Education and the First Amendment's Religious Clauses," *West Virginia Law Review*, 75 (1975), 213; cited in Ball, pp. 7–8.

43. Wisconsin v. Yoder, 406 U.S. 205.

44. Prince v. Massachusetts, 321 U.S. 158 (1944), cited in Smith v. Organization of Foster Families, 431 U.S. 816 (1977).

45. 268 U.S. 510 (1925).

46. Everson v. Board of Education, 330 U.S. 1.

47. See Leo Pfeffer, *Church, State and Freedom*, 2nd ed. (Boston: Beacon Press, 1953), pp. 518–520.

48. For a discussion of this see William D. Valente, "Overview of Constitutional Developments Affecting Individual and Parental Liberty Interests in Elementary and Secondary Education," published address delivered to the Lawyer's Clinic on Parental Liberty in Education sponsored by the Koch Foundation, Washington, D.C., 1978, pp. 17–18.

49. Carol B. Franklin, "House Panel Airs Conflict Over IRS School Proposal," *Report from the Capital*, 34, No. 3 (March 1979), p. 8.

50. For a discussion of these matters see Ball, pp. 9–13.

51. National Labor Relations Board v. The Catholic Bishops of Chicago, 440 U.S. 490 (1979).

52. See Sorauf, pp. 114–120.

53. 47 Ohio St. 2d. 181 (1976).

54. See Valente, pp. 19–20.

55. See Ball, p. 12, for hints at counsel's role.

56. For a history of these matters see Anson Phelps Stokes, *Church and State in the United States*, 3 vols. (New York: Harper and Brothers, 1950). Stokes is a separationist, but his work is a solid source for basic documents and includes most relevant events.

57. 330 U.S. 1 (1947).

58. For a discussion of these matters see Sorauf, pp. 190–200.

59. Ibid., pp. 200–204.

60. See a reference to these promises in Daniel P. Moynihan, "Government and the Ruin of Private Education," *Harpers*, April 1978, p. 28.

61. See Bob Packwood, "The Accessible Dream: Financing Educational Needs," *Common Sense*, 1 (Summer, 1978), 39–62, and Moynihan, pp. 28–38.

62. Stan L. Hastey, "Congress Defeats Tuition Tax Credits," *Report from the Capitol*, 33, No. 10 (November-December, 1978), p. 8.

63. Stanley Elam, ed., *A Decade of Gallup Polls of Attitudes Toward Education, 1969–78* (Bloomington, Indiana: Phi Delta Kappa, 1978), pp. 196 and 336–337.

64. See Walfred H. Peterson, "Confusion Confounded: Government Aid to Private Education in the Burger Court," *Christian Scholar's Review*, 9 (1980), 145–214.

65. Wolman v. Walter, 433 U.S. 299 (1977).

66. Valente, pp. 10–20.

67. See Table I, Chapter Four, p. 104.

68. See his dissents in Earley v. Decinso, 403 U.S. 602 (1971) and Committee v. Nyquist, 413 U.S. 756 (1973).

69. See their dissents in Committee v. Nyquist, 413 U.S. 756 (1973) and Meek v. Pittenger, 421 U.S. 349 (1975).

70. Justice White goes out of his way to make aid cases policy matters. See his dissent in Committee v. Nyquist, 413 U.S. 756 (1973).

71. For a summary on this see Leo Pfeffer, *God, Caesar, and the Constitution* (Boston: Beacon Press, 1975), pp. 256–257.

72. For a discussion of this last right, see Chapter Three.

73. Committee v. Nyquist, 413 U.S. 756 (1973).

74. Sloan v. Lemon, 413 U.S. 875 (1973).

75. See their dissent in the *Nyquist* and *Sloan* opinions cited immediately above.

76. For a discussion of this see Sorauf, pp. 308–312. See also Wheeler v. Barrera, 417 U.S. 402 (1974) in which the Supreme Court forced Missouri, contrary to its strict "separationist" constitution, to spend federal funds from a federal education program in church-related schools if it wished to participate in a federally funded program that benefited both private and public school pupils.

77. Carl J. Friedrich, "Rights, Liberties, Freedoms: A Reappraisal," *American Political Science Reveiw*, 57 (1963), 841–854.

78. Ibid., 851.

79. Egon Schwelb, *Human Rights and the International Community* (Chicago: Quadrangle Books, 1964), p. 85.

80. Ibid.

81. Ohio v. Whisner, 47 Ohio St. 2d 181 (1976).

82. 411 U.S. 1 (1973).

83. Elam, p. 196.